Reassessing
the Henrician Age

Reassessing
the Henrician Age

Humanism, Politics and Reform
1500–1550

ALISTAIR FOX
& JOHN GUY

Basil Blackwell

© Alistair Fox and John Guy 1986

First published 1986

Basil Blackwell Ltd
108 Cowley Road, Oxford OX4 1JF, UK

Basil Blackwell Inc.
432 Park Avenue South, Suite 1503,
New York, NY 10016, USA

British Library Cataloguing in Publication Data

Fox, Alistair
  Reassessing the Henrician Age: humanism,
  politics and reform 1500–1550.
  1. Humanism—History   2. Philosophy, English
  —16th century
  I. Title   II. Guy, John
  144'.0942   B778
  ISBN 0-631-14614-8

Library of Congress Cataloging in Publication Data

Fox, Alistair.
  Reassessing the Henrician Age.
  Bibliography: p.
  Includes index.
  1. Great Britain — Civilization — 16th century
  — Addresses, essays, lectures.   2. Renaissance —
  Great Britain — Addresses, essays, lectures.
  3. Great Britain — Politics and government —
  1507–1547 — Addresses, essays, lectures.
  4. Reformation — Great Britain —Addresses,
  essays, lectures.   5. Henry VIII, King of England,
  1491–1547 — Addresses, essays, lectures.
  I. Guy, John, 1949–   II. Title.
  DA320.F68   1986   942.05   85–22966
  ISBN 0-631-14614-8

Typeset by Katerprint Typesetting Services Ltd, Oxford
Printed in Great Britain by Billing & Sons Ltd, Worcester

Contents

Acknowledgements   vii

Abbreviations   viii

Introduction   *Alistair Fox*   1

PART ONE   Humanism

1   Facts and Fallacies: Interpreting English Humanism
    Alistair Fox   9
2   English Humanism and the Body Politic   *Alistair Fox*   34
3   Sir Thomas Elyot and the Humanist Dilemma
    Alistair Fox   52

PART TWO   Politics

4   Prophecies and Politics in the Reign of Henry VIII
    Alistair Fox   77
5   Thomas More and Christopher St German: The Battle
    of the Books   *John Guy*   95
6   The King's Council and Political Participation
    John Guy   121

PART THREE   Reform

7   Thomas Cromwell and the Intellectual Origins of the
    Henrician Revolution   *John Guy*   151

8 Law, Equity and Conscience in Henrician Juristic
   Thought   *John Guy*   179
9 Scripture as Authority: Problems of Interpretation in
   the 1530s   *John Guy*   199

Select Bibliography   221

Index   233

Acknowledgements

The authors thank Anaig Fenby and Mary Sullivan of the Department of English, University of Otago, and Mrs Rachel Guy for proof-reading the text; and the University of Otago for a travel grant and the British Council for a Visitorship that enabled Alistair Fox to examine manuscripts in the United Kingdom. Debts to fellow scholars are many and are acknowledged in footnotes and bibliography, but some call for particular mention. In respect of chapter 6, John Guy is indebted to Dr David Starkey's unpublished papers read at Bristol University and the Folger Institute, which set him thinking upon altered lines concerning the Pilgrimage of Grace, the Council, and the role of the nobles at Court at the time of the Eltham Ordinance and during the 1530s. Dr Starkey kindly provided access in advance of publication to his contributions to C. Coleman and D. R. Starkey, eds, *Revolution Reassessed* (Oxford University Press, 1986). Also Folger seminar papers by Professor Thomas F. Mayer upon Thomas Starkey and aristocratic political thought, and by Mr Frederick Conrad upon Sir Thomas Elyot, were illuminating. In respect of chapter 7, John Guy thanks Dr Virginia Murphy and Dr Graham Nicholson for generous permission to cite their unpublished dissertations. Dr Nicholson's article, 'The Act of Appeals and the Henrician Reformation', is forthcoming. Lastly the authors express gratitude to the steering committee, visiting speakers, and members during autumn 1984 of the Center for the History of British Political Thought at the Folger Institute, Washington DC, who discussed the ideas of this book in a generous and stimulating atmosphere. Professor Sir Geoffrey Elton kindly scanned the page proofs at a busy time; his prodigious learning spared the authors several errors.

Abbreviations

Throughout the notes, the following abbreviations have been used, for which fuller details are given in the Bibliography.

Cal. SP Spanish	*Calendar of State Papers, Spanish*, ed. G. A. Bergenroth and others, 13 vols
LP	*Letters and Papers, Foreign and Domestic, of the Reign of Henry VIII*, ed. J. S. Brewer and others, 21 vols and Addenda
More, *CW*	*The Yale Edition of the Complete Works of St Thomas More*, 14 vols
SP	*State Papers during the Reign of Henry VIII*, 11 vols
STC	*A Short-Title Catalogue of Books Printed in England, Scotland and Ireland, and of English Books Printed Abroad, 1475–1640*, by A. W. Pollard and G. R. Redgrave and others, 2 vols, 1926
STC²	*A Short-Title Catalogue . . .*, 2nd edn, ed. W. A. Jackson, F. S. Ferguson and K. F. Pantzer, 1976, vol. II

Introduction

Alistair Fox

It has been evident for some time that the Henrician Age has begun to undergo a thorough reassessment. The Protestant Reformation no longer appears as spontaneous and popular a movement as was once supposed, nor does anticlericalism prove as widespread as was once claimed.[1] Similarly, our understanding of major figures has been drastically revised as they have come under the scrutiny of scholars prepared to look at the actual evidence. Recent studies of Thomas More, for example, have modified once and for all the saintly image manufactured by the Marian hagiographers.[2] Some figures, such as Christopher St German, have assumed much greater prominence as their thought, work, and deeds have begun to be properly analysed.[3] Even the Tudor political revolution, our understanding of which was shaped by the earlier revisionist studies of G. R. Elton, is itself coming under renewed scrutiny. Elton showed

[1] See Christopher Haigh, *Reformation and Resistance in Tudor Lancashire* (Cambridge, 1975).

[2] See, in particular, G. R. Elton, 'Sir Thomas More and the opposition to Henry VIII', in *Studies in Tudor and Stuart Politics and Government* (3 vols, Cambridge, 1974, 1983), vol. I, pp. 155-72; his 'Thomas More, Councillor', ibid., vol. I, pp. 129-54; his 'The real Thomas More?', ibid., vol. III, pp. 344-55; John A. Guy, *The Public Career of Sir Thomas More* (Brighton, 1980); Alistair Fox, *Thomas More: History and Providence* (Oxford, 1982); and Richard Marius, *Thomas More* (New York, 1984).

[3] See John Guy, *Christopher St German on Chancery and Statute*, Selden Society, suppl. series, vol. 6 (London, 1985).

in a succession of books how fundamentally radical the political
changes of Henry VIII's reign were, and explained these
changes as part of an orchestrated design conceived by Thomas
Cromwell.[4] Further research suggests that this view, too, may
need to be modified.[5]

In spite of the work already done, it is unlikely that a new
synthesis will emerge until much more ground has been covered.
New areas of importance still have to be identified and explored,
and new hypotheses tested. Above all else, there is a need for
much more detailed work on particular cases. Only when this
has been achieved will it be possible to make new generalizations to replace the distorting simplifications of the old. This
book of essays has been compiled in order to contribute to the
process of reassessment by offering new perspectives on major
issues, by drawing attention to material that has been hitherto
neglected, and by suggesting new emphases.

Part One concentrates on English humanism as a political
influence, and seeks to modify conventional assumptions. The
author questions whether English humanism was ever the
unified movement it is commonly depicted as being, and suggests that distortions have arisen because of imprecise definitions of 'humanism' and the inclusion of too many non-humanist
figures under that heading. Further questions are raised as to
whether 'Erasmianism' was the common commitment of English humanists, as is usually assumed, and, finally, whether
those humanists who, like Sir Thomas Elyot, were truly Erasmian had any real influence on Henrician politics at all. Conversely, it is suggested that English humanism was a multifarious movement, and that any political influence it exerted
came from varieties of humanism that were not Erasmian, but

[4] See G. R. Elton, *The Tudor Revolution in Government: Administrative Changes in
the Reign of Henry VIII* (Cambridge, 1953); his *England under the Tudors* (London,
1955); his *Policy and Police: The Enforcement of the Reformation in the Age of Thomas
Cromwell* (Cambridge, 1972); his *Reform and Renewal: Thomas Cromwell and the
Common Weal* (Cambridge, 1973); and his *Reform and Reformation: England 1509-
1558* (London, 1977).

[5] See *Revolution Reassessed: Revisions in the History of Tudor Government and
Administration*, ed. C. Coleman and D. R. Starkey (Oxford, 1986), and John
Guy, chapter 7 below.

based on very different principles and aims. The three essays in this section have been designed to be complementary. The first identifies persistent errors in the traditional view of English humanism at a general level, pinpointing faulty syncretism and slackness of definition as the main causes. The second essay discusses five particular humanists – Erasmus, Thomas More, Richard Pace, Thomas Elyot, and Thomas Starkey – in order to draw distinctions that might provide the basis for a new descriptive typology. The third essay examines the political writings and career of Sir Thomas Elyot as a case study illustrating why Erasmian humanism was ineffectual as a force in Tudor politics.

Part Two presents three papers that highlight various political concerns of the period and elucidate some of the forces at work behind them. The essay on prophetic literature in the period establishes the importance of prophecies as a register of popular aspirations and fears, showing why they became so dangerous in the later years of Henry VIII's reign. In his essay on Thomas More and Christopher St German, Dr Guy identifies the real issues motivating their polemical exchange of 1533, which has baffled scholars for so long. He shows that St German was seeking to foster a new theory of law which would effectively displace the notion that canon law was the common law of Christendom. Recognizing that such a displacement would seriously impair the powers and status of the church in England, More wrote his *Apology* and *Debellation of Salem and Bizance* in an attempt to refute the king's secondary propaganda, rather than simply as pious effusions. The final essay in this part traces the defeat of the representative ideal and the medieval case for participation in government through counsel. It reveals one of the motivating forces behind the Pilgrimage of Grace to have been a concern to arrest the narrowing of the Council to an inner body chosen solely for its members' willingness to enact the king's will. These findings modify the idea that Cromwell's commitment to the supremacy of Parliament and the rule of law sprang from an interest in the *res publica* rather than the *res privata* of the ruler, as he appeared to some people to have been instrumental in the creation of a 'private' council that was absolutist in its workings.

Part Three comprises three final papers that trace the intellectual origins of Henrician reform and various responses to it.
Concerning the political revolution, Dr Guy argues that Thomas
Cromwell was not the sole architect of the notion of national
sovereignty, and that Henry VIII, continuing a process that had
been begun by Henry VII, was determined from near the outset
of his reign to control the English Church. Policy was neither
cohesive nor fully co-ordinated, but called into being as the
politics of the divorce required. The last two papers in this
section return to the juristic issues underpinning Henrician
reform. Once again, Christopher St German is shown to have
been a more significant theorist than was once allowed. In his
essay on 'Law, Equity and Conscience' Dr Guy examines St
German's *Doctor and Student* and *A Little Treatise Concerning Writs
of Subpoena* to show why his understanding of conscience and
equity precluded separate courts and special procedures: equity
was not outside the law but resident within it, therefore what
was void in law was void in equity; conversely, equity could not
run against the law. Commitment to these principles, Dr Guy
shows, was what prompted St German's attacks on the ecclesiastical jurisdiction. In his final paper Dr Guy demonstrates
that reform was inextricably tied to the question of the authority
of scripture and the further question of who had power to
interpret it. Even though Henry VIII relied upon scripture as
authority for his jurisdictional revolution, there was, nevertheless, no single 'Henrician' position on this issue, not even
amongst those who denied the church's authority. Arguing from
St German's *An Answer to a Letter* and his unpublished 'Dyalogue', which is deposited in Cromwell's papers, Dr Guy elu-
cidates the stages by which St German grew progressively
disquieted over Henry VIII's caesaropapism and the power to
interpret scripture it implied. Advocating first a theory of con-
sensual exegesis under the king-in-parliament as representing
the whole church in England, St German later switched to the
belief that authority should reside in a general council. Although
this was not a viable policy option in the 1530s, the very fact that
St German entertained it should remind one that there were
aspects of Henrician reform policy that even his partisans found
hard to accept.

The essays collected in this book had sundry origins. Several of them were first presented at a seminar at the Folger Institute on 'Political Thought in the Henrician Age'; others have been written for the present book. Neither severally nor collectively do they purport to offer a complete revision of the Henrician Age – that will require the combined findings of many scholars and more than one discipline – but they do indicate where some of the main problems to be resolved lie, and take some steps, as bold as can be ventured now, towards answering them. Thus it is hoped that these papers, themselves participating in a process that is only yet gathering momentum, will stimulate further reassessment in the future.

PART ONE

Humanism

1

Facts and Fallacies:
Interpreting English Humanism

Alistair Fox

When historians began to re-examine the idea of the Renaissance nearly half a century ago, one consequence was an upsurge of interest in English humanism. From the late 1930s a succession of books confronted the issue,[1] but far from dispelling uncertainties, they provoked two new questions for every one they had tried to resolve. It is timely, now that scholarly activity in this area has all but died away, to examine why the older studies failed to reach consensus, and work towards a new one.

One sympathizes with the modern student who tries to make sense of the views laid before him. On the one hand he will be told that humanism was 'arrested' with the deaths of More and Fisher,[2] or submerged under the Protestant

[1] The most important studies are R. W. Chambers, *Thomas More* (London, 1935); Douglas Bush, *The Renaissance and English Humanism* (Toronto, 1939); W. G. Zeeveld, *Foundations of Tudor Policy* (Cambridge, Mass., 1948); Fritz Caspari, *Humanism and the Social Order in Early Tudor England* (Chicago, 1954); Robert P. Adams, *The Better Part of Valor: More, Colet, and Vives, on Humanism, War, and Peace, 1496-1535* (Seattle, 1962); Arthur B. Ferguson, *The Articulate Citizen and the English Renaissance* (Durham, N.C., 1965); James Kelsey McConica, *English Humanists and Reformation Politics under Henry VIII and Edward VI* (Oxford, 1965); Elton, *Reform and Renewal*; and Quentin Skinner, *The Foundations of Modern Political Thought*, 2 vols (Cambridge, 1978).

[2] Chambers, *Thomas More*, p. 379; for a vigorous rebuttal, see Douglas Bush, 'Tudor humanism and Henry VIII', *University of Toronto Quarterly*, 7 (1937), pp. 162-7.

Reformation,[3] then on the other hand that the Henrician religious settlement was the fulfilment of Erasmianism,[4] and that northern humanism 'grew up largely in the service of the Reformation'.[5] By some he will be told that the humanists shared a common social doctrine presupposing aristocratic supremacy,[6] by others that they were a diverse group united only by dissatisfaction with the existing state of society and 'a nebulous sense that human deficiencies could be remedied by human action'.[7] With regard to individual humanists, he will find Colet characterized as an enemy to *humanitas* in his hostility to human wisdom and his fear of nature,[8] and alternatively as the pioneer of humanist education, and a liberal theologian.[9] With Thomas More, he will find the issues more contentious still. While no one, as yet, has denied that More was a humanist in his earlier career, there is no agreement as to whether he retained that humanism in his later years. The editor of More's *Treatise upon the Passion of Christ* in the Yale edition finds it redolent of humanism in style and form,[10] while another commentator sees the Tower works as evidence of a radical change in More which rendered the term 'humanist' inappropriate, if not totally meaningless.[11] Just as disconcerting as the violent contradictions in the world of scholarship at large are the occasional studies that see no problems at all, disguising all difficulties under the harmonious symmetry of various patterns and paradigms; these studies usually offer visions of a humanist

[3] Frederic Seebohm, *The Oxford Reformers, John Colet, Erasmus, and Thomas More*, 2nd edn (London, 1869), p. 505; see also Adams, *Valor*, p. 4.

[4] McConica, *English Humanists*, p. 199.

[5] Bush, *The Renaissance and English Humanism*, p. 69.

[6] Caspari, *Humanism and the Social Order*, pp. 1, 11, 18, *et passim*.

[7] Elton, *Reform and Reformation*, p. 15.

[8] See Eugene F. Rice, 'John Colet and the annihilation of the natural', *Harvard Theological Review*, 45 (1952), pp. 141-63, and the same author's *The Renaissance Idea of Wisdom* (Cambridge, Mass., 1958), pp. 125, 127.

[9] See Kalyan K. Chatterjee, *In Praise of Learning: John Colet and Literary Humanism in Education* (New Delhi, 1974); and Adams, *Valor*, pp. 21-8.

[10] More, *CW*, XIII, pp. li, lxxxii-lxxxiii, cxxii, clxxx.

[11] Craig R. Thompson, 'The humanism of More reappraised', *Thought*, 52 (1977), pp. 231-48.

movement so coherent and united as to defy credibility.[12] In short, modern scholarship has presented a picture of English humanism that is blurred in its outlines and confusing in the illusions and distortions it produces in the eyes of the beholder.

It is not necessary to conclude, however, that the case is hopeless, that, as some exasperated scholars have declared, the word 'humanism' should be banished from accounts of early modern thought; but it is essential to re-examine the grounds of its usage and come to terms with the main sources of current confusion.

An excessive, and sometimes exclusive, reliance on extrinsic rather than intrinsic evidence causes some of the mischief in studies of English humanism. On the one hand it leads to the inclusion of those who should not be treated as humanists at all, and on the other it obscures significant differences between humanists, making essential discriminations impossible. Both consequences can be seen in one modern study of the role of humanists in government which, identifying as humanists those who both attended one of the universities and also enjoyed royal patronage, treats men like Stephen Hawes, John Skelton, and Alexander Barclay as if they were generically the same as figures like Thomas Linacre, John Cheke, and Thomas Smith.[13] While the biographical facts of the former three indeed suggest that avenues were open for learned, literary men to find advancement at court, it is begging the question to assume automatically that humanism had anything to do with that advancement; closer inspection reveals that neither Hawes nor Skelton were humanists at all, while Barclay was the kind of man who was influenced by the practices of humanism without ever understanding its aims or imbibing its spirit.

For details of Hawes's life we must rely on the testimony of John Bale who, several decades after Hawes's death, wrote that 'Stephen Hawes, a man of distinguished family, was eager from

[12] This tendency is present in the works of Ferguson, McConica, and Skinner listed in n. 1 above.

[13] Arthur J. Slavin, 'Profitable studies: humanists and government in Early Tudor England', *Viator: Medieval and Renaissance Studies*, 1 (1970), pp. 307-25.

his youth to develop his mind through humane studies. Having left his family he went to various universities in different countries to seek to become a man of letters.'[14] No evidence exists to corroborate these vague assertions, and even if Bale were correct, the humane studies Hawes is presumed to have cultivated certainly left no traces on his own literary output. He is apparently unaware of the classics. In *The Pastime of Pleasure* he does cite Plato, but it has been convincingly demonstrated that he drew upon the *Margarita philosophica* of Gregorius Reisch for his information, and did not know Plato's works at first hand.[15] Neither the content nor the forms of classical literature appealed to him; instead, he preferred to write in the tradition of medieval dream allegory as represented by Guillaume De Guilleville's *Le pèlerinage de la vie humaine* and Lydgate's *The Assembly of the Gods*. Similarly, he was entirely indifferent to the new system of education being propounded by Colet and Erasmus. The lengthy account in *The Pastime of Pleasure* of how Grand Amour, the hero, meets the Seven Liberal Arts in the Tower of Doctrine is based upon Lydgate's similar exposition in *The Assembly of the Gods* and, in the words of one authority, 'may be styled a tractate on medieval education'.[16] The prevailing medievalism of the work is so pervasive that it disqualifies Hawes from entering the ranks of the humanists altogether. Hawes's advancement can have owed nothing to his non-existent humanism; if anything, he gained his position as groom of the chamber because of his talent for versifying fashionable moralistic and amatory sentiments, and his usefulness as a propagandist who could celebrate the Tudor dynasty with suitably ornate poetic embellishments.[17]

The career of John Skelton produces the same kind of *trompe-l'oeil* if viewed only in its outer manifestations. To all appearances he seems the exemplary English humanist; indeed, he has

[14] I quote the translation given by A. S. G. Edwards, *Stephen Hawes* (Boston, 1983), p. 1.

[15] *The Pastime of Pleasure by Stephen Hawes*, ed. William Edward Mead, Early English Text Society, original series, no. 173 (London, 1928, for 1927), p. 111/2864; cf. pp. lxiv-lxxvi.

[16] See ibid., pp. xliv-lxxvii.

[17] For an account of Hawes's works as pro-Tudor propaganda, see Alistair Fox, 'Stephen Hawes and the political allegory of *The Comfort of Lovers*', forthcoming in *English Literary Renaissance*.

been described, together with More, as casting a 'giant shadow' over all the rest.[18] The external evidence is persuasive: Skelton was granted the title of 'laureate' not only by the universities of Oxford and Cambridge, but of Louvain as well, which indicates that he had a high degree of expertise in rhetoric;[19] he served as tutor to Prince Henry, for whom he wrote a *speculum principis*; he engaged in translation, producing an English version of the *Bibliotheca historica* of Diodorus Siculus; and he wrote verse in Latin elegiacs. His major works, however, tell another story. Far from espousing the humanist promotion of curricular reform, Skelton actively opposed it. In *Speke Parott*, his virulent attack on Wolsey written about 1520, Skelton denounced the institution of courses in Greek at Oxford and Cambridge, the new humanist method of teaching Latin in the grammar schools, and even the humanists' general concern with eloquence:

> In *Achademia* Parrot dare no probleme kepe,
> For *Greci fari* so occupyeth the chayre,
> That *Latinum fari* may fall to rest and slepe,
> And *silogisari* was drowned at Sturbrydge Fayre;
> Triyvyals and quatryvyals so sore now they appayre,
> That Parrot the popagay hath pytye to beholde
> How the rest of good lernyng is roufled up and trold.
>
> Albertus *De modo significandi*
> And Donatus by dryven out of scole;
> Prisians hed abroken now, handy-dandy,
> And *Inter didascolos* is rekened for a fole;
> Alexander, a gander of Menanders pole,
> With, '*Da causales*', is cast out of the gate,
> And '*Da racionales*' dare not shew his pate.
>
> Plautus in his comedies a chyld shall now reherse,
> And medyll with Quintylyan in his Declamacyons,
> That *Pety Caton* can scantly construe a verse,
> With, '*Aveto*' in *Greco*, and such solempne salutacyons,

---

[18] Slavin, 'Profitable studies', p. 309.

[19] See H. L. R. Edwards, *Skelton: The Life and Times of an Early Tudor Poet* (London, 1949), pp. 34-5.

Can skantly the tensis of his conjugacyons;
Settyng theyr myndys so moche of eloquens,
That of theyr scole maters lost is the hole sentens.[20]

In the war between the 'Greeks' and the 'Trojans' Skelton had chosen the opposite side to that of the true humanists, such as Thomas More.[21] For Skelton, good learning meant scholastic logic and grammar taught by rule and precept in the old way, not by imitation and example. His conservatism was thus not merely social and political – he could never forgive Wolsey for aspiring to rise above his class – it was intellectual as well, and absolutely inimical to the Erasmian programme in almost every respect. Elsewhere in *Speke Parott*, for example, he attacks Erasmus's *Novum instrumentum*, his new Latin translation of the New Testament with its parallel Greek text:

Our Grekys ye walow in the washbol *Argolycorum*;
For though ye can tell in Greke what is *phormio*,
For ye scrape out good scrypture, and set in a gall
Ye go about to amende, and ye mare all.[22]

As far as matters of religious and pedagogical reform are concerned, it is very misleading to describe Skelton by the same term that is associated with the aims and activities of Colet, Erasmus, and More.[23] And if his own vernacular writings are taken into account, Skelton's distance from genuine humanism is quite explicit. Like Hawes, he writes in the older medieval forms such as the dream allegory, the didactic lament, and the flytyng, and his style alternates between high Lydgatean ornation and the low semi-doggerel known as the Skeltonic. Nothing about these poems reveals the slightest influence of humanism; a comparison between Skelton's *Why Come Ye Nat to Courte* and

[20] *John Skelton: The Complete English Poems*, ed. John Scattergood (New Haven and London, 1983), p. 235/162-82.

[21] For More's defence of the 'Greeks', see his Letter to Oxford University of 1518, in *St Thomas More: Selected Letters*, ed. Elizabeth Frances Rogers (New Haven and London, 1961), pp. 95-103.

[22] *John Skelton: The Complete English Poems*, ed. Scattergood, p. 235/150-4.

[23] For similar conclusions, see John M. Berdan, *Early Tudor Poetry, 1485-154?* (New York, 1920), p. 234; and Edwards, *Skelton*, pp. 20-3.

Thomas Wyatt's Horatian *Satires* will underline the difference between mere invective and true classical imitation. Skelton knew many of the classics – he was the first to express the Platonic theory of poetic inspiration in England (in his *Replica-cyon*) – but his classical knowledge did not impinge significantly upon his views or practice, nor was he concerned to make it do so.

Alexander Barclay reveals the existence of yet another variety of sub-humanist concealed by the clumsiness of the extrinsic approach. As with Skelton, his credentials as a humanist seem impeccable. He was the first to introduce the classical pastoral into English with his *Egloges* of about 1514; he translated Sallust's *Jugurtha* into English prose; and he frequently, like a good Erasmian, urged the necessity for children to receive a sound education.[24] In the 'Prologe' to the *Egloges* he shows that he knows about the history of the pastoral by referring to Theocritus and Virgil, and cites Horace as his authority on poetic decorum; elsewhere he occasionally displays his classical knowledge in a bravura flourish of classical exempla.[25] Yet Barclay's humanism is only skin deep. He is a writer who mimics what he sees others around him doing without ever understanding why they are doing it. Consequently, his works are hostile to humanism in content, even while they reflect its influence in their form. For example, in the *Egloges* Barclay misses the tone of the classical pastoral altogether, so overloading his poems with sententious allegory that the rustic setting becomes grotesquely mismatched with the main themes.[26] Moreover, Barclay's basic indifference to classicism is reflected in his choice of sources. Although he knew, or at least knew of, the pastorals of Theocritus and Virgil, he chose to versify the *Miseriae curialium* of Aeneas Silvius (1405-1464) and the *Eclogues* of Baptista Spagnolo, or Mantuanus (1448-1516), inferior works by second-rate, late

---

[24] See *Stultifera nauis, qua omnium mortalium narratur stultitia. The ship of fooles* (London, 1570), fo. 12 (*STC*, no. 3346); cf. *The myrrour of good maners* (London, ?1518), sig. B6ᵛ (*STC²*, no. 17242).

[25] See, for example, ibid., sigs. D12ᵛ-D13.

[26] See C. S. Lewis, *English Literature in the Sixteenth Century Excluding Drama* (London, 1954), p. 131.

medieval writers. Similarly, Barclay's major work, *The Shyp of Folys*, was translated from a poem by Sebastian Brandt that owed nothing to humanism whatsoever. Brandt, a conservative professor of jurisprudence at Basel, wrote *Das Narrenschiff* in colloquial German octosyllabic couplets. Locher subsequently gave it a pseudo-classical appearance by translating it into Latin elegiacs and substituting classical characters for Brandt's original biblical ones, and it was Locher's version that Barclay turned into English verse.

Barclay's lack of taste can be readily explained: it was the matter, not the manner, that drew Barclay to his sources. Eloquence was not one of his main concerns, for, as one scholar has well put it, Barclay was not a poet but a preacher, and his works are little more than versified sermons.[27] He merely used those forms in vogue to command an audience. Thus, even though Barclay was influenced by humanism, one should not casually refer to him as a humanist without first making it clear that he was atypical if, indeed, he really qualified for that title at all.

If neither learning nor humanistic pretensions make a true humanist without a conscious commitment to humanist aims and an animating humanist ethos, neither do simple involvement in politics nor 'civic concern' unless there is further corroborating evidence. An interesting test case can be found in the example of Christopher St German who, it has been alleged, was a member of a large group of official writers induced 'to flood the countryside with Erasmian literature' because of 'the coincidence of royal policy with the traditional interests of the Erasmian community in England' after Wolsey's fall from power.[28] In the early 1530s St German was an aging lawyer, distinguished as the author of *Doctor and Student*, enthusiastic for reform, and sufficiently respected to be enlisted as a government pamphleteer by about 1534, if not earlier.[29] He cannot, however, be considered a humanist in any but a loose, anachronistic

---

[27] Berdan, *Early Tudor Poetry*, p. 251.

[28] McConica, *English Humanists*, pp. 166-7.

[29] See *St German's Doctor and Student*, ed. T. F. T. Plucknett and J. L. Barton, Selden Society (London, 1974), p. xii; and Guy, *St German*, pp. 21-5.

sense, and even then the appellation does not carry conviction. In none of his writings does he show any interest in ancient sources outside of Aristotle and Augustine; he is devoid of any stylistic eloquence; and he regularly reverts to the old *quaestio* method of the schoolmen in preference to humanistic literary forms. Although he does attempt the dialogue form several times, as in *Salem and Bizance*, his dialogues derive not from the philosophical or expository types of Plato and Cicero, and far less from the dramatized dialogues of Lucian, but rather from the old debate forms of the native tradition. To call these works 'dialogues', in any case, is to misname them; the dialogue is a rhetorical pretext, the decorum of which St German finds hard to sustain.

Yet it has recently been proven that St German was the author of a remarkably enlightened parliamentary draft of 1531 advocating wide-sweeping social reform.[30] The measures proposed are so radical that one scholar was tempted to identify its architect as Thomas More.[31] Along with proposals for a vernacular Bible, for the creation of a great standing council, and for the reform of the clergy, this document urges measures for poor relief that are reminiscent of *Utopia*: a programme of centrally organized state works on the highways so as to eliminate idleness and vagabonds, to be funded through a system of income tax ('common chestes'), and investigation by the great council of prices and incomes, based upon the assumption of a just minimum wage.[32] Nevertheless, St German's proposals are not the product of humanist doctrine, but of legal rationalism and common sense, which should provide an object lesson against leaping to the assumption that any political writing with a reformist bent proves its author to be a humanist, Erasmian or otherwise. One scholar committed this error when, believing the 1531 reform document to have been written by William Marshall, an undisputed humanist, he contended that it proved 'the

[30] See Guy, *St German*, pp. 25-31. For the text of this document, see ibid., pp. 127-35.

[31] J. J. Scarisbrick, 'Thomas More: the king's good servant', *Thought*, 52 (1977), pp. 249-68; see also Elton, *Reform and Renewal*, pp. 71-6.

[32] See below, p. 113.

capacity of the humanist mentality for constructive thought'.[33]
It does no such thing; rather, it demonstrates the capacity of a
common lawyer's practical realism for constructive thought.
Once scholars cease including in their discussions of humanism
and humanists figures who are not properly humanists at all, it
will go a long way towards dispersing the mists that beshroud
the whole issue.

Apart from an excessive reliance on extrinsic evidence, confusion arises also from attempts to make broad generalizations
about humanism as a movement. It has been characterized
variously as neo-Stoic, depending upon the belief 'that all men
form a single society which is, or should be ruled by one Natural
Law';[34] as Platonic, upholding the goal of 'a good and just state
which is ruled by an elite of guardians and philosophers';[35] and
as practical, utilitarian, and realistically pragmatic.[36] Whatever
the social doctrine imputed to the humanists, it is almost invariably described as 'Erasmian'.[37] The problem with all such
generalizations is that exceptions can always be found to the
general rule, so that none of them can do justice to the total
array of evidence. Consequently, these generalizations distort
through over-simplification, selectivity, or exaggeration. The
real problem lies deeper still – in an almost universal assumption that humanism was a coherent and unified movement.
Demonstrably, all humanists did share an interest in classical
learning as an alternative to medieval scholasticism, but as soon
as modern scholars try to extend that common concern to social,
political, or even moral philosophies, no generalizations will
work.

The attempt to make humanism conform with prefabricated
assumptions has produced two contradictory myths: on the one
hand the idea that humanism was 'arrested' in the 1530s as

---

[33] Ferguson, *Articulate Citizen*, p. 336.

[34] Adams, *Valor*, p. 9.

[35] Caspari, *Humanism and the Social Order*, pp. 10-11.

[36] Ferguson, *Articulate Citizen*, p. 166, *et passim*.

[37] As by, for example, Ferguson, ibid., p. 39, and McConica, *English Humanists, passim*.

Henry VIII axed classical scholarship along with its main proponents and spoliated the universities,[38] and on the other, that humanism continued substantially unchanged, its spirit and vision being 'applied' and 'adapted' by later, more civic-minded men.[39]

The 'arrest' theory will not bear serious scrutiny: it depends upon ignorance of the historical facts, as Bush conclusively proved,[40] and the fallacious assumption that the first-generation humanists shared a common discernible viewpoint. Hagiography has played a part in the creation of this myth. Scholars who are partial to More and Erasmus have tended to identify the two men and then equate 'humanism' with both. Perceiving the setbacks both suffered in their later careers, scholars assume that humanism itself must also have suffered a setback.[41] What they overlook are the facts that More had parted company from Erasmus, and perhaps from humanism itself, long before his own political demise, and that the two men suffered disappointment for very different reasons.

At least as early as 1516, More had developed fundamental doubts about aspects of the Erasmian programme, in spite of his friendship for Erasmus and his vigorous defence of the latter's *Moria* and New Testament. While he supported Erasmus's enthusiasm for *bonae litterae* and his concern for reform, More had come to mistrust certain of Erasmus's aims and methods. As the ironies of *Utopia* show, he was ambivalent about the wisdom of adopting a moral stance that was so arbitrary it could make things worse by provoking a reaction, and his doubts were fuelled by his own deepening pessimism about the irremediable imperfection of the human condition, a pessimism that ran counter to Erasmus's much more optimistic world view.[42]

[38] See J. S. Phillimore, 'The arrest of humanism in England', *Dublin Review*, 153 (1913), pp. 1-26; Chambers, *Thomas More*, p. 379; and Adams, *Valor*, pp. 4, 87, 260.

[39] Caspari, *Humanism and the Social Order*, pp. 42, 75; Ferguson, *Articulate Citizen*, p. 165, *et passim*.

[40] Bush, 'Tudor humanism and Henry VIII', pp. 162-7.

[41] See Adams, *Valor*, pp. 85-7, 260.

[42] For a detailed discussion of More's world view, see Fox, *Thomas More*; see also below, chapter 2.

More's decision to enter the king's service in 1517 (possibly earlier), and his reluctance to inform Erasmus of it,[43] suggest that he had embarked upon a role that he knew would incur his friend's disapproval – as indeed it did, judging by the letter Erasmus wrote to More in April 1517 lamenting his desertion of good letters. More knew that politics could not be conducted according to the moral absolutes preached by Erasmus, but required a much shrewder recognition of political realities; in any case, once he had joined the Council, even though he continued to nurture his friendship with Erasmus for some time, More progressively went his own separate way, both intellectually and in action.

Once the Lutheran Reformation had forced men to take sides, there are, furthermore, signs that More's differences with Erasmus became still more fundamental. They are revealed in his uneasy equivocation over Tyndale's charge that, to be consistent, he should have attacked Erasmus as well as the reformers because of his emendation of the Vulgate and his exposure of clerical abuse in *Moriae encomium*. In reply, More excuses Erasmus on the grounds that he found 'no such malycyouse entent wyth Erasmus my derlynge' as he declared he found in Tyndale.[44] This is a remarkably tepid and non-committal defence: it allows for the possibility that Erasmus may indeed have erred, in More's opinion, but was not blameworthy because of his good will (and, it is implied, his naivety). Moreover, he is at pains to emphasize that no matter what the contents of *The Praise of Folly* might have been, they should not be taken to represent his own views, 'the boke beynge made by a nother man though he were my derlynge neuer so dere'.[45] The bad-tempered iteration in this passage shows that More knew Tyndale had hit the mark, and that his own position was very far removed from the Erasmian humanism he had once let the world believe he supported. In his final declaration of willingness to burn not only Erasmus's earlier books, but also some of his own, More reveals that he had arrested his own humanism long before anyone else did it for

[43] See Elton, 'Thomas More, Councillor', in *Studies*, vol. I, pp. 129-54.
[44] More, *CW*, VIII, part I, p. 177.
[45] Ibid., p. 178.

him. Thus by 1533 More had little in common with Erasmus that can be ascribed to a mutual commitment to humanism. He did still long for the European nations to be at peace so that they could present a united front against the Turks, but one did not need to be a humanist to have that desire.

More's fall, too, owed nothing to his humanism. It occurred because he backed a conservative cause that ran counter to the revolutionary tide of the times. Specifically, he became entangled in the political manoeuvring that was triggered by the king's desire for a divorce, backed the wrong side, and lost. In contrast, Erasmus's influence waned because his moralized precepts and exhortations, however well-intentioned, were too impractical to have any lasting effect on the princes to whom they were addressed, and because his attacks on religious abuse were superseded by others who were more vigorously determined to remedy it. Erasmus was unable to follow the radical implications of his own policies to the limits that others had chosen to do, and so was left behind, resented by both sides in the Reformation conflict.[46]

The 'arrest' theory also presupposes a greater degree of identity between Colet and the other humanists than the evidence will support. Colet was essentially a theologian who became a humanist because he found the neo-Platonic doctrine of the Florentine humanists compatible with his Christian belief, and humanistic exegetical methods useful for elucidating the meaning of scripture. Consequently, he developed into an educator because he believed that the cultivation of eloquence and lexical and grammatical training could more effectively lead to a true understanding of the Bible than could the traditional methods of the scholastic theologians.[47] That, together with his distress at the immorality and worldliness vitiating the clergy and a loathing of war – natural enough in any pious preacher – was about as far as his commitment to any so-called humanist 'programme' went. He certainly did not have any detailed, comprehensive vision of wide-ranging political reform like that

---

[46] For the most potent statement of this view, see Johan Huizinga, *Erasmus and the Age of Reformation* (New York, 1957).

[47] See Chatterjee, *In Praise of Learning*, pp. 93-4.

expounded by Erasmus; rather, he expected that interior spiritual reformation in individual men would eventually lead to renovation of the existing order: 'this in truth will be done passing well, if men, now turned away from God, return to him, and if all things belonging to man have, so far as they can, an upward direction.'[48] Colet's thought on these matters was very similar to that of Erasmus, but his lack of interest in the wider spectrum of Erasmus's concerns makes them humanists of a very different kind: humanism, for Colet, was an instrument for assisting men to turn away from the world; for Erasmus, it was also to be, in the short term, a source of moral instruction and a mine of precepts for worldly reforms of which Colet would have been most suspicious.

Once the differences between Colet, More, and Erasmus have been properly acknowledged, it is hard to see that they formed any 'movement' that could ever have been arrested as such. This impression can only be created by the amalgamation of the distinctive features of each separate humanist into a homogeneous composite which is then taken to represent them all. Ironically, the two things they really *did* share in common were not arrested: an enthusiasm for the new learning, and a belief in the need to recover a purified Christianity, even if those twin interests tended to bifurcate among their successors into the separate preoccupation of pedagogues (like Ascham and Cheke) on one hand, and of the Protestant reformers (like Tyndale, Frith, or Barnes) on the other.[49]

The counter-argument – that there was an unbroken continuity as Erasmian humanism evolved from theory to application – is equally ill-founded. According to this view, classically inspired education made available a new source of precept and precedent that spawned a new secular ideal.[50] Because the humanist movement had 'far outgrown the academic confines of its earlier

---

[48] *Joannis Coleti enarratio in epistolam S. Pauli ad Romanos: An Exposition of St Paul's Epistle to the Romans*, ed. J. H. Lupton (London, 1873), p. 59.

[49] On the survival of humanism in the later part of Henry VIII's reign, see in particular Zeeveld, *Foundations*, and Elton, *Reform and Renewal*.

[50] See Ferguson, *Articulate Citizen*, pp. 147-8; cf. p. 162.

years', the younger humanists of the second quarter of the century, their minds 'quickened' and 'broadened' by their classical studies, were able to apply the wisdom they had derived from the writers of antiquity in a practical way.[51]

This argument has the appeal of seeming to reconcile all the evidence into a smooth, harmonious synthesis, but on close inspection it proves to be begging the very questions it should be answering. Did scholars in the 1530s and 1540s 'apply' classical precepts in the proposals they offered for social, political, and economic reform? Was their inspiration Erasmian? And is there any evidence that their thinking, as distinct from their literary style, was in fact shaped by their humanist studies? Overriding all these questions is a still larger one: was there really a continuity of humanism as practised variously and severally by Colet, More, and Erasmus, or did humanism itself undergo a significant transformation as certain expectations and preoccupations of the older generation were discarded and became replaced by new ones?

The main weakness of the continuity theory is that it requires the definition of 'humanism' and 'humanist' to be broadened to the point where they cease to be useful as descriptive terms. Humanism, for instance, has been defined as 'the conscious reinterpretation of the literature and history of Greece and Rome . . . made within the specific context of a society in the process of transition', and a humanist as 'one whose mind has been shaped by study of this reinterpreted antiquity and who has in consequence become able to make a characteristically fresh approach to the problems of life'.[52] The qualifying phrases in these definitions, by which the semantic sense of the words is enlarged, beg the very questions they assume to have been resolved. If humanism consciously reinterpreted classical literature and history within the specific context of a society in the process of transition, what, precisely, did that reinterpretation involve? Did it really mean that humanists 'applied' the ideas they had found in the classics, or did it mean that they rejected them as impractical and substituted their own new criteria

[51] Ibid., pp. 158-9, 162.
[52] Ibid., pp. 162-3.

instead? Further, if scholars were employing new criteria, were those criteria necessarily derived from their classical study at all? It serves no useful purpose to assert simply that 'the humanist intellectual found his principles in the moral philosophy of the ancients, tempered of course by Christian tradition, and his data in history and in the direct observation of society',[53] when that 'tempering' may have been so fundamental as to render the classical principles irrelevant. Similarly, was the ability to make a fresh approach to the problems of life necessarily a consequence of the shaping influence of reinterpreted antiquity at all? One thinks of Christopher St German or Clement Armstrong, who certainly offered fresh approaches to the problems of life by offering extremely radical schemes to remedy social and economic diseases, but neither of whom was in any sense influenced by the study of antiquity. The real defect of such loose definitions is that they blur the issue by indiscriminately incorporating non-humanist thinkers and thought into the data by which they define humanism itself.

A further sleight of hand is produced by generalizing upon the basis of particular instances. More often than not, judgements concerning humanism in the younger generation amount to little more than extrapolations from the cases of either Thomas Elyot, or Thomas Starkey or, sometimes, a fusion of both. This tendency can be seen in one particular study in which Elyot and Starkey are treated as proof that the younger humanists, determined to take humanism out of the coterie, 'sought to draw upon all that was best in both the classical and the Christian traditions', and to apply that wisdom practically in the governance of the 'weal public'.[54] Close inspection of the works of Elyot and Starkey shows, however, that two diametrically opposed approaches to the problem of governance have been artificially linked. It is Elyot alone, not Starkey, who draws upon classical sources. Indeed, Starkey at one point specifically rejects Plato's ideal commonwealth as a model because of its impracticality; he is far more influenced by the example of various contemporary

---

[53] Ibid., p. 167.
[54] Ibid., p. 168ff.

Italian city states than by classical antiquity.[55] Elyot is content to parade classical precepts and examples with relentless optimism; Starkey prefers to work rationally and empirically, using the findings of experience and common sense. It is Elyot alone who is Erasmian; Starkey's political theory may not have derived from his humanistic training at all. It is unhelpful to quote Elyot's concluding remark in *The Governour* that consultation is 'the last part of morall Sapience, and the begynnyng of sapience politike',[56] for it merely draws attention to the fact that Elyot was never able to offer any practical advice – which is probably why he failed so dismally in his own political career.[57] *The Image of Governance*, which Elyot belatedly issued a decade later in an attempt to fulfil his promise to describe 'all the remnant of what pertains to a just public weal',[58] still presents only a series of moralized exempla that strain credibility in their pictures of idealized virtue and unmitigated vice, as remote from the reality of Tudor politics as it is possible to be. Significantly, in a chapter dealing with 'Remedy and Policy: The Humanist Approach', the author of the study in question is forced to leave Elyot out: he discusses only More, Starkey, and Marshall – inevitably so, as Elyot never offered any specific remedies or policies.

Further examples of false generalizations resulting from the desire to present English humanism as a coherent movement can be found in the standard authorities. Caspari, for example, maintained that the humanists advocated a rational and largely secular education, and that they evolved a social doctrine to defend and justify the aristocracy.[59] Neither of these contentions is wholly true. The educational system Colet prescribed for his grammar school at St Paul's was certainly not secular in its bias.

---

[55] *England in the Reign of Henry the Eighth: Life and Letters and A Dialogue between Cardinal Pole and Lupset by Thomas Starkey*, ed. Sidney J. Herrtage, Early English Text Society, extra series, nos 12, 32 (London, 1878, repr. 1927), p. 163.

[56] *The Boke Named the Governour*, ed. H. H. S. Croft, 2 vols (London, 1883), vol. II, p. 447; cf. Ferguson, *Articulate Citizen*, p. 170.

[57] This matter is discussed fully in chapter 3 below.

[58] *The Governour*, ed. Croft, vol. I, p. 24.

[59] Caspari, *Humanism and the Social Order*, pp. 1, 15, 18.

Quite apart from good literature in Latin and Greek, Colet declares that the boys are to study 'specially Cristyn auctours that wrote theyre wysdome with clene and chast laten other in verse or in prose, for my entent is by thys scole specially to incresse knowledge and worshipping of god and oure lorde Crist Jesu and good Cristen lyff and manners in the Children'.[60] Starkey, too, considered that the system of public education he was proposing needed to be perfected by the enhancing effect of Christian doctrine.[61] Likewise, the view that the humanists uniformly supported the aristocracy and the existing order will not bear close scrutiny. It may be true with a theorist like Elyot, but an ambitious political aspirant like Richard Morison could argue, possibly with an eye to his own advancement, 'that trewe nobilitie is neuer, but where vertue is', and that promotion should be determined according to virtue only, not birth.[62] Only if 'aristocracy' were to be defined in its Platonic sense as 'government by the best' could Morison be regarded as sanctioning an aristocratic structure for the governance of England. If one looks at Starkey's view of kingship, the same kind of qualifications have to be made. Unlike Elyot, he did not believe that kings are untouchable, since 'the hartes of princes be in goddes owne handes and disposition',[63] but rather that 'thys ys in mannys powar, to electe and chose hym that ys both wyse and iust, and make hym a prynce, and hym that ys a tyranne so to depose.'[64] The parliamentary sovereignty that Starkey goes on to propose, based on the power of statute and the trimming of royal prerogatives,[65] argues against the idea that all humanists were prepared to see England governed by an hereditary elite.[66] The theory

[60] 'Statuta Paulinae Scholae', repr. in Chatterjee, *In Praise of Learning*, Appendix B, p. 104.

[61] *Starkey*, ed. Herrtage, pp. 202-7.

[62] *A remedy for sedition* (London, 1536), sigs. B1^v−B2^r (*STC*^{2}, no. 18113.5); see also Ferguson, *Articulate Citizen*, pp. 226-7.

[63] *The Governour*, ed. Croft, vol. I, pp. 23-4.

[64] *Starkey*, ed. Herrtage, p. 167.

[65] Ibid., pp. 168-9, 179, 181.

[66] For a further critique of Caspari's thesis, see H. R. Trevor-Roper, 'Tudor humanism', *History Today*, 6 (1956), pp. 69-70. For an argument to the contrary, see Thomas F. Mayer, 'Faction and ideology: Thomas Starkey's *Dialogue*', *Historical Journal*, 28.1 (1985), pp. 1-25.

really only applies to Elyot, who, while he may have been the 'apostle of humanism to the English governing class',[67] was by no means as representative of the second-generation humanists as is commonly supposed. It is time to turn away from such amorphous, syncretic generalizations, to recognize that differences between individual humanists exist, and trace the much more complicated patterns of relationship that emerge as a result.

A final source of obfuscation arises from imprecise handling of the relationship between humanism and religion. Ever since the term 'Christian humanist' was coined to describe the blend of learning and piety found in men like Colet and Erasmus, the distinction between those who were genuine humanists and those who were religious reformers with substantively different commitments has been blurred.

Part of the problem is the usual tendency to describe as 'humanist' figures who were either not humanists at all, or had ceased to be humanists. Stephen Gardiner provides a case in point. He was very well grounded in humane letters, having studied the classics and Greek at Trinity Hall, Cambridge; he supported humanistic curricular reforms in the universities; he pursued an active political career as Wolsey's secretary, as an ambassador, and finally as lord chancellor in the reign of Mary. He thus appears to be the very epitome of a humanist as conceived by the popular myth. Once he became caught up in promoting the king's divorce and the royal supremacy, however, his earlier humanism ceased to be a relevant influence on his activities. His *De vera obedientia* shows no trace of humanism in its form, style, or substance, so that there is little purpose in continuing to regard him as a humanist at that later stage in his career. Even Ferguson, who aimed to prove that humanism was not arrested in the 1530s, concedes that Gardiner was distracted from humanist concerns by the dictates of expediency.[68] Humanism was not a dye with which men were indelibly stained for life; it was a practice and set of assumptions that could be

[67] Ferguson, *Articulate Citizen*, p. 168.
[68] Ibid., p. 242.

repudiated or neglected at will. In Gardiner we can discern a pattern that is common enough in the second half of Henry VIII's reign: a willingness to let humanistic interests slide into recess in the face of more urgent pressures on the political and religious scenes.

Equally faulty is the common belief that Christian humanism involved an harmonious synthesis. Too often, scholars appear to have been taken in by the propaganda of humanists like Erasmus who asserted an unequivocal compatibility between humanism and Christian doctrine. In reality, however, the synthesis was fraught with tensions. Even with Erasmus, a potential rejection of secular learning as 'unnecessary' was implicit in his thought from the outset. For him, as for Colet, the forms, modes, and even the style of the pagan classics served essentially to sugar-coat a didactic pill; as he said in his *Letter to Martin Dorp* defending the manner of *Moriae encomium*, 'Evangelical truth sinks in more pleasingly and takes firmer hold in souls when dressed up in these little enticements than if it is simply stated as naked truth.'[69] Once the truth had taken hold, the manner of presenting it became redundant: like a husk, it might be discarded once the kernel had been safely extracted. Erasmus never fully allowed for the fact that humanist learning might point men's attention in the opposite direction from the transcendental, and make claims that were not rendered obsolete by the findings of faith, but he was, on the other hand, prepared, if pushed, to give learning over altogether. As he said to Dorp: 'if you hold the view that human learning should be despised out of love for true piety, and that one arrives at this wisdom much more quickly through a certain transformation in Christ, and if it is your judgement that everything else worth learning can be seen more fully in the light of faith than in the books of men, I would gladly agree with your opinion.'[70] In this statement,

---

[69] *Christian Humanism and the Reformation: Selected Writings of Erasmus*, ed. John C. Olin, rev. edn (New York, 1975), p. 60.

[70] Ibid., p. 80. For the counter-view that there was a teleological harmony in Erasmus's thought, see Brendan Bradshaw, 'The Christian humanism of Erasmus', *Journal of Theological Studies*, new series, 32.2 (1982), pp. 411-47.

Erasmus foreshadows what did indeed occur, particularly in those who espoused Luther's doctrines: a realization that humanism was not adequate for promoting the kind of spiritual renovation for which they longed.

The same kind of repudiation of humanism took place on the other side, as the case of Thomas More demonstrates. From the outset he was alternately enthusiastic and ambivalent about humanism, just as he was torn between a desire for the contemplative life and an equally strong urge towards the active one. In his *Letter to Oxford University* of March 1518, while he does not hesitate to recommend a liberal education, he does equivocate over endorsing the idea that secular learning and theology can be readily accommodated by means of a neo-Platonic scale of transcendence. There are some, he says, 'who through knowledge of things natural (i.e. rational) construct a ladder by which to rise to the contemplation of things supernatural; they build a path to theology through philosophy and the liberal arts . . . they adorn the queen of heaven with the spoils of the Egyptians!'[71] However, while acknowledging that *others* construct such a ladder, More refrains from stating that *he* does, and if one looks at his own humanistic writings, it appears that he never tried to use his humanism tendentiously in the cause of piety as Erasmus did, for example, in the *Enchiridion militis christiani*. More would later argue in his *Dialogue Concerning Heresies* (1529) that there was no disharmony between faith and reason, or between a liberal education and theology, but that was in a polemical context when he was faced with the need to refute those who had rejected humanism altogether.[72] By the time of *A Dialogue of Comfort against Tribulation*, however, he had reaffirmed a more sceptical position: even though the pagan moral philosophers were not utterly to be refused, 'all their comfortable counsaylles are very farre vnsufficient' in matters of faith, and their 'erronyouse receytes' needed to be corrected by reference to 'the great phisicion god'.[73]

[71] *Selected Letters*, ed. Rogers, p. 99.
[72] See More, *CW*, VI, p. 132.
[73] More, *CW*, XII, pp. 10-11.

There was always, therefore, an incipient fracture in the
Christian-humanist synthesis, and under the stresses of the
1520s and 1530s the two components tended to separate. Moreover, there is some truth to the contention that the Reformation
was 'both the culmination and the ruin of humanism'.[74] On one
hand the Protestant reformers, having used humanist methods
of textual scholarship and exegesis to recover the spirit of scripture, found the message more important than the means by
which they had attained it; on the other hand, those who
opposed the Reformation were forced to reject the instruments
that had precipitated it. One can see this taking place in
Thomas More in the time between his confident call for an
English translation of scripture in 1528-9, and his support of the
1530 proclamation against heretical books declaring that such a
translation was 'not necessary'.[75]

Not all humanists retreated in this manner, and humanism as
such was not arrested, but in the context of the Reformation,
Erasmus's belief that humanism could be comfortably synthe-
sized with the doctrines of the church was shown to be naive.
From 1530 onwards, humanism and religion tended to be pursued as contiguous, though separate, interests in different
spheres of human life. Elyot, for example, remained fervently
committed to humanism, but only at the cost of eschewing
direct religious comment altogether. Similarly, humanists like
Ascham and Cheke found it safer to restrict themselves to
educational matters. An analogy might be drawn between the
separation of humanist and religious preoccupations and the new
conception of the relationship between spiritualty and temporalty
after the Henrician revolution: each had their separate and clearly
defined spheres of jurisdiction. At any rate, for practical purposes one needs to recognize when presumed 'Christian humanists' are acting as humanists, and when they are acting simply
as Christians (of one persuasion or another). Unless such a
distinction is made, nearly every religious polemicist or contro-
versialist of the period may be deemed a 'humanist' depending

[74] Roberto Weiss, 'Learning and education in Western Europe from 1470-
1520', in *The New Cambridge Modern History* (Cambridge, 1957), vol. I, p. 126.

[75] More, *CW*, VI, pp. 331-2; see also Guy, *Public Career*, pp. 171-2; cf. More,
CW, IX, p. 13.

on whether or not they had a learned background. Such inclusiveness would render the term 'humanist' practically meaningless.

Having identified the major sources of confusion – excessive inclusiveness, forced generalizations, and over-simplified pattern-making – one must be careful not to throw the baby out with the bathwater. If this is to be avoided, however, a more exact definition of humanism must be recovered. The root problem with the current use of the term is its propensity to escape beyond its proper bounds and invade territory in which it does not belong. This occurs when it is used to describe political philosophies of one complexion or another, or is taken to represent a general attitude to life. To reinvest it with useful meaning requires a return to a definition that is semantically and historically based, as Kristeller has long argued.[76]

The term 'humanist', as has been well attested, evolved in Italy during the late fifteenth century to denote variously a teacher of classical literature or a student of classical learning.[77] Thereafter, it slowly became diffused around Europe. In the *Epistolae obscurorum vivorum* (1515) there occurs a mock-satiric reference to 'isti humaniste [qui] nunc vexant', and the spleen of the schoolmen is directed against 'omnes poetas et humanistas'.[78] Clearly, the term was used to distinguish proponents of the new learning from the practitioners and devotees of the old, which should never be forgotten when the term is used today. Without a specific commitment to the idea that classical learning is valuable or efficacious, no Tudor figure should be considered a 'humanist'.

The term 'humanism' is more problematical. It was first used in 1808 by a German educator to describe a programme and

[76] Paul Oskar Kristeller, *Renaissance Thought and its Sources*, ed. Michael Mooney (New York, 1979), p. 22; cf. Kristeller's review article, 'Studies on Renaissance humanism during the last twenty years', *Studies in the Renaissance*, 9 (1961), pp. 7-30.

[77] See Augusto Campana, 'The origin of the word "humanist"', *Journal of the Warburg and Courtauld Institutes*, 9 (1946), pp. 60-73, from whom the following information is drawn.

[78] *Ep.* I, 7, II, 58, quoted by Campana, ibid., p. 69.

ideal of classical education.[79] Subsequently, it was used in the sense of an historical event by Hagen (1841-3) and Voigt (1859).[80] Since then it has been broadened, with vexing consequences for scholarship, to designate any kind of philosophical attitude which emphasizes human values.[81] Again, it seems most profitable to adhere strictly to the semantic connotations of the word, and not to succumb to the temptation of applying it to the humane concerns that classical study may have promoted, but did not promote by itself, in the early sixteenth century. Otherwise, one will sooner or later be forced to concede that every impulse, deed, and intention directed towards change in the sphere of human morality and institutions was in some sense 'humanist', thus rendering the term useless as a tool of historical description. It is certainly true that a desire to replace outworn medieval institutions, conventions, and methods lay at the very heart of Tudor humanism, but so too did it animate lawyers and lollards, and many others who were untouched by the influence of classicism. Thus, unless the classical component is present, one is not dealing with humanism, but with something else.

The second necessity is to recognize the diversity of Tudor humanism, which was not monolithic as is usually depicted, but a multifarious phenomenon. The cultivation of classical studies led to a variety of expectations and preoccupations which in turn depended upon the diverse theological, political, and moral assumptions of those who espoused it. Someone like More, for instance, who believed that both human nature and the human situation were providentially imperfect, was never likely to entertain seriously either the idealism or the optimism of a man like Erasmus, who held that human nature could be significantly ameliorated by education. Similarly, an Aristotelian, Italianate humanist like Starkey, who believed that politicians had to deal with practical exigencies in terms of what experience

[79] See Kristeller, *Renaissance Thought*, p. 22.

[80] See Campana, 'Origin of the word "humanist"', p. 72.

[81] For the most detailed study of the connotations of the word 'humanism', see Vito R. Giustiniani, 'Homo, humanus, and the meanings of "humanism"', *Journal of the History of Ideas*, 46 (1985), pp. 167-95. Giustiniani's study, which appeared after this book went to press, reaches conclusions similar to those of the present writer.

proves to be actually possible, was not likely to present advice based on abstract moral absolutes in the way that a Platonist like Elyot did. Humanism was not a philosophy of life, but a tool by which men hoped to make their philosophies efficacious in the active life.

One should distinguish, too, between the different spheres in which humanism had any lasting influence, and not assume that it spread promiscuously to all. The main influence was in culture and education, and there can be no doubt that humanism furnished a new ideal of what constituted a gentleman, and that humanistic education prepared young men for public life by training them in manners, virtue, and eloquence. But whether humanism itself exercised any direct – as distinct from indirect – influence on political decisions is seriously to be doubted. After the fall of Cromwell, humanism had very little relevance to politics at all in the remainder of Henry VIII's reign, except to qualify men for careers as secretaries and pedagogues, or for writing propaganda.

The safest conclusion to be drawn is that most of the prevailing generalizations about English humanism need to be either discarded or radically revised. There was a strong element of piety in most humanists, some of them did believe that wisdom derived from humanistic study could be put to use in the commonweal, and many of them were actively concerned with reform, but no statement about any individual or group applies to them all. In fact, the differences between them are more interesting than superficial similarities, and the task of scholarship for the next twenty years should be to identify these differences and account for their origins precisely, in order to trace more accurately the lineaments of the phenomenon.

2

English Humanism and the Body Politic

Alistair Fox

Two decades ago James K. McConica argued that Henrician reform policy was influenced by a group of English humanists whose characteristic commitment was Erasmian humanism.[1] Response to this thesis was equivocal: while recognizing that intellectual influences did help to shape policy, some scholars were reluctant to concede that the term 'Erasmian humanism' adequately explained the nature or origins of this influence.[2] 'Erasmian' and 'humanism' had been defined in terms too broad to describe the complex mixture making up English humanism. Closer definitions and distinctions were required, and in this chapter I shall try to develop some. By comparing the writings of Erasmus himself with those of four leading English humanists, Thomas More, Richard Pace, Thomas Elyot, and Thomas Starkey, one can see that Erasmian humanism had little direct influence on Henrician politics, and that English reform drew its substance from a type of humanism based on very different assumptions.

Erasmus's humanism, like other types, was founded upon an enthusiasm for good letters: *studia humanitatis*, or the study of

---

[1] McConica, *English Humanists*.

[2] See the reviews of McConica's book by G. R. Elton, *Historical Journal*, 10 (1967), pp. 137-8; and by A. G. Dickens, *History*, 52 (1967), pp. 77-8.

grammar, rhetoric, history, poetry, and ethics in the classical texts in preference to the old emphasis on logic, natural philosophy, and metaphysics.[3] Erasmus differed from others, however, in the degree of fervour with which he believed in the reforming power of *bonae litterae*. As early as the *Antibarbari* (1487-8) he was declaring that the influence of a man who is both eloquent and learned must necessarily be widespread and pervasive.[4] In particular, the learned man could benefit the state by inculcating good precepts into the prince, 'now by a suggestive thought, now by a fable, now by analogy, now by example, now by maxims, now by a proverb'.[5] Indeed, the very safety of the state depended upon the good education of the prince, the effectiveness of preachers, and the schoolmasters, and good letters had a vital bearing on all three.[6] Once good education secured good morals, all other benefits would flow from that.

Erasmus's humanism was complicated by his attempts to marry it to Christian piety. Learning was not to be an end in itself, even for secular purposes, but, as Erasmus asserted in the *Enchiridion militis christiani* (1503), the pagan poets and philosophers were useful as a *preparation* for the Christian life.[7] One should pick out from pagan books whatever is best, imitating a bee flying about the garden.[8] By pursuing liberal disciplines, 'we may arrive at last by a long circuitous route at the place to which the Spirit led the Apostles in a very short time.'[9] Thus, the real importance of the new learning was to be in helping to guide men through 'the labyrinth of this world into the pure light of the

---

[3] For definitions of humanism, see William Bouwsma, *The Interpretation of Renaissance Humanism*, 2nd edn (Washington, 1966), p. 12.

[4] *Opera omnia Desiderii Erasmi Roterodami*, ed. J. H. Waszink and others, I-1 (Amsterdam, 1969), p. 103/22-5; for an English translation, see *Collected Works of Erasmus*, 23-1 (Toronto, 1978), p. 82/29-32.

[5] *The Education of a Christian Prince*, tr. and ed. Lester K. Born (New York, 1968), pp. 144-5.

[6] *Antibarbari*, *Opera omnia*, I-1, p. 53/23-5; *Collected Works of Erasmus*, p. 30/20-2.

[7] *The Essential Erasmus*, tr. and ed. John P. Dolan (New York, 1964), p. 36.

[8] Ibid., p. 39.

[9] *Antibarbari*, *Opera omnia*, I-1, p. 136/29-30; *Collected Works of Erasmus*, 23-1, p. 121/2-4.

spiritual life'.[10] The bias of Erasmus's Christian-humanist synthesis was Platonic and transcendental, and involved a spiritual
progression away from the life of the body and visible things,
which are imperfect, towards the invisible world and 'those
things that are real'.[11] There have been attempts to deny the
incipient dualism in Erasmus by claiming a teleological harmony between the orders of nature and grace in his thought, but
all such accounts depend upon the notion that 'in order to make
sense of the text [i.e. Erasmus's] . . . the reader must finally be
able to decode the rhetoric' – in other words, ignore what
Erasmus actually wrote.[12] As it is, the otherworldly tendency in
Erasmus's thinking worked counter to the type of experience a
humanist was bound to encounter in the (often sordid) world of
Tudor politics. This can be seen in Erasmus's advice to Colet
after the latter had complained about the trouble he was in after
having delivered his famous sermon before Convocation:

> I'd like to see you withdrawn to as great a distance as
> possible from the world's affairs: not because I fear this
> world may entangle you in her allurements and claim
> possession of you as her own, but because I'd rather see
> your distinguished talents, eloquence and learning wholly
> devised for Christ. But if you can't completely get clear,
> still beware of sinking daily deeper in that bog. Perhaps
> defeat would be better than victory at such a cost; for the
> greatest of all blessings is peace of mind.[13]

Erasmus himself never had to encounter the reality of court
politics at first hand, but those of his disciples who did often
manifested the very response he urges here: retreat into a withdrawn spirituality once the affairs of the world threatened to
impinge upon one's peace of mind.

[10] *Enchiridion, The Essential Erasmus*, pp. 51-2.

[11] Ibid., pp. 59, 61-3.

[12] Bradshaw, 'The Christian humanism of Erasmus', esp. pp. 420, 446.
Bradshaw argues (unconvincingly to this reader) that all apparent dualistic
tendencies in Erasmus can be explained away as exigencies of the particular
polemical argument of each work concerned.

[13] Erasmus to Colet, 11 July 1513, printed in *Humanism, Reform, and Reformation in England*, ed. Arthur J. Slavin (New York, 1969), p. 8.

How did this distinctive blend of humanism and piety strike the humanist community in England? In the spheres of pedagogy and religion the influence was considerable. It can be traced in Erasmus's relations with English friends such as Colet and More, and with Cambridge men such as Henry Bullock, Richard Croke, Thomas Lupset, Richard Fox, and many others. Unquestionably, Erasmus had a great effect on education in the schools and universities.[14] He was equally responsible for leading many to a new kind of spiritual experience through their reading of his *Novum instrumentum*, his restored Greek New Testament with its new Latin translation. Thomas Bilney, later burnt as a heretic, affirmed that he had been 'allured rather by the Latin than by the word of God'.[15] But many of the English were suspicious of the political implications of Erasmian humanism from the outset.

Chief among the doubters was Thomas More. His reservations can be inferred from a comparison of *Utopia* with Erasmus's *Institutio principis christiani*. The two books are companion works, written at the height of the friendship between More and Erasmus. In early 1515 Erasmus had been invited to join the court of the future emperor, Charles V, and the *Institutio* was designed as advice for that prince. More began *Utopia* some time in July or August of the same year during a lull in diplomatic negotiations in Flanders. What is sometimes overlooked is that Erasmus visited England in the spring of 1515, from where he mentioned in a letter to Domenico Grimani that he was busy on the treatise he intended for Charles.[16] It is thus likely that More could have read a draft of the *Institutio*, or at the very least could have heard Erasmus discuss it, for there are enough resemblances between Utopian polity and Erasmus's image of the ideal state to lead one to suppose that *Utopia* was written as his response to the latter. Just as Erasmus argues that a prince

[14] See McConica, *English Humanists*, pp. 48-51, 89ff.; H. C. Porter, *Reformation and Reaction in Tudor Cambridge* (Cambridge, 1958), p. 31ff.; and Caspari, *Humanism and the Social Order*, pp. 32-3.

[15] Quoted by Porter, *Tudor Cambridge*, p. 39.

[16] *Opus epistolarum Des. Erasmi Roterodami*, ed. P. S. Allen and others (Oxford, 1906-47), p. 334, ll. 170-2.

should cut off useless extravagances, avoid wars, resist seeking to extend the boundaries of his kingdom;[17] that a very few laws suffice, and that they should be set forth very simply and provide not only punishments but also rewards;[18] that idleness and the exaltation of wealth is the source of much crime, and that simple theft should not be punished by death while more serious crimes go almost unscathed;[19] so, too, does More present a state whose institutions embrace those very ideals in order to avoid the same vices. The correspondences extend even to agreement that the incorrigible and recalcitrant must finally be put to death.[20] But the dialogue form of *Utopia* makes it a much more ambiguous work than the straightforward *speculum principis* of Erasmus. It is Raphael Hythlodaeus, the idealistic 'speaker of nonsense', who has been to Utopia, describes it, and believes he has seen an ideal state which is actually attainable in this world. Morus, the other main character, does not agree with him, and multiple ironies in the work suggest that only the outer appearance of things has changed in Utopia; the reality of human sinfulness and the need to adopt a *modus operandi* that takes it prudently into account, remains.[21] *Utopia* is, in fact, a 'put-case' in which More the lawyer tests what it would be like if Erasmus's idealistic exhortations could be realized in an actual state, and the test shows the proposition to be wanting.

It is wanting chiefly because the proposer is the victim of a degree of self-deception, shown, in turn, as springing from a naive blend of optimism and moral absolutism that can quickly turn into crippling, and equally distorting, pessimism. Hythlodaeus, although not identical with Erasmus, has a certain unnerving resemblance to him: in his restless need to travel unencumbered by fixed responsibilities;[22] in his exclusive preference for the Greek writers over any others;[23] and most clearly in his determination to deal uncompromisingly with the root cause

[17] *The Education of a Christian Prince*, ed. Born, pp. 215-16.
[18] Ibid., pp. 221-3, 234.
[19] Ibid., pp. 225, 228.
[20] Ibid., p. 224; *Opera omnia*, IV-1, p. 197/931-3; More, *CW*, IV, p. 190/25-7.
[21] These ironies are fully described in Fox, *Thomas More*, ch. 2.
[22] More, *CW*, IV, pp. 51, 55-6.
[23] Ibid., p. 181/4-6.

of abuse. In the *Querela Pacis*, for example, Erasmus offers very few practical suggestions as to how peace can be promoted; instead, he insists that 'we must look for peace by purging the very sources of war, false ambitions and evil desires. As long as individuals serve their own personal interests, the common good will suffer.'[24] Hythlodaeus's enthusiasm for Utopian polity springs from his belief that the root cause has been remedied: the abolition of money has 'extirpated the roots of ambition and factionalism along with all the other vices'.[25] Tragically, the ironies of the fiction show what Hythlodaeus cannot see: that his claim is not entirely true. *Utopia* shows More acknowledging that there is a great gap between the Erasmian sense of what 'ought' to be, and the cruel reality of what *can* be. While he was drawn to Erasmus's fervent idealism, More reluctantly conceded that as far as political realities were concerned, it was practically, if not totally, irrelevant.

There could be no real reconciliation between their respective inclinations as long as More was committed to a political career. This is shown most forcibly by More's treatment of the metaphor of life as a play, drawn from Lucian's *Menippus*, compared to Erasmus's handling of the same *topos* in *Moriae encomium*. For Erasmus, human life is a play in which the characterization and make-up which hold the audience's eye is mere folly. Anyone who tries to take the masks off the actors and show their true faces to the audience would spoil the illusion and be thought a madman.[26] Moria's exhortation to men to adapt themselves to things as they are and have an eye for the main chance is heavily ironic, for it is exactly what Erasmus did not do. He habitually acted like the wise man in his own fiction whom he imagines dropping down from heaven to expose the truth of what is taking place in the human drama. In *Moriae encomium* the skyman's imagined observations merge into Folly's satiric attack on contemporary abuses, and both become indistinguishable from Erasmus's own voice as expressed in his other works.

[24] *The Essential Erasmus*, p. 193.
[25] More, *CW*, IV, p. 245/9-10.
[26] *Praise of Folly*, tr. Betty Radice with an introduction by A. H. T. Levi (Harmondsworth, 1971), pp. 104-5.

Morus in *Utopia*, on the other hand, approves of the play-acting, without irony: 'whatever play is being performed, perform it as best you can, and do not upset it all simply because you think of another which has more interest', he urges Hythlodaeus.[27] At the heart of this divergence lies a different understanding of the human situation. For Erasmus, its imperfection is an aberration; for More, its imperfection was instrumental, and thus unavoidable, because God, in his wise providence, had made the world willingly, and not naturally, that is, not 'to the vtterest poynt of souerayne goodnes' that he could have done, but only as good as it suited him, so that its very imperfections might act as a check to human pride.[28] Whereas for Erasmus the play-acting was part of the corruption to be remedied, for More it constituted the most efficacious way of ensuring that what could not be made perfectly good was made as little bad as possible.[29]

Given the fundamental disagreement between their respective world views, it is not surprising to find that More's sense of the benefits of humanism differed subtly from Erasmus's as well. In his *Letter to the University of Oxford* of 29 March 1518, More defended a liberal education on the grounds that 'animam ad virtutem praeparat'.[30] The Erasmian-minded translator will render this as Erasmus himself might have read it, as 'train the soul in virtue'.[31] Erasmus's own compilations of *adagia, apophthegmata,* and *parabolae* imply how he thought this training was effected: by selectively extracting pills of moral wisdom from the classical writers, sweetened by a refined and elegant style. More's *Letter to Oxford*, however, does not say what the translator says it does: a liberal education does not train the soul *in* virtue, it 'prepares' the soul *for* virtue, by imparting to it a wise sense of the meaning of the human situation ('rerum humanarum prudentia'), which is best gained from the poets, orators, and

[27] More, *CW*, IV, p. 99/27-9.

[28] See More, *CW*, VI, I, p. 74/26ff.; also Fox, *Thomas More*, pp. 147-51.

[29] More, *CW*, IV, p. 100/1 -2.

[30] *The Correspondence of Sir Thomas More*, ed. E. F. Rogers (Princeton, 1947), pp. 115-16.

[31] *Selected Letters*, ed. Rogers, p. 98.

historians.[32] More is clearly echoing Cicero here, but Cicero's word is 'sapientia', and the semantic difference between 'sapientia' and 'prudentia' is significant.

The non-Erasmian cast of More's thought is revealed even more clearly in the *Dialogue Concerning Heresies*: 'reason is by study / labour and exercyse of Logyk / Phylosophy and other lyberall artes corroborate and quyckened / and the iudgement bothe in them and also in oratours / lawes & storyes moche ryped.' Poets, moreover, do 'moche helpe the iudgement / and make a man amonge other thynges well furnyshed of one specyall thynge / without which all lernynge is halfe lame . . . a good mother wyt.'[33] Humanistic learning, for More, does not prepare for spiritualized transcendence, but prepares a man for action by quickening the faculties and equipping him with a realistic sense of the way things actually are in this world. Thus, while the two friends shared a great deal in common, they were not saying precisely the same things, although only More seems to have been aware of that fact.

If More showed signs of scepticism, the same scepticism was displayed, albeit unintentionally, by Richard Pace in his treatise *De fructu qui ex doctrina percipitur* ('On the benefit of a liberal education') of 1517. Pace appears to have been a scatterbrain (he died insane), and *De fructu* is an embarrassing display of bad taste and intellectual feebleness; nevertheless, he was actively involved in politics, first as secretary to Christopher Bainbridge, the king's agent in Rome in 1509, then as Wolsey's secretary from 1515, and finally as principal secretary to the king,[34] and hence, as the modern editors of *De fructu* note, 'the relevance of his book to the general predicament of the court humanist in the Renaissance cannot be ignored'.[35] Pace wrote *De fructu* to give himself publicity and secure his place within the international

[32] *Correspondence*, ed. Rogers, pp. 115-16; *Selected Letters*, ed. Rogers, p. 99.

[33] More, *CW*, VI, I, p. 132/6-16.

[34] For Pace's life, see Jervis Wegg, *Richard Pace: A Tudor Diplomatist* (London, 1932).

[35] *De fructu qui ex doctrina percipitur* (*The Benefit of a Liberal Education*), tr. and ed. Frank Manley and Richard S. Sylvester (New York, 1967), p. xxiii.

humanist circle.[36] It is a eulogy of the new learning designed for
the boys of Colet's school at St Paul's, chiefly interesting for the
way that it undermines the praise it is ostensibly offering. Wherever Pace extols an art, his satirical sense of contemporary
conditions subverts the supposed benefits he is claiming for it.[37]
Rhetoric, for example, having listed the conventional reasons for
her pre-eminence – that no one can be praised, persuaded, or
dissuaded without her – laments the contrast between the old
days when Demosthenes ruled Athens and Cicero Rome and her
own times: 'for in this age . . . not only eloquence, but also all the
other arts are like some worthless, but rare thing. If we look at it
for half an hour, more or less, we don't care if we ever see it
again.'[38] Transparently, Pace does not feel that a liberal education has any real utility at all. When he recounts the tale of a
nobleman who angrily claimed that learning was good for
nothing but poverty, and that his son should sooner be hanged
than be a student, all that Pace can answer is that someone
brought up merely to hawk and hunt would not be able to reply
fittingly to a foreign ambassador.[39] Almost everything Pace or
one of his personified arts says is unwittingly designed to put
schoolboys off: the references to Erasmus's poverty undermining
the claim that learning leads to preferment;[40] the everlasting
disagreement Geometry alleges in all other fields of learning but
her own;[41] and, finally, the inexperienced schoolmasters, beat-
ings, and other troubles the boy will encounter before his work
finally ends up in honorable pleasure.[42] Unless the work is some
kind of *jeu d'esprit*, Pace is patently insincere in asserting the
benefit of a liberal education: it is of no practical utility in a
world in which advancement is procured more readily through
flattery than virtue, and where ambassadors are sent abroad to

[36] See Wegg, *Richard Pace*, p. 120.

[37] This point is developed at length by Sylvester and Manley in their edition
of *De fructu*, pp. xx-xxiii.

[38] Ibid., p. 91.

[39] Ibid., p. 23.

[40] Ibid., p. 117.

[41] Ibid., pp. 61-3.

[42] Ibid., p. 123.

lie for the good of their country.[43] And can Pace have been aware of the most pungent irony of all: that *De fructu* was written hard upon his energetic attempts on Wolsey's behalf to raise a Swiss army against the French, exactly the kind of practice that Erasmus was deploring?[44] Pace's Erasmianism, if it existed at all, was only a thin veneer.

Despite the doubt of More and the scepticism of Pace, Erasmianism did have its committed followers in England. Chief among them was Sir Thomas Elyot. His works are imbued with both the manner and substance of Erasmus, and his career demonstrates the dilemma of any Erasmian humanist who might chance to find himself in office.

Allowing for differences of temperament and some minor differences of opinion, *The Boke Named the Governour* may be regarded as Elyot's version of Erasmus's *Institutio principis christiani*. For Elyot, as for Erasmus, monarchy is the best form of government;[45] the qualities required of governors are similar for both: kindliness, clemency, courtesy, wisdom, integrity, self-restraint, liberality;[46] merit, not fancy, should be the basis of reward for servants of the state, and no good counsellor should be omitted or passed over.[47] Elyot's prescription for the education of a gentleman is little more than an expanded reworking of the system Erasmus described in the *Institutio*, *De ratione studii*, and *De pueris instituendis*, spiced with other gleanings from continental writers such as Patrizi and Castiglione.[48] Elyot also adopts Erasmus's method of using classical texts, which is to select didactic precepts and examples. Histories, like the classical poets and philosophers, furnish 'preceptes, exhortations,

[43] See Sylvester and Manley, ibid., p. xxiii.

[44] See Wegg, *Richard Pace*, pp. 65-113.

[45] *The Governour*, ed. Croft, vol. I, pp. 8-24; *The Education of a Christian Prince*, ed. Born, p. 173.

[46] *The Education of a Christian Prince*, ed. Born, p. 209; *The Governour*, ed. Croft, vol. II, pp. 38-119.

[47] *The Education of a Christian Prince*, ed. Born, p. 219; *The Governour*, ed. Croft, vol. II, p. 436.

[48] See John M. Major, *Sir Thomas Elyot and Renaissance Humanism* (Lincoln, Nebr., 1964), pp. 39-76, 78-83.

counsayles, and good persuasions, comprehended in quicke sentences and eloquent orations'.[49] They are 'the mirrour of mannes life, expressinge actually . . . the beaultie of vertue, and the deformitie and lothelynes of vice'.[50] Such statements highlight the essential difference between the humanism of Elyot and Erasmus and that of More. For the former two, to read the ancient writers is to excerpt them, to extract moral *sententiae*, to pillage material so as to give ideal abstractions a local habitation and a name. That is why Erasmus was compelled to warn the prince not to read histories at face value, because they show some things which are by no means to be approved for a Christian prince; the morally edifying bits, however, are to be rescued 'as you would a jewel from a dung heap'.[51] Similarly, Elyot warned 'that it were better that a childe shuld neuer rede any parte of Luciane than all Luciane'.[52] The utility of books lay in the paradigms of vice and virtue that could be constructed out of them to illustrate the 'fourmes' of things, and the motive for reading them was not to enlarge experience, but to censor and control it. For More, reading served to widen experience so that the reality of it could be more completely comprehended as the foundation for positive action. In his own humanistic works, *Utopia* and *The History of King Richard III*, he preferred to show it whole, not didactically and piecemeal.

The idealistic, didactic intent in Erasmian humanism rendered it ineffectual as a force in Tudor politics, however respected its arch-priest may have been. The final pages of *The Governour* reveal the source of its limitations. Elyot closes the work satisfied that he has treated the last part of 'morall Sapience'; but he also admits that the last part of moral wisdom is the *beginning* of 'sapience politike'.[53] Ironically, the work ends just at the point where one is interested to see how the precepts are to be turned into practice. Earlier, Elyot had promised to

[49] *The Governour*, ed. Croft, vol. II, p. 387.
[50] Ibid., vol. II, p. 401.
[51] *The Education of a Christian Prince*, ed. Born, p. 201.
[52] *The Governour*, ed. Croft, vol. I, p. 58.
[53] Ibid., vol. II, p. 447.

divide his book into two volumes, one treating the best form of education of noble children, and the other treating 'all the reminant . . . apt to the perfection of a iuste publike weale'.[54] A decade later, Elyot tried to fulfil that promise by publishing his *Image of Governance* (1541), purportedly compiled from a biography of the Emperor Alexander Severus by his secretary, Eucolpius, but it is a feeble affair, in no way answering to the requirements. Elyot chooses to present his ideal of good governance by assembling the 'actes and sentences notable' of Alexander Severus into 'a paterne to knyghtes, an example to iudges, a myrrour to prynces, a beautiful ymage to all theym that are lyke to be gouernours'.[55] The pattern lacks credibility, however. Alexander himself is as ideally virtuous as his predecessor, Heliogabalus, was exaggeratedly evil: he is 'moderate and sobre', showing 'constance and grauitie', and 'an incomparable mansuetude' and humility, yet is 'meruaylouse merye and pleasant' in recreation and 'amiable in communication'. He despises rich apparel and ostentation, so hates flattery that he refuses to hear orators or poets speak anything in his praise, yet 'so moch estemed and fauoured lerning that he ordeyned greatte salaryes to be gyuen to rhetorycians, teachers of grammar, phisitions, astronomers, geometricians, musiciens, deuisers of buildings and ingines'.[56] Elyot's ideal state, in fact, is a humanist wish-fulfilment fantasy. One supreme governor delegates authority to many counsellors in reward for their learning and virtue; youths are educated according to the order prescribed in *The Governour*, while maidens are 'brought vp in shamefastnes, humblenesse, and occupation necessary for a housewyfe'; idleness is extirpated; and salubrious libraries 'decked with pleasant imagerye' and conversation galleries provide recreation for those of high estate while soft music plays.[57] In its own way this humanist utopia is quite charming, but it is very remote from the problems

---

[54] Ibid., vol. I, p. 24.

[55] *The Image of Governance*, in *Four Political Treatises by Sir Thomas Elyot*, ed. Lillian Gottesman (Gainsville, Florida, 1967), p. 422.

[56] Ibid., pp. 228-33.

[57] Ibid., pp. 280-96.

and issues of Tudor politics in the 1530s. Moreover, Elyot seems
unaware of the fundamental irony of the story he is presenting:
that Alexander's moral rigour was so extreme that it provoked
his soldiers to murder him. Far from justifying the ideal of
governance it espouses, Elyot's work serves unintentionally as a
cautionary exemplum depicting a political failure.

The gap between Elyot's Platonic forms and Tudor reality
was highlighted by his dismal failure in office. After earlier
disappointment at being edged out of position as clerk to the
Council in 1530, Elyot got his big chance when he was
appointed ambassador to Charles V in early September 1531,
his mission being to promote Henry VIII's position concerning
the divorce. Secretly opposing the divorce, Elyot must have
found that the conflict between his beliefs and his brief effec-
tually neutralized him, especially as he appears to have been
playing a double game.[58] In any case, Henry had grown discontented with him by January 1532, and he was quickly replaced
by Cranmer.[59] Although he did not remonstrate with the king
about the divorce until after his return to England, Elyot later
expressed his belief that his integrity and outspokenness had
been responsible for his downfall; more likely it was his ineffecti-
veness, but either way his case shows the dilemma of the Erasmian humanist: idealism of the abstract and absolute moral
kind seldom survived the encounter with political reality. Either
the participant was forced to compromise, or else he disqualified
himself from office. Elyot tried unsuccessfully to compromise,
but was then driven back into his absolutist stance, as his two
dialogues of 1533, *Pasquil the Playne* and *Of the Knowledge which
Maketh a Wise Man*, vividly attest.

Elyot's case shows the point at which Erasmian humanism
reached the end of a cul-de-sac as far as English politics were
concerned. Elyot himself wryly acknowledged as much: 'diuerse

[58] Upon his return to England, Elyot sent a detailed report in cipher to
Gonsalvo De Puebla, son of the Spanish Ambassador, who had helped arrange
Catherine's marriage: see Stanford E. Lehmberg, *Sir Thomas Elyot, Tudor
Humanist* (Austin, Texas, 1960), p. 107.

[59] See ibid., pp. 100-2.

there be which do not thankfully esteme my labours, dispraysinge my studies as vayne and vnprofitable, sayinge in derision, that I haue nothing wonne therby, but the name onely of a maker of bokes.'[60] For the real humanist contribution to English politics one must look elsewhere: to a radically different type of humanism, evident in the circle of scholars fostered by Thomas Cromwell.

Thomas Starkey's *Dialogue between Lupset and Pole* exemplifies the differences. Starkey, one of the scholars enjoying the patronage of Reginald Pole in Padua during the early 1530s,[61] wrote to Cromwell towards the end of 1534 eager to be preferred to the king's service.[62] His bid was successful, for in February 1535 he was appointed chaplain to Henry VIII, after which he sent Cromwell a 'lytyl scrole', presumably that work entitled 'What ys pollycye aftur the sentence of Arystotyl', which was Part I of the *Dialogue* worked over for the occasion.[63]

Starkey himself did not recover from the disgrace he suffered when Pole finally displayed his resistance to the king's cause with *De unitate ecclesiastica* (1536), but his *Dialogue* may have had some influence on the drafting of reform legislation, as Elton has demonstrated.[64] It is therefore illuminating to anatomize the ways in which Starkey's assumptions and methods diverge from those of Erasmus.

In the first place, the dialogue form itself contributes to the meaning. Truth is not self-evident, and dialogue answers to the need for 'reasonyng and dowtyng for the cleryng of the truth'.[65] Moreover, the terms in which it is grasped are not definitive for all time, but convenient for the time, place, and circumstances. One of the most startling features of the *Dialogue* is Starkey's

---

[60] *The Image of Governance*, in *Four Political Treatises*, ed. Gottesman, p. 206.

[61] For a full account of this circle, see Zeeveld, *Foundations*.

[62] *Starkey*, ed. Herrtage, pp. ix-x.

[63] See G. R. Elton, 'Reform by statute', *Proceedings of the British Academy*, 54 (1968), p. 169; and Mayer, 'Faction and ideology', pp. 1-25, esp. p. 24.

[64] Elton, 'Reform by statute', pp. 174-5. The extent of this influence is questioned, however, by Mayer, 'Faction and ideology', pp. 24-5.

[65] *Starkey*, ed. Herrtage, p. 11; cf. p. 27.

willingness to allow for legitimate diversity. Lupset, for example, noting that 'the Turke, Sarasyn, Jue, and Chrystun man, and other dyuerse sectys and natyon[ys], dyssent and dyscorde in the maner of pollycy', nevertheless argues that so long as their laws are ordered according to the law of nature, they shall not be damned, 'seyng the infynyte gudnes of God hathe no les made them aftur hys owne ymage and forme, then he hath made the Chrystun man'.[66] Diverse forms of government, for Starkey, are instrumental, not definitive, therefore neither rule by king, council, nor democracy is inherently better than any other so long as the type adopted agrees to the nature of the people and is directed towards the common good.[67] Even the state of Christendom, he allows, although it is 'the most perfayt and sure, and most conuenyent to the nature of man', might not be the most perfect and flourishing that *could* be, 'for as much as hyt lakkyth . . . worldly prosperyte'.[68] Far from seeking his patterns and paradigms from the classics and the past, Starkey looks forward to what might be achieved in the future. There is a much greater sense of the possibility of historical progress in the *Dialogue* than in any of the other works discussed so far. In spite of recent attempts to disprove the prevailing view of Starkey as a liberal,[69] the optimistic tone and homocentric bias of the *Dialogue* seem the very opposite of medieval conservatism.

Starkey is, in fact, far more of a 'humanist' in the broader, anachronistic, modern sense. He replaces the old medieval *contemptus mundi*, still forcefully present in Erasmus, with an Italianate sense of the dignity of man and a secular excitement at 'the wonderful workys of man here apon erth . . . the gudly cytes, castellys, and townys, byllyd for the settyng forth of the polytyke lyfe . . . meruelus gud lawys, statutys, and ordynancys . . . infynyte strange artys and craftys . . .'.[70] His belief in the incomparable excellence and dignity of man makes Starkey resist the

---

[66] Ibid., pp. 18-19.
[67] Ibid., p. 53.
[68] Ibid., p. 60.
[69] See Mayer, 'Faction and ideology', esp. p. 2.
[70] *Starkey*, ed. Herrtage, p. 12.

transcendental drift of Erasmian doctrine. The spiritual life has its place in Starkey's commonwealth, as is dramatized in the episode where Lupset and Pole break off their discourse so that they might hear mass, 'and wyth pure hart and affecte cal for that lyght of the Holy Spryte, wythout the wych mannys hart ys blynd and ignorant of al vertue and truthe'.[71] But the life of spirit does not supersede concern with the things of this world, it animates and guides man's attempts to develop their life in it. Men need not despise material benefits in order to reach heaven: 'worldly felycyte and prosperouse state in thys lyfe present, excludyth not man from the most hye felycyte of the lyfe to come, but rather, yf he vse hyt wel, hyt ys also a mean wherby he the bettur may attayne to the same.'[72]

Starkey's assumptions thus freed him from both the Erasmian and Morean types of pessimism. Erasmus's political idealism was always liable to promote embittered withdrawal in those who tried to act by it in politics, like Hythlodaeus or Elyot, and found the attempt futile. Starkey rejected the attempt from the outset. He has Lupset dismiss Plato's commonwealth as a dream, 'for man by nature ys so frayle and corrupt, that so many wyse men in a commynalty to fynd, I thynke hyt playn impossybul'. Pole rejoins that one should not look for such heads as Plato describes, but ones 'aftur a more cyuyle and commyn sort'.[73] So far, Starkey's political philosophy sounds very reminiscent of that of Morus in Book I of *Utopia*, but Starkey went a lot further than More. Whereas More concluded that there was not much more men could do other than try to make what could not be perfected as little bad as possible, Starkey believed that a great deal could be done: because of the legislative and compulsive power of the state.

At the heart of Starkey's position was a radical political positivism that neither Erasmus nor More could ever have countenanced. Acknowledging that 'man, by instructyon and gentyl exhortacyon, can not be brought to hys perfectyon', Pole

[71] Ibid., p. 144.
[72] Ibid., p. 42.
[73] Ibid., p. 163.

argues that he can nevertheless be constrained to follow the course of right reason 'by feare of punnyschment', until 'by long custume' he might be 'induced to folow and dow that thyng for the loue of vertue wych befor he dyd only for feare of payne or desyre of reward'.[74] The power of framing and enforcing necessary laws was not to reside with the prince alone, but with Parliament, whose sovereignty was ultimately supreme.[75] Starkey himself would have preferred a mixed government, consisting of an elected monarch and a system of delegated councils, but recognized that perhaps it was best for England, in the circumstances, to take its prince by succession.[76] Nevertheless, his central idea of the effectual power of statute was shared by others among Cromwell's pamphleteers, notably Christopher St German, and became the lynch-pin of Henrician reform.[77]

It only remains to observe that Starkey, having found an effectual instrument for achieving reform, one that did not depend solely upon moral exhortation and pious hope, proceeded to give an acute analysis of the causes of existing faults, and proposed a whole series of practical remedies, many of which were taken up by the administration and enacted in statute.[78] His proposals are distinctive in dealing with what is and can be, rather than with what ought to be.

Erasmianism, then, was only one strand in English political humanism, and rather a minor one at that, however instrumental it may have been in furthering the cause of educational and religious reform. As far as secular politics were concerned, Englishmen tended either merely to pay lip service to it, or respectfully by-passed it in favour of other options. Those espousing it proved unsatisfactory politicians. At the heart of the English reticence appears to have been a mistrust of the transcendental

---

[74] Ibid., p. 147.

[75] Ibid., pp. 167-9.

[76] Ibid., pp. 104-7; 168-70.

[77] See G. R. Elton, 'Thomas Cromwell redivivus', *Archiv für Reformationsgeschichte*, 68 (1977), pp. 198-203.

[78] See Elton, 'Reform by statute', p. 174ff.

bias of Erasmus's humanism, with its emphasis on ideal forms. Erasmianism, being insufficiently concerned with practicalities, looked in the other direction from that in which most English humanists wanted to gaze as they sought to translate wisdom into political action. It is not without significance that true Erasmians favoured monarchy over alternative political systems; the notion of a good prince by-passed the need to face the exacting task of evolving a polity in which dominion was mixed, being more political than regal. In this, too, they were out of step with the times. The logical exemplar of Erasmian political theory in the future was to be James I, the philosopher prince, but what he represented, as history soon proved, did not find lasting favour with Englishmen.

3

Sir Thomas Elyot and
the Humanist Dilemma

Alistair Fox

Perhaps the most outstanding humanist of his generation was Sir Thomas Elyot.[1] The list of his achievements is impressive by any standards: he was the first writer in England to fashion the idea of an educated gentleman, in *The Boke Named the Governour*; the first to translate direct from Greek into English, in *The Doctrinal of Princes*; and the first to compile a comprehensive Latin/English *Dictionary*. His literary range extended to a collection of adages (*The Bankette of Sapience*), an extremely popular medical treatise (*The Castel of Helth*), an ideal commonwealth (*The Image of Governance*), and other works of political and moral philosophy. Throughout his literary career he was an early champion of the use of the vernacular for serious writing, personally introducing a vast range of new words into the language from Latin and Greek. In the nature of his interests, Elyot epitomizes Renaissance humanism. It is all the more interesting, therefore, to find that his career illustrates a dilemma central to the experience of all humanists who sought to enter political life: how to turn knowledge into action, and theory into practice.

Elyot's case shows why Erasmian humanism, in particular, had very little influence on political affairs in England. Its

---

[1] For the standard accounts of Elyot's career, see Lehmberg, *Sir Thomas Elyot*, and Pearl Hogrefe, *The Life and Times of Sir Thomas Elyot, Englishman* (Ames, Iowa, 1967).

combination of Platonic idealism and Stoic moral absolutism contained no theory of legitimate action that could allow the Erasmian humanist to act effectively in a corrupt world. Erasmus himself never had to wrestle with this problem at first hand, but Elyot, his most notable English disciple, did, and when the brutal reality of political failure shook his complacency, he discovered that his humanist doctrine offered him no help. Elyot, in fact, found himself actually living through both reactions to the humanist dilemma that Thomas More had imaginatively prophesied in *Utopia*. In order to attain a position of political influence, Elyot at first acted in a way remarkably like the 'civil philosophy' advocated by Morus in Book One of *Utopia*, by disguising his true beliefs for the sake of political expediency. But he soon discovered Hythlodaeus's objection to the indirect approach – that it is impossible to maintain one's moral integrity when beliefs and actions are in conflict – to be painfully valid. However when he tried the alternative course of outright plain-speaking, he found equally that Morus had been right in foreseeing that such advice would not be listened to. Nothing confirms the accuracy of More's prophetic analysis more vividly than Sir Thomas Elyot's real-life experience of the ironies it identifies.

Elyot's earlier career was not particularly noteworthy. Until he lost his position at court because of Wolsey's fall, he appears to have lived a life which was both sheltered and complacent. Born about 1490, he was educated at home in Wiltshire until his admission to the Middle Temple, his father's Inn, in 1510.[2] As he himself attests in the preface to the first edition of his *Dictionary*, he received no formal education after his twelfth year, but was 'led by himself into liberal studies and both sorts of philosophy'.[3] One biographer has suggested that he was placed in one of the Inns of Chancery between 1503 and 1510, but there is no evidence for this.[4] Others have argued that Elyot studied under

---

[2] Lehmberg, *Sir Thomas Elyot*, p. 3ff.; Hogrefe, *Sir Thomas Elyot*, p. 49ff.

[3] Lehmberg, *Sir Thomas Elyot*, p. 10.

[4] Hogrefe, *Sir Thomas Elyot*, p. 53.

Thomas More at this time,[5] but this case, too, rests upon unfounded conjecture. According to Stapleton, it was Margaret, Elyot's wife, who studied in More's school, not Elyot himself.[6] It is possible that Elyot attended Oxford; there was a 'Thomas Eliett' who took the degrees of Bachelor of Arts and Bachelor of Civil Law in 1519 and 1524 respectively,[7] but the identification is far from certain, and it is hard to reconcile with Elyot's own avowal that he received no formal instruction after his twelfth year.

We are presented, then, with a man who was 'bookish' by training and inclination, but without notable ambition. In spite of his entry to the Middle Temple, there is no evidence that Elyot was ever called to the bar or practised law.[8] Instead, he appears to have been content to enjoy whatever advantages his father could secure for him, while giving rein to his amateur enthusiasm for good letters.

As far as the active life was concerned, Elyot was rather a slow and late starter. His first position, that of clerk to the Justices of Assize of the Western Circuit (of whom his father was one), was probably gained for him by paternal influence. Elyot remained in this job from 1510 until about 1526 when Wolsey persuaded him to give it up.[9] It was not until several years after his father's death that Elyot gained a position on his own initiative, that of assistant clerk to the King's Council, to which he was sworn in on 4 May 1526.[10] By this time, Elyot was in his mid-thirties, a fact that suggests a fair degree of either passivity or complacency in his earlier life. Having drifted through life so

[5] Ibid., p. 59; Lehmberg, *Sir Thomas Elyot*, pp. 14-15.

[6] Ibid., p. 16.

[7] Registrum H (Registrum congregationis 1518-1536) of the Oxford University Archives, fo. 1ʳ, a transcript of which is printed in Lehmberg, *Sir Thomas Elyot*, p. 13. For the opposite conclusion, see *The Governour*, ed. Croft, vol. I, pp. xxiii-xxvi; and Hogrefe, *Sir Thomas Elyot*, pp. 49-50.

[8] Lehmberg, *Sir Thomas Elyot*, p. 11.

[9] Ibid., pp. 22, 28.

[10] Although Lehmberg claims that Elyot was named to the senior clerkship, it was in fact to the junior clerkship; see J. A. Guy, *The Court of Star Chamber and its Records to the Reign of Elizabeth I*, Public Record Office Handbooks, no. 21 (London, 1985), pp. 11, 83 n. 68.

comfortably, Elyot must have found it a huge shock when he was abruptly discharged from his post in 1530.

Elyot describes what happened in a letter written to Thomas Cromwell on 8 December 1532. He had been advanced to the clerkship by Wolsey 'for some goode oppynion that he conceyved of me'.[11] Elyot may have attracted Wolsey's attention with the *Hermathena*, a Lucianic dialogue in praise of eloquence written by one Papyrius Geminus Eleates, possibly a pseudonym playing on the correspondences between 'Thomas' and 'Geminus', 'Elyot' and 'Eleates', and 'clerk' and 'Papyrius'.[12] The work is dedicated to Richard Pace, Wolsey's secretary, with whom Elyot was sufficiently well acquainted to buy a sermon by John Fisher more because it had been translated into Latin by Pace 'than for the author or mater'.[13] Whatever the initial reason, Wolsey thought sufficiently well of Elyot to create an extraordinary clerkship for him. He persuaded him, furthermore, to resign his clerkship of the Assizes so that he could be continually present at the Council, 'promysing . . . that by his meanes the king shold otherwise shortly promote me bothe to more worship and profite'.[14] As junior clerk, Elyot found himself doing the lion's share of the work – recording statements of defendants and witnesses during examinations in the Star Chamber – while Richard Eden, the senior clerk, collected the stipend.[15] Elyot seems to have been prepared to put up with this state of affairs for four years because, one assumes, of his trust in Wolsey's promises of advancement. Neither the advancement nor an adequate fee were forthcoming. Wolsey did not give Elyot a patent until 1528, when he finally devised one granting the senior clerkship to Elyot, but conditionally upon Richard Eden's surrender of the patent granted to him in 1512.[16] Eden refused to relinquish his

[11] K. J. Wilson (ed.), *The Letters of Sir Thomas Elyot*, Studies in Philology, 73.5 (1976), p. 12.

[12] On Elyot's authorship of the *Hermathena*, see Constance W. Bouck, 'On the identity of Papyrius Geminus Eleates', *Transactions of the Cambridge Bibliographical Society*, 2, Part 5 (1958), pp. 352-8.

[13] Letter to Cromwell, 6 March 1536, *Letters*, ed. Wilson, p. 27.

[14] Ibid., p. 13.

[15] See Guy, *Star Chamber*, p. 13; Lehmberg, *Sir Thomas Elyot*, pp. 28-9.

[16] Guy, *Star Chamber*, p.11.

patent and, after Wolsey's fall, reasserted his right to the clerkship. A new patent of 20 April 1530 granted the principal
clerkship to Richard Eden and his nephew, Thomas Eden, in
survivorship, and Elyot was discharged from his post under
More's authority, being rewarded, as he complained, 'onely
with the order of Knighthode' which he found more costly and
onerous than agreeable.[17] In one fell stroke, ill fortune had
deprived Elyot of his patron, his position, his influence, and any
chance of recovering the financial rewards that were justly
owing to him. In effect, he had to start on the road to advancement all over again, and he was impatient.

It had taken him fourteen years to gain his previous position,
and Elyot must have realized that he could not afford to wait
that long a second time. He therefore chose political expediency
over principle, transferring his allegiance to the ascendant faction, even though he knew its aim was to secure the king's
divorce, which he secretly opposed. Possibly without realizing it,
Elyot had begun to act according to the advice Morus had
offered Hythlodaeus in *Utopia*: to be politically effective, one
needed to choose an appropriate part in the play at hand, acting
discreetly so as not to antagonize the other protagonists, in the
hope of being able indirectly to influence things for the better. To
achieve this, Elyot first sought to regain a place at court by
attempting the route tried by almost every other ambitious
scholar in the 1530s: he displayed his credentials by writing a
book, and he attached himself to the rising star in Henry VIII's
administration, Thomas Cromwell.

The Boke Named the Governour, published in 1531, was designed
to impress Henry VIII with Elyot's merit as a potential counsellor. The 'Proheme' is addressed to Henry, and the opening
praise of monarchy in the first three chapters is pitched to flatter
him. Elyot asserts the need for 'one soueraigne gouernour' in a
public weal on the grounds that all things are divinely fixed into
an hierarchical order: 'For who can denie but that all thynge in
heuen and erthe is gouerned by one god, by one perpetuall
ordre, by one prouidence? One Sonne ruleth ouer the day, and

[17] Ibid., p. 84 n. 75; cf. Letter to Cromwell, 8 December 1532, *Letters*, ed.
Wilson, p. 14.

one Moone ouer the nyghte.'[18] By implication, the king's power is absolute. Elyot emphasizes this point by declaring himself incompetent to write on the office or duty of a sovereign governor, 'holy scrypture affirmyng that the hartes of princes be in goddes owne handes and disposition'.[19]

It has been argued credibly that Elyot did not originally compose *The Governour* as a political work at all, but rather as an educational treatise that was later adapted for political purposes.[20] Certainly, there is a basic inconsistency between the unlimited power ascribed to the prince in the opening chapters of the work and the severe limitations imposed on that power by the virtues described in Book Three which the prince, along with other inferior governors, is supposed to embody.[21] Whether or not the opening praise of monarchy was a later addition or part of the original conception, it was contrived to appeal to the king's own growing belief in his imperial powers. Did Elyot have inside knowledge of the strategies afoot to procure Henry his divorce? This, too, seems likely, especially given Elyot's own close relationship with Thomas Cromwell.

Elyot had known Cromwell since 1519, as he reminds his mentor in a letter of 1538 copied on to the flyleaf of a copy of his *Dictionary*. The terms in which he addresses Cromwell suggest a friendship of considerable warmth: 'you will be very fond of me because I have kept the laws of friendship . . . You will clearly see that I am telling the truth if you will remember our first meeting, which was nineteen years ago, because the great feeling of kindness which I then conceived toward you has never diminished in the least.'[22] Moreover, Elyot's surviving letters to Cromwell suggest that he was accustomed to seeking Cromwell's aid and receiving his advice. After his dismissal from the

[18] *The Governour*, ed. Croft, vol. I, pp. 11-12.

[19] Ibid., vol. I, pp. 23-4.

[20] See Lehmberg, *Sir Thomas Elyot*, pp. 37-9; for counter-arguments see Major, *Sir Thomas Elyot*, pp. 3-35, and Hogrefe, *Sir Thomas Elyot*, p. 141.

[21] Lehmberg, *Sir Thomas Elyot*, p. 37.

[22] *Letters*, ed. Wilson, p. 36: 'me multum amplexabere, quod leges amicitiae retinuerim. . . Quod non mentior tute iudicaueris, primi congressus nostri memor a quo hic quidem annus est vndeuigesimus, quod maxuman erga te concoeptam beneuolentiam, non tandidem relaxarim' (ibid., p. 33).

clerkship, he not only looked to Cromwell for the recovery of his fee,[23] but also relied upon him to further his interests with the king: 'My lorde for as moche as I suppose that the kinges moste gentill communicacion with me . . . procedid of your afore remembrid recommendacions, I am animate to importune your goode lordship with moste harty desyres to contynue my goode lorde in augmenting the kinges goode estimacion of me.'[24] It was Cromwell, too, who discreetly warned Elyot that his desire to become a counsellor was futile, as Elyot acknowledged in a letter of 1533: 'according to your wise and frendely aunswere unto me, I can not compelle men to esteme me as I wolde that thei sholde.'[25] Given the long-standing friendship between Elyot and Cromwell, together with the later signs that Cromwell was repeatedly willing to act in Elyot's interest, it is entirely probable that he could, and would, have alerted Elyot to what would gain him favour in 1530. Cromwell was promoted to the Council in late 1530, having (according to Pole) proposed to the king a strategy for increasing his power by abolishing the authority of the Pope in England, thereby eliminating the divided loyalty of the clergy.[26] He would also have known of the theory of imperial sovereignty being devised by Edward Foxe and Thomas Cranmer for Henry VIII. The document containing this theory, the *Collectanea satis copiosa*, was shown to Henry in September 1530.[27] While Elyot hesitated to venture into the debate over ecclesiastical liberty, he did allow it to appear that *The Governour* supported an absolute regal sovereignty.

It worked. Henry and Cromwell must have believed that they could use Elyot to further the divorce, for in early September 1531, Elyot was appointed ambassador to Charles V. His brief was to 'fish out and know in what opinion the Emperour ys of us, and whether, dispairing of our old freindship towards him, or

[23] Letter to Cromwell, 8 December 1532, *Letters*, ed. Wilson, pp. 11-15.

[24] Letter to Cromwell (Autumn) 1536, ibid., p. 30.

[25] Ibid., p. 22.

[26] *Apologia ad Carolum V*, in *Epistolae Reginaldi Poli S. R. E. Cardinalis et aliorum ad se*, ed. A. M. Quirini (Brescia, 1744-57), vol. I, pp. 120-1.

[27] See below, pp. 156-61.

fearing other neewe communication with France, he seeketh
wayes and meanes that might be to our detriment or noe'. He
was also to remind Charles not to 'medle' in 'our great cause
between us and the Q'.[28] Elyot's mission was clearly one of the
utmost delicacy; that he was given it implies a large degree of
trust on the part of the administration. Yet we know, *post facto*,
that Elyot was violently opposed to the divorce on the grounds
that Henry was surrendering to bestial 'affects' in pursuing it.[29]
How, then, did he come to be given the job?

The answer is one which Elyot's biographers have been reluctant to believe: that Elyot, for the sake of political advancement,
initially dissembled the true nature of his feelings. They deduce,
a posteriori, that because Elyot opposed the divorce, he could not
possibly have been affiliated with Cromwell and the Boleyn
faction. The evidence, however, shows clearly that he was. In
fact, whether by design or accident, Elyot found himself acting
as a double agent, serving his own interests and those of Queen
Catherine as well as the king's, until the impossible conflict
between his beliefs and his brief caught up with him.

Apart from dressing up *The Governour* to appeal to Henry
VIII, Elyot also allied himself with the court faction most likely
to further his advancement. On 10 September 1531 Chapuys,
the imperial ambassador in London, wrote to Charles V naming
Elyot as the new English ambassador, remarking that 'Maystre
Vullyot . . . a este au cardinal et maintenant est [à] la dame,
laquelle ainsy que l'on m'a dit, la promen a ceste charge quant
et luy partira le maystre des rolez': Elyot currently belongs to
the party of Anne Boleyn (la dame), who has promised to
procure for him the position of Master of the Rolls as soon as the
incumbent retires.[30] Lehmberg assumed that Chapuys was
'quite incorrect' in thinking that Elyot was a follower of Anne

[28] British Library Cotton MS Vitellius B. xxi, fo. 60; Lehmberg, *Sir Thomas Elyot*, pp. 96-8.

[29] Hogrefe, *Sir Thomas Elyot*, pp. 136, 139-40, rightly draws attention to the reflection of Elyot's disapproval of Henry VIII's conduct in his harping on sexual morality in *The Governour*.

[30] *Cal. SP Spanish*, IV, ii, 239f.; Lehmberg, *Sir Thomas Elyot*, p. 30.

Boleyn,[31] but given Elyot's connections with Cromwell and the
fact that he was appointed ambassador at all, there is no reason
to doubt the truth of Chapuys's report. It is entirely feasible that
Elyot would have thought it worth appearing to be in the pro-
Boleyn camp if, on one hand, it ensured the advancement that
had so rudely been snatched from him by Wolsey's disaster,
and, on the other, if it could allow him to further Catherine's
cause through the kind of indirect action that Thomas More had
urged in *Utopia*.

Further despatches from Chapuys confirm that Elyot did
indeed act covertly on the Queen's behalf. After returning to
England in June 1532, Elyot not only briefed Chapuys on the
conversation he had had with Henry VIII upon his arrival, but
also sent a detailed report in cipher to Gonsalvo De Puebla, the
emperor's chaplain. De Puebla's father had helped to arrange
the marriage between Catherine and Henry in the first place,
and De Puebla himself in 1529 had been trying to arrange a
military alliance between Charles V and the Earl of Desmond in
Ireland against England.[32] If not downright treasonous, therefore, Elyot's actions could have been construed as such, had he
been caught, and it was probably fortunate for him that Cromwell did not have a key to De Puebla's cipher in 1532.[33] To
Chapuys, at least, Elyot seemed to be someone working very
much in the interests of Catherine. He reported to Charles V
that Elyot's conversation with Henry VIII on his return from
the continent had been greatly to Catherine's benefit, and that
he would continue to cultivate Elyot to advance Catherine's
cause.[34] One can infer that Chapuys and Charles would have
greatly preferred Elyot to remain ambassador; his pro-
Aragonese sympathies served their purposes better than those of

---

[31] Lehmberg, *Sir Thomas Elyot*, p. 30; cf. Hogrefe, *Sir Thomas Elyot*, p. 157; for
further evidence that Chapuys was right in placing Elyot in the Boleyn circle,
see McConica, *English Humanists*, pp. 122-3.

[32] *LP*, V, no. 1077; *Cal. SP Spanish*, IV, ii, 453; see also *LP*, IV, nos. 5322,
5323, 5501, 5620, 5938, and Hogrefe, *Sir Thomas Elyot*, pp. 174-6.

[33] Lehmberg, *Sir Thomas Elyot*, p. 108.

[34] *LP*, V, no. 1077; *Cal. SP Spanish*, IV, ii, 453.

Henry himself. Henry, however, had very quickly grown discontented with Elyot's performance, and he was recalled in January 1532, to be replaced by Cranmer.

Neither Elyot nor Chapuys fully understood the reasons for Elyot's recall. In a letter of 22 January 1532, Chapuys, announcing that Cranmer would take over as ambassador in a few days, expresses puzzlement: he does not know 'why they are discontented with the present ambassador'.[35] In another letter of 5 February 1532, Chapuys, having evidently tried to probe to the heart of the matter, reports that 'le roy m'a coloré la revocation de l'autre ambassadeur sur la requeste de sa femme': the king had pretended that Elyot had been recalled at his wife's request (presumably Elyot's wife, not the Queen).[36] Clearly, however, Chapuys did not believe that he was being told the full truth, since his ironic word 'coloré' implies a recognition that the king was dissembling. Elyot, too, was baffled, as he complained to Cromwell in a letter of 18 November 1532: 'I perceyve the kinges opynion mynisshed toward me ... and I ... hadd in lass estimation than I was in whan I servid the king first in his Counsayle.'[37] Upon returning to England, Elyot – so he told Chapuys – had remonstrated with the king, and the two dialogues he published in 1533 imply that Elyot ascribed his disfavour to this remonstrance. But Elyot had been recalled long before he remonstrated with the king, and Chapuys doubted whether his words had been effective in any case.[38] Besides, Elyot cannot have expressed his objections very forcefully, for his name appears in the list of knights and gentlemen to be servitors at the coronation of Anne Boleyn.[39] Unlike More, who refused to attend the coronation, he was not prepared to let his objections to the marriage become so plain as to threaten his own safety.

[35] *LP*, V, no. 737.
[36] Ibid., no. 773; *Cal. SP Spanish*, IV, ii, 898.
[37] *Letters*, ed. Wilson, p. 9.
[38] Chapuys to Charles V, 5 June 1532, *Cal. SP Spanish*, IV, ii, 453; Lehmberg, *Sir Thomas Elyot*, p. 107.
[39] *LP*, VI, no. 562, pp. 247, 249; see also Hogrefe, *Sir Thomas Elyot*, p. 187.

The real cause of Elyot's dismissal was probably his ineffec-
tuality. It is hard to imagine how he could have been anything
other than ineffectual when his personal views clashed so violently with the position he was obliged to represent on behalf of
Henry. Even though he had chosen to temporize, the very nature
of the neo-Stoic, Erasmian, moral absolutism that his other
works show him to have espoused, must have rendered it impossible for him to temporize effectively. To his cost, he experienced
the potency of Hythlodaeus's objections to the 'civil philosophy'
urged by Morus in *Utopia*:

> At court there is no room for dissembling, nor may one shut
> one's eyes to things. One must openly approve the worst
> counsels and subscribe to the most ruinous decrees. He
> would be counted a spy and almost a traitor, who gives
> only faint praise to evil counsels.
>   Moreover, there is no chance for you to do any good
> because you are brought among colleagues who would
> easily corrupt even the best of men before being reformed
> themselves. By their evil companionship, either you will be
> seduced yourself or, keeping your own integrity and inno-
> cence, you will be made a screen for the wickedness and
> folly of others. Thus you are far from being able to make
> anything better by that indirect approach of yours.[40]

Elyot's flirtation with the Morean indirect approach had not
influenced things for the better, nor had it secured for him the
advancement he craved. He was too moral to be a Machiavel,
but too weak to be a martyr, and to his own consternation he
found himself thrust into the political wilderness yet again,
having come no nearer to resolving the problem of how to turn
theory into action.

Having failed a second time to secure permanent advancement,
Elyot fell back upon the certitudes of his own moral vision. From
playing the part of Morus, in other words, he adopted the stance

[40] More, *CW*, IV, p. 103.

of Hythlodaeus. From discreet dissimulation, he switched to defiant assertion of his moral integrity and the preaching of absolute ethical standards he thought were being affronted by Henry VIII and his counsellors. Above all else, he sought to justify this extreme reaction and, at the same time, his failure to find a way of exercising his wisdom for the good of the public weal, as he believed a good humanist should. In short, he duplicated the response of Hythlodaeus to frustration, and thereby confirmed the acuteness with which More had foreseen the fate of Erasmian idealistic humanists once they encountered the harsh realities of political life.

Apart from lamenting his loss of favour to Cromwell and complaining at being out of pocket,[41] Elyot expressed his disappointment by publishing two dialogues in 1533: *Pasquil the Playne* and *Of the Knowledge which Maketh a Wise Man*.

His tenor of mind when writing these two works may be gauged from a letter he sent to John Hackett, the English ambassador in the Low Countries, on 6 April 1533. Having cryptically referred to the imminent annulment of the marriage between Henry and Catherine as 'a grete kloude which is likely to be a grete storme whan it fallith', Elyot reports that the king is in good health, and prays that 'truthe may be freely and thankfully herd', adding, 'for my part *I am finally determyned* to lyve and dye therin. Neither myn importable expences unrecompencid shall so moche feare me, nor the advauncement of my Successor the busshop of Caunterbury so moch alure me that I shall euer deklyne from trouthe or abuse my soveraigne lorde unto whome I am sworne.'[42] The wording of this passage is highly significant. In the phrase 'I am finally determyned', the word 'finally' implies that Elyot had not always been prepared to live and die in the truth in the past, but has now fortified himself sufficiently to abide by it in the future. Similarly, his protestation that he would not allow the advancement of Cranmer, his successor as ambassador, to tempt him to decline from the truth, suggests that he had indeed been tempted to do so. It manifestly galled

[41] Letters to Cromwell of 18 November 1532 and 8 December 1532, *Letters*, ed. Wilson, pp. 7-15.

[42] Ibid., p. 17. My italics.

Elyot to see others, like Cranmer, advanced because they were prepared to play the game. This resentment surfaces in his letter to Cromwell of 18 November 1532: 'I perceyve other men avauncid openly to the place of Counsaylors which neither in the importaunce of service neither in chargis have servyd the king as I have doone.'[43] In any case, the letter to Hackett betrays a lingering temptation on Elyot's part to ingratiate himself by concealing the full extent of his opposition to the divorce. Once this is recognized, the rigid moral positions Elyot asserts in his dialogues of 1533 become more explicable: they represent the resolution of a struggle within Elyot himself to resist the urge to temporize for the sake of promotion. Having 'finally' turned his back on that option, he decided to speak out with savage indignation at those who lacked, as he thought, either the integrity or the courage to imitate him.

The personal bearing of these dialogues upon Elyot's own situation has not been properly recognized hitherto because of a false belief that they were written 'to enlist support for More in his distress'.[44] This notion depends upon a supposed similarity between More's circumstances in 1533 and those of Pasquil and Plato in the dialogues: 'A "grave, wise Councelour" had been dismissed by the king because he refused to forsake a counselor's duty, which was to render to the king wise and honest advice, no matter how unpalatable.'[45] Such an identification, however, is not supported by the facts. First, More was not dismissed from office, he resigned on grounds of ill health, and however transparently disingenuous More's excuse was, it destroys the precision of the parallel. Second, More explicitly declined to meddle in the divorce after having given his initial reaction to Henry VIII in late September 1527. As he reminded Cromwell in a letter of 5 March 1534, 'after this I did never nothing more therein, nor never any word wrote I therein to the impairing of his Grace's part neither before nor after, nor any man else by my procurement, but settling my mind in quiet to serve his grace in other things, I would not so much as look nor wittingly let lie by

[43] Ibid., p. 9.
[44] Major, *Sir Thomas Elyot*, p. 97.
[45] Ibid., p. 96.

me any book of the other part.'[46] More had not been dismissed
because he rendered unpalatable advice to Henry as Plato had
done to Dionysius – but Elyot had, or at least believed he had,
when he had remonstrated with the king in June 1532. A second
argument alleged to prove that the dialogues are a veiled allegory on More's resignation involves the similarity between the
passage in William Roper's *Life of More* describing Charles V's
reaction to the news of More's death and a passage in Elyot's *Of
the Knowledge which Maketh a Wise Man.* According to Roper, the
emperor summoned Elyot and said: 'if we had bine maister of
such a servante . . . we wold rather haue lost the best city of our
dominions then haue lost such a worthy councellour.'[47] In *Of the
Knowledge* Elyot has Aristippus, the interlocutor, ironically
remark that if Plato can justify why God gives men sharper
tribulation than they deserve, then he is very wise indeed; if he
can explain away that problem, he, Aristippus, will affirm that
Dionysius was more liberal than wise when he gave Plato to
Polidis: 'For he hadde bene better to haue gyuen to hym six the
beste cities in Sicile, than to haue departed from suche a counsayllour.'[48] Again, Elyot was far more likely to have been allud-
ing to himself than More. In the first place, Elyot was not on the
continent in 1535 when More died, and considering that *Of the
Knowledge* was published in 1533, the words could not possibly
have referred to More's death. It is further argued that the
words were really spoken on the occasion of More's resignation
in 1532.[49] Elyot, however, had left the emperor's court in early
April 1532, a month before More resigned,[50] so that he could not
have heard the emperor make that remark even if he had done
so. The answer is quite simple: Roper clearly purloined what he

[46] *Selected Letters*, ed. Rogers, no. 53, pp. 207-8.

[47] William Roper, *The Lyfe of Sir Thomas Moore, Knighte*, ed. Elsie Vaughan
Hitchcock, Early English Text Society, original series, no. 197 (London, 1935),
pp. 103-4.

[48] *Of the Knowledge which Maketh a Wise Man*, ed. Edwin Johnston Howard
(Oxford, Ohio, 1946), p. 143.

[49] H. W. Donner, 'The Emperor and Sir Thomas Elyot', *Review of English
Studies*, new series, 11 (1951), pp. 55-9; see also Hogrefe, *Sir Thomas Elyot*, pp.
158-201.

[50] Lehmberg, *Sir Thomas Elyot*, p. 106.

thought was a well-turned sentiment suitable for his hagiographical, myth-making purposes. In this instance, the appeal of the fiction became more alluring than the historical fact.

Elyot, therefore, was writing in 1533 not to aid More covertly, but to express his own feelings towards the dilemma he recognized he was in. His purpose in *Pasquil the Playne* and *Of the Knowledge which Maketh a Wise Man* was threefold: to justify his own failure to gain a position of counsel, to lash out at those who had achieved such positions through hypocrisy, and to assert the truth concerning the king's conduct as he saw it.

Pasquil the Playne is primarily a justification of Elyot's decision to abandon political discretion for plain-speaking. He had come to believe that temporizing promoted more ills than it could remedy; moreover, as his own example proved, it could not guarantee political survival in any case. The time had come, therefore, for him to speak with the forthrightness of Hythlodaeus. The dialogue is cast as a dramatic parable in which 'plainnes and flateri do come in trial' when Pasquil, 'an image of stone / sittinge in the citie of Rome openly', encounters two 'cosen germanes', Gnatho, a courtier, and Harpocrates, a priest-confessor, both of whom have been called to counsel.[51] Gnatho believes in 'holdyng thy tonge wher it behoueth the. And spekyng in tyme that whiche is conuenient.'[52] Harpocrates is one who 'speketh littell or nothyng / but formynge his visage in to a grauitie with silence / loketh as if he affirmed all thynge, that is spoken.'[53] Through his mouthpiece, Pasquil, Elyot rejects both forms of action. When Gnatho cites Aeschylus in support of his attitude, Pasquil alleges that he has distorted Aeschylus's meaning. To hold one's tongue where it behoves does not mean compromise, but rather that one should simply await the appropriate time and place:

> Whan thou perceiuest thy Maister to be resolued in to wrath or affections dishonest. Before wrathe be increased

[51] *Pasquil the Playne*, in *Four Political Treatises*, ed. Gottesman, pp. 42, 62.
[52] Ibid., p. 49.
[53] Ibid., p. 63.

in to fury, and affection into beastly enormitie: As oportunitie serueth the, reuerently and with tokens of loue tow-
arde hym, speke suche wordes as shalbe conuenient.

Oportunitie consisteth in place or tyme, where and whan
the sayd affections or passion of wrath be some dele mitigate and out of extremitie. And wordes be called conue-
niente, whiche haue respecte to the nature and state of the
person, vnto whom they be spoken . . . For oportunitie and
tyme for a counsayllour to speke / do not depend of the
affection and appetite of hym that is counsayled.[54]

Here is a radical redefinition of the 'civil philosophy' Morus
offered in *Utopia*, which involved oblique action and role-play-
ing, with a necessary compromise between principle and practice. Like Hythlodaeus, however, Elyot now declared himself
unwilling to compromise, as if morality were a Lesbian rule of
lead and not an absolute rule.

In response to Harpocrates, Pasquil/Elyot endeavours to prove
that for a man to remain silent when he knows his master to be
infected with 'capytall synnes' is like failing to warn someone
who has a naked sword drawn at his back.[55] Besides, he argues,
silence is no guarantee of surety, since circumstances can alter,
and 'seldome is the maister in ieopardie / and the seruantes at
libertie / specially they whiche be next about hym' – as Elyot
well knew to his own cost from the shattering consequences of
Wolsey's fall which had wrecked his own career.[56]

The fiction of *Pasquil the Playne* shows that even while Elyot
was asserting this Hythlodaean stance, he was painfully aware
of the likely cost to hopes of advancement of adopting it. His
own remonstrance to the king had proved that waiting for the
convenient time and place did not necessarily work; either that,
or that he had monumentally miscalculated the appropriateness
of the occasion. Furthermore, plain-speaking had irreparably
damaged his own chances of advancement, or so he thought. In

[54] Ibid., pp. 55-6.
[55] Ibid., p. 66.
[56] Ibid., pp. 69-70.

Gnatho's comments on Pasquil's dilemma, one can detect a
veiled allusion to Elyot's own: 'thou wylt neuer leue thyn old
custome in railing, yet hast thou wyt inough to perceiue what
damage and hindrance thou hast therbi susteined: & more art
thou likely & with greatter peryll, if thou haue not good awayte,
what, and to whome, and where thou spekist.'[57] Conversely,
Elyot knew what he needed to do if he were to gain promotion;
Gnatho sums it up: 'leue nowe at the last thin yndiscrete libertie
in speche, wherin thou vsest vnprofitable tauntes and rebukes, I
may well calle them vnprofytable, wherby nothynge that thou
blamist, is of one iote amended, and thou losest therby preferment whiche thyn excellent wit doth require.'[58] Were Pasquil to
act as he advises, Gnatho promises, within two years he would
be 'newe paynted and gylt / and haue mo men wondryng at the,
than at any other ymage in Rome.'[59] Like Gnatho, he is to 'laye
apart the lesson of gentiles, called humanitie', and instead, 'sens
thou mayst haue good leysour / beinge not yet called to counsaile, pike out here and there sentences out of holy scripture to
fournysshe thy reason with authoritie.'[60]

   This last passage is particularly instructive. It shows that
Elyot knew what was really at stake: the validity of his own type
of humanism, and the moral wisdom it embodied, as a qualification for political life. Erasmian as he was, Elyot believed that the
wisdom he had gleaned from the ancients equipped him ideally
to be a counsellor; Gnatho, to the contrary, is saying that, in the
reality of court politics, such wisdom is irrelevant. In effect,
Elyot was caught in a bind. Humanistic study had furnished
him with a wealth of moral precepts, and all his ancient sources
emphasized the need for politics to be governed by philosophy;
but the very nature of the wisdom Elyot had gathered ensured
that he would not be listened to in a world dominated by corrupt
'affects'. Moreover, Elyot had rejected the alternative philosophy of political action which had tempered his neo-Stoic absolutism in favour of practicality. Nevertheless, there are signs in
Pasquil the Playne that Elyot felt ambivalent about the position in

[57] Ibid., p. 47.
[58] Ibid., p. 48.
[59] Ibid., p. 59.
[60] Ibid., p. 61.

which he found himself trapped. However loquacious Pasquil seems in the dialogue, he himself stresses that he only babbles 'but ones in a yere'.[61] Implicitly, Elyot is acknowledging that in spite of the theory of plain-speaking he is propounding, the occasions on which he is prepared to practise it are few and far between. At one point he plays on the fact that Pasquil is, after all, a *stone* statue; if everything were not 'so farre out of frame / that stones doo grutche at it', Pasquil would 'speake neuer a worde, but sit as styll as a stone, like as ye se me.'[62] The images suggest that Elyot, too, is normally as silent as a stone, being moved now to break his silence only because of the extreme danger he sees in developments at Henry VIII's court.

One reason for Elyot's Pasquil-like outburst in 1532 was his indignation that others, lacking both his wisdom and his scruples, were succeeding where he had failed. He admits as much when Harpocrates asks: 'Sens thou profitest so lyttel, why arte thou so busy?' To which Pasquil replies: 'To thintent that men shal perceiue, that theyr vices, whiche they thinke to be wonderfull secrete / be knowen to all men. And that I hope alwaye / that by moche clamoure / and open repentance, whan they see the thing not succede to theyr purpose / they wyl be ashamed.'[63] To some extent, therefore, he was trying to even the scales of justice. Elyot thought that he had couched his fable in terms so general that he could not be accused of attacking anyone in particular, 'for I haue sayd nothynge / but by the waye of aduertisement / withoute reprochyng of any one person / wherwith no good man hath cause to take any dispeasure.'[64] Elyot's protestation was as naive as it was dishonest. While Gnatho could indeed be any one of a number of Henry VIII's counsellors, it is not too difficult to discern in Harpocrates a thinly disguised portrait of Cranmer, Elyot's arch-rival.

Elyot discovered once again that worthy intentions were not enough to protect him from the displeasure of those in power. As the 'Proheme' to *Of the Knowledge which Maketh a Wise Man*

[61] Ibid., p. 97.

[62] Ibid., p. 98.

[63] Ibid., p. 99.

[64] Ibid., p. 100. Elyot repeated this defence in the 'Proheme' to *Of the Knowledge which Maketh a Wise Man*, ed. Howard, p. 9.

attests, *Pasquil the Playne* brought him into further disfavour. He
complains that some have maliciously conjectured that he had
written to rebuke some particular person: 'Thus vnthankfully is
my benefyte receyued / my good wyll consumed, and all my
labours deuoured.'[65] As far as grasping the ways of the political
world was concerned, Elyot was a very slow learner. He seems to
have been genuinely surpised to find that plain-speaking, even
mitigated by the indirectness of fiction, as his Pasquillade had
been, was no more effectual than his earlier discreet dissimulation.

Of the Knowledge which Maketh a Wise Man is Elyot's final
attempt to come to terms with the vicious circle in which his
philosophy had placed him. Whereas *Pasquil the Playne* was a
satirical Lucianic dialogue, *Of the Knowledge* is, as the title page
of the second edition declares, a 'disputacion Platonicke' consisting of five dialogues. Being essentially dialectical rather than
satiric, it serves as Elyot's own consolation of philosophy against
his realization that his Pasquillian pose, however heroic, was
doomed to failure. He concludes, finally, that no matter how
disastrous the consequences are, the wise man is obliged by
definition to speak the truth. In its own way, this disputation
identifies the dilemma of the idealistic humanist as brilliantly as
Thomas More had done nearly two decades earlier.

As a vehicle for the disputation Elyot chose an apposite
historical fable drawn from Diogenes Laertius – that of Plato's
disastrous experience in Sicily when he tried to warn Dionysius
that the latter was becoming a tyrant. Dionysius, inflamed with
fury, had given Plato to Polidis, who in turn sold him into
slavery, from whence he barely escaped with his life. The story
lent itself admirably to the purpose. Implicit parallels between
Dionysius and Plato on one hand, and between Henry and Elyot
on the other, allowed Elyot to express indirectly his feelings
concerning his exclusion from the Council. Certainly, the terms
in which Dionysius is described recall the unnamed 'master' in
Pasquil the Playne just as readily as they do the historical Dionysius, and Henry VIII most of all: 'he was a man of quicke &

---

[65] Ibid., pp. 4-5.

subtile wit, but therwith he was wonderfull sensuall, vnstable, & wandring in sondrye affections. Delytinge sometyme in voluptuous pleasures, an other tyme in gatheryng of great tresure and rychesse, oftentymes resolued into a bestly rage and vengeable crueltie / Aboute the publicke weale of his countraye alwaye remysse, in his owne desyres studious and diligent.'66 Likewise, when he makes Aristippus declare Dionysius's folly in dismissing Plato, Elyot has in mind his own dismissal: 'he hath moste folishly lost the[e]Plato, in puttynge the[e] from him, which by thy counsaile shuldist haue ben to hym so royall a tresure.'67 Elsewhere, Elyot's expressions of frustration at being denied the chance to render counsel are so frequent as to make it improbable that he had anyone else in mind, particularly as he was concerned to demonstrate his merit as a philosopher in the very act of writing this Platonic disputation.68 The figure of Aristippus was also very appropriate for Elyot's purpose, because as well as being a voluptuary, Aristippus was one of the flatterers of Dionysius. Hence, he is comparable to Gnatho and the contemporary flatterers in Henry's court whom he represents. In attempting to persuade Aristippus that he could not act in any way other than he did, Plato is thus presenting Elyot's own apology to any of his peers who had the wit to discern the analogy.

Having described how he came to be in rags and on the road, Plato proceeds in the first four dialogues to define the principles which led him to act as he did towards Dionysius. The difference between men and animals, he declares, is that men have knowledge and beasts remain ignorant.69 Ignorance consists in not knowing oneself, while knowledge consists of understanding what constitutes the similitude of God in man. When a man allows himself to be ruled by carnal 'affects' he surrenders his

---

66 Ibid., pp. 203-4.

67 Ibid., p. 231.

68 See, for example, *The Bankette of Sapience*, in *Four Political Treatises*, ed. Gottesman, p. 187; and *The Castel of Health*, Book III, cap. 12. As early as *The Governour* of 1531, Elyot had devoted a whole chapter to the topic 'Of repulse or hynderaunce of promotion' (Book III, cap. xiii).

69 *Of the Knowledge which Maketh a Wise Man*, ed. Howard, p. 71.

intelligible, God-like part and declines from his pre-eminence.[70]
The rebuke of the sensible part reactivates understanding, and
that is why God has providentially furnished many obstacles to
men's will, such as sickness, adversity, and vexation, so as to
check its corruption and help prevent him from falling into
ignorance.[71] By this point in the argument, Plato and Aristippus
are, symbolically as well as literally, near the end of their
journey.[72] Having proved dialectically that wisdom consists of
knowledge, Elyot goes on in the fifth dialogue to argue that
'none may be called a wise man, excepte vnto that knowlege,
wherin is wysedome, he ioyneth operation'.[73] That is why Plato
was obliged to rebuke Dionysius for his tyranny. Dionysius had
desired to see whether Plato's countenance, speech, and form of
living did express his reputed wisdom. Since Plato believed that
wisdom must be expressed in action, and since by believing
Plato to be a wise man Dionysius bound him not to deceive
him,[74] Plato had no option but to point out how far short
Dionysius fell from the true excellency of a king, or else he would
have proved himself 'to haue ben a foole and no wyse man'.[75]

Ironically, in demonstrating the logical inevitability of Plato's
action and its disastrous consequences, Elyot was confirming yet
again the ultimate insolubility of the dilemma confronting his
particular kind of idealistic, absolutist humanism. Plato knew in
advance that Dionysius was an unstable and vengeful tyrant,
and, as Pasquil urged, he tried to wait for the right moment,
'abydynge oportunitie to speake, which mought ryse of some
speciall demande of kyng Dionise' before trying to amend him
through sage counsel. Nevertheless, when that occasion arose
(when Dionysius asked him to declare the state and pre-eminence of a king), Dionysius was still enraged, in spite of all
Plato's tact. Plato had tried to make his point obliquely, by first

---

[70] Ibid., pp. 120-1.
[71] Ibid., p. 126ff.
[72] Ibid., p. 191.
[73] Ibid., p. 197.
[74] Ibid., p. 220.
[75] Ibid., p. 226.

describing an ideal king, and then a tyrant, in much the same way that Erasmus had in the *Institutio principis christiani*.[76] Dionysius, however, had refused to listen, and accused Plato of preaching folly, which prompted Plato to tell him his words savoured of tyranny.

The whole mimesis is invested with a tragic irony. As Plato observes, he had been put in a situation in which he had to satisfy Dionysius, but in which, if the king were not to understand, his words would have been futile at the same time as they destroyed Plato's credibility with the king.[77] Moreover, 'if he had not bene a Tyraunt in dede / he wolde neuer haue bene discontented.'[78] Ironically, however, Dionysius was, and was therefore bound to be discontented. Plato was in a situation in which he could not possibly hope to win, and by depicting it, Elyot seems to be acknowledging that the Hythlodaean stance he had asserted in *Pasquil the Playne* was suicidal, no matter how correct it was morally. *Of the Knowledge which Maketh a Wise Man* is invested with a strong overtone of Stoic fortitude.[79] Ultimately, Elyot was forced to concede that perhaps that was the only redress which the humanist-philosopher had.

In part, *Of the Knowledge* was a theoretical exercise, putting Elyot's case in its most absolute, uncompromising terms. One half of his mind, it seems, remained with the sceptical and doubting Aristippus, who still doubts the wisdom of offering oneself to peril without hope of benefit.[80] At the end of the disputation, although he has been somewhat persuaded to change his Epicurean viewpoint, Aristippus nevertheless declares: 'Wel Plato in such experience of wysdome I wyl not folow the[e]',[81] and perhaps that suggests that Elyot, too, was not fully prepared in reality to travel the full extent of the road down which his idealistic principles led.

[76] Ibid., pp. 204-11.
[77] Ibid., p. 212.
[78] Ibid., p. 217.
[79] See, for example, ibid., pp. 173, 185.
[80] Ibid., p. 225.
[81] Ibid., p. 229.

PART TWO

Politics

4

Prophecies and Politics in the Reign of Henry VIII

Alistair Fox

Manuscripts from the early Tudor period contain a surprising number of political prophecies, and frequent references in contemporary documents attest to their widespread use.[1] Most of the prophecies had circulated in the fifteenth century and even earlier, but after the accession of Henry Tudor in 1485 they seem to have been collected and refurbished with particular zeal. Indeed, several of the most important extant compilations date from the last three decades of Henry VIII's reign.[2]

Why should prophecies have been so popular during this time? What was their function and significance? There have been sporadic attempts to answer some of the questions, but no one has yet explained why this sub-literary genre had such widespread appeal and such an apparently potent life.[3] The

[1] For a descriptive survey see Rossell Hope Robbins, 'Poems dealing with contemporary conditions', in *A Manual of the Writings in Middle English, 1050-1500*, ed. Albert E. Hartung (New Haven, 1975), pp. 1516-36; 1714-25.

[2] Bodleian Library, MS Rawlinson C. 813; British Library, MS Lansdowne 762; and British Library, MS Sloane 2578.

[3] The standard work on political prophecy is Rupert Taylor, *The Political Prophecy in England* (New York, 1911; repr. 1967), which gives a general survey and examines prophecies as a literary form; Madeleine Hope Dodds shows that prophecies were used to foment rebellion during the Pilgrimage of Grace, 'Political prophecies in the reign of Henry VIII', *Modern Language Review*, 11 (1916), pp. 276-84; and Erwin Herrmann considers the English prophecies as part of a wider European movement, 'Spätmittelälterliche englische Pseudo-prophetien', *Archiv für Kulturgeschichte*, 57 (1975), pp. 87-116.

author of the only book on the subject (written in 1911) summed up the main difficulty: 'a thorough study of the material is too scanty and the whole field too large.'[4] The lamentably pedestrian quality of the prophecies as literature offers a further impediment; as one critic has put it: 'many of them, including the unpublished items, are such doggerel that they lack interest even as *literaria curiosa*.'[5] Nevertheless, the prophecies had a far greater social and political importance than is often supposed.[6] Socially, they provided a means for Englishmen to objectify their fears and hopes concerning developments in Henry VIII's reign. Indeed, the political prophecy was exploited to create a myth of destiny which foreshadowed, and perhaps even promoted, the later idea of England as the elect nation. Politically, they were important because both supporters and opponents of Henry's reform policy used them as propaganda. Eventually the administration found them so dangerous that an energetic attempt was made to suppress them.[7] All the main characteristics of the prophecies can be demonstrated from two important manuscript compilations: Oxford Bodleian Library MS Rawlinson C. 813, and British Library MS Lansdowne 762. Both typify a kind of manuscript collection popular at the time, containing a wide variety of material ranging from lyric verses to satirical *facetiae* (such as the distinction between a harlot, a hunter, and a whore).[8] Both are products of the period leading up to the break with Rome.[9] In particular, prophecies form the bulk of the

[4] Taylor, *The Political Prophecy*, p. ix.

[5] Robbins, 'Poems dealing with contemporary conditions', p. 1516.

[6] Elton, *Policy and Police*, analyses the impact of prophecies and the administration's response to them.

[7] See ibid., pp. 78-82.

[8] Rawlinson C. 813, fo. 35^r.

[9] The Rawlinson MS refers to the execution of the Duke of Buckingham, and so must have been compiled after 1521, the Lansdowne MS quotes a passage from Skelton's *Colin Clout*, and so must have been written after 1519-20, and both seem to be earlier than 1534, since the different orders of friars and their quarters in London are mentioned as still existing. On the dating of the Lansdowne MS see James A. H. Murray (ed.), *The Romance and Prophecies of Thomas of Ercildoune*, Early English Text Society, original series, no. 61 (London, 1875), p. lvix; for the dating of Rawlinson MS C. 813 see Sharon L. Jansen Jaech, 'English political prophecy and the dating of MS Rawlinson C. 813', *Manuscripta*, 25 (1981), pp. 141-50.

material, and a remarkable number of prophecies are duplicated
in each. Given that the two manuscripts were compiled independently (substantive variants in the shared texts prove that),[10]
the prophetic material in them gives us a clear idea of what was
circulating in England during the 1520s and early 1530s.

The prophecies fall into several groups differentiated according to the seer to whom they are ascribed. The most numerous
are those attributed to Merlin. Usually beginning with a formu-
laic phrase such as 'Of all the merveles off merlion howe
he makes his mone take tende to his talking . . .', they are loose
imitations of 'The Prophecies of Merlin' in Geoffrey of Monmouth's *Historia regum Britanniae* and the prophetic passages in
his *Vita Merlini*. Characteristically, they use symbolism which is
heraldic or totemistic, involving animals and plants. In one
recurrent type a lion is banished to Berwick, and fierce contention rages between such creatures as a young bull and a bastard,
a wolf and a bear, while a dragon destroys a city and puts a king
to flight for fear. Anarchy reigns until a young prince restores
the temporalty and spiritualty to peace.[11] Alternatively, the
prophecy describes a struggle involving a lily, a lion, an eagle
from the east, and a son of a man bearing wild beasts in his
arms, whose kingdom is in the land of the moon. The son of a
man joins with the eagle, the lily loses his crown, fierce battles
rage, and the greater part of the world is destroyed, with the
head of the world being cast down. Then the son of a man is
crowned, goes to the holy land, makes an alliance with the eagle,
and universal peace and plenty are achieved for the world.[12]

A second kind of prophecy is that loosely based upon the
writings of the Pseudo-Methodius (St Methodius was a bishop
in Lycia who died about A.D. 311).[13] It, too, picks up details from

[10] See, for example, the texts of 'The Prophisies of Rymour, Beid, and
Marlyng', Rawlinson C. 813, fo. 72[r]ff., and Lansdowne 762, fo. 75ff.

[11] See, for example, the 'Prophecia Johannis Merlyon', Rawlinson C. 813,
fos. 88[v]-89[v].

[12] 'A prophesye off Marleon', Rawlinson C. 813, fos. 94[v]-95[r].

[13] Rawlinson C. 813, fos. 90[v]-94[v]; see also Taylor, *The Political Prophecy*, p. 35.
On the Pseudo-Methodius and his influence, see Paul J. Alexander, 'The
diffusion of Byzantine Apocalypses in the medieval West and the beginnings of
Joachimism', in *Prophecy and Millenarianism: Essays in Honour of Marjorie Reeves*,
ed. Ann Williams (Harlow, Essex, 1980), pp. 55-106, esp. pp. 62-5.

Geoffrey of Monmouth. We have similar ominous warnings of castles to be destroyed, seas rising up in storms, famines, planetary changes, an invasion of the Scots, and the advent of a national deliverer. The mode of presentation, however, differs from the Merlin, or Galfridian, type, and belongs to the tradition of the Sibylline oracles.[14] Instead of using figurative allegory, the writer describes these events as literal, in order to evoke as powerful an image of apocalyptic disaster as possible. Yet another group consists of prophecies attributed to John of Bridlington, alias John Thwenge, prior of Bridlington. Even before he died (in 1379), Bridlington had become associated with a Latin prophecy, *'Febribus infectus'*.[15] In the mid-fifteenth century material from this prophecy was combined with Merlin material to produce 'The Cock in the North', one of the most widespread of all the prophecies, of which there are versions in both the Rawlinson and the Lansdowne manuscripts. There occur many of the familiar symbolic figures (a dreadful dragon, a bull and a bastard, a mole and a mermaid, the eagle and the antelope); fierce battles are to leave wives and maidens mourning; and a dead man is to rise and make peace, after which he will win the holy cross and be buried in the vale of Jehoshaphat.[16]

Originally these prophecies had an allusive, topical meaning. The context for Geoffrey of Monmouth's vaticinations was the civil discord from the dynastic quarrel between Stephen and Matilda, the invasion of David I of Scotland, and the rise of adventurers.[17] The 'two moons in the air' which are found in the *Vita Merlini* and recur in the sixteenth-century prophecies, originally signified the two Matildas: Stephen's queen, and the Empress Matilda, claimant to the English throne.[18] Once the symbols and *topoi* had lost their original meaning, later periods adapted them to their own purposes. For example, the 'cock' in

[14] On Sibylline literature, see Alexander, ibid., pp. 56-62.

[15] See Robbins, 'Poems dealing with contemporary conditions', p. 1522; Taylor, *The Political Prophecy*, pp. 51-8.

[16] Rawlinson C. 813, fo. 121^r; Lansdowne 762, fos. 62^r-63^r.

[17] See Basil Clarke (ed.), *Life of Merlin: Geoffrey of Monmouth, Vita Merlini* (Cardiff, 1973), p. 6.

[18] Ibid., pp. 133, 154.

the north originally referred to the Black Prince as future king of France through a pun on 'galli' (cocks) and 'Galli' (Gauls); however, in the early fifteenth century the faction comprising the Percys, Glendower, and Mortimer used it to signify Sir Henry Percy (Hotspur) in its attack on Henry IV.[19] Still later versions used other animal symbols to refer to the Wars of the Roses. In the Rawlinson 'Prophecia Johannis Merlyon' the boar and the bull are made to stand for Oxford and Clarence, while the female griffin and the antelope signify Margaret of Anjou and her son.[20] Clearly, the ingredients in the prophecies were valued not for any fixed meaning, but because their meaning was fluid and indeterminate.

It is all the more interesting, therefore, to find that there was a concerted effort in the 1520s and 1530s to synthesize all the prophecies that had been circulating since the fourteenth century into one grand design having a contemporary national and international relevance. The synthesis appears in its most ambitious form in 'The Prophisies of Rymour, Beid, and Marlyng', a lengthy pseudo-romance that occurs in both Henrician manuscripts under discussion.[21] In turn, this synthesis was made possible by an earlier work, the romance called *Tomas of Ersseldoune*, composed in the border area some time after 1388. Widely circulating throughout the fifteenth century, this romance introduced prophetic elements of yet another seer, Thomas of Erceldoune, commonly known as 'the Rhymer' (notable for having prophesied the death of Alexander III of Scotland). Erceldoune's prophetic images are more powerful than the Galfridian ones, being less simply figurative and more expressionistic, and carrying with them a feeling of the supernatural:

[19] See Dodds, 'Political prophecies', p. 280; Taylor, *The Political Prophecy*, p. 54; Charles Lethbridge Kingsford, *English Historical Literature in the Fifteenth Century* (New York, 1913), p. 236; and Robbins, 'Poems dealing with contemporary conditions', p. 1519.

[20] Kingsford, *English Historical Literature*, p. 237.

[21] Rawlinson C. 813, fos. 72^v-88^r; Lansdowne 762, fos. 75^r-88^v. The Lansdowne text is printed in *Ercildoune*, ed. Murray, Appendix II, pp. 52-61. Murray collates this text with that in Rawlinson C. 813, but the collation is unreliable and inaccurate. A Scottish version occurs in *The Whole Prophesie of Scotland* (1603; repr. for the Bannatyne Club, vol. 44, Edinburgh, 1833).

> iij crowned kinges, with dyntes sore
> shalbe slayne, & vnder be.
> a Raven shall comme ouer þe moore
> and after him a crowe shalle flee,
> to seke þe moore, without reste,
> after a cross is made of stone,
> ouer hill & dale, bothe easte & weste.[22]

This prophecy of a fearsome battle at Gladesmoor left an indelible impression in the imagination of later compilers, as did the pervasive suggestions of the supernatural. Even more crucially, *Tomas of Ersseldoune* furnished a narrative framework capable of containing all the disparate elements of other prophecies in a pattern that could be comprehended.

The romance draws upon the conventions of the traditional dream allegory as developed by poets such as Chaucer and Lydgate. In the Thornton manuscript of *Tomas of Ersseldoune* Thomas is depicted as wandering by Huntley banks one glad May morning when he sees a lovely lady riding on a dapple-gray horse. Discovering that she is not the Virgin Mary as he first suspected, Thomas makes love to her seven times, whereupon her beauty is transformed into hideous ugliness and she takes him with her to dwell at her lord's castle in middle earth for three years. At the end of this time the lady gives Thomas prophetic visions referring to Scottish history, past and future, and returns him to Eildon tree in Huntley banks. Although her prophecies at first allude to actual events during the minority of David II, they quickly turn into a fanciful amalgam of the main *topoi* from Geoffrey of Monmouth's *British History*. As one might anticipate, the prophecy ends by predicting the advent of a bastard out of the west who will unite Britain, hold a grand parliament, overcome all his foes, and die in the holy land.

However bizarre *Tomas of Ersseldoune* might seem to us now, it was one of the most popular romances of the fifteenth century

---

[22] *Tomas of Ersseldoune* , in *Ercildoune*, ed. Murray, p. 38/567ff. of MS Sloane 2578. For the date of the poem, see Taylor, *The Political Prophecy*, p. 70. In transcribing quotations from this edition and the manuscripts themselves, I have silently expanded all contractions except the ampersand.

and proved very useful to the pseudo-prophets of the early sixteenth century. It not only allowed a lot of disparate material to be held together within a coherent whole, but it also had a beginning, a middle, and an end capable of suggesting a firm shape to events in a sequence of historical time. The prophet-seers in the early Tudor period seized upon these advantages, and in 'The Prophisies of Rymour, Beid, and Marlyng' came up with a new synthesis that ordinary Englishmen found enormously persuasive as a vision of what their past, present, and future might mean.

With a brilliant stroke, the Tudor poet grasped what none of his predecessors had fully realized: that the pattern inherent in Geoffrey's prognostications and *Tomas of Ersseldoune* could be made to conform very easily to the pattern in the Book of Revelation. He may have been influenced by pseudo-Joachimist writings in this respect, although the apocalyptic treatment is less elaborate than in Joachim's scheme, and may have been derived independently.[23] At every point he arranged and added to his source material to strengthen the resemblance. Whereas Thomas, in the earlier romance, had found that his holy-seeming lady was really a witch, the Tudor poet makes her a 'crowned quene' and encourages an identification between her and the Virgin Mary by surrounding her 'with a companye off Angeles ffree' and giving her 'a holi water spingele in hur hande' with which she hallows the ground.[24] Her appearance thus matches that of the woman in Revelation 12 with a crown of twelve stars, who is herself a type of the New Eve, and hence of the Virgin. Several lines later, when the lady intervenes to separate St George and St Andrew, who are engaged in combat, she explicitly says:

> . . . ffrom my dere Son commyn am I
> to take the ffelde you twoo betwene
> where ever itt ffall in burghe or bye.[25]

---

[23] On Joachimite prophecy, see Marjorie Reeves, *The Influence of Prophecy in the Later Middle Ages: A Study in Joachimism* (Oxford, 1969).

[24] Rawlinson C. 813, fos. 73ʳ-73ᵛ.

[25] Ibid., fo. 74ʳ.

The second major change the Tudor poet makes is to deloca-
lize the battle of Gladesmoor, a fierce conflict predicted in the
Ercildoune prophecies that recurs frequently in the later versions.[26] Once she has 'halowed the gronde with hur hande', the
lady declares:

> here shalbe gladesmore þat shall glade vs all
> that shalbe glading of our glee
> þer shalbe gladesmore where euer itt falle
> butt not gladesmore by the See.[27]

Originally this prophecy referred to Gladsmuir in East Lothian,
a wide uncultivated moor which derived its name from its being
the resort of vast numbers of kites; however, the Tudor poet
develops the potential pun in the name, 'glad-us-more', so as to
suggest that this battle, when it occurs, will in some way be a
cause of joy to the people. He also denies the place any literal
relevance: Gladesmore is not the geographical location known
by that name, but some indeterminate place 'wher euer itt falle'.
The name is thus turned into an arcane prognostication of an
event that will bring about peace and happiness, not unlike the
millennial peace promised in the Book of Revelation.[28] By the
time the prophecy has concluded, we are able to match this
expectation with the universal peace achieved by the 'childe
with a chaplett' after his crusade to the holy land.

In making Gladesmoor figurative rather than literal, thus
linking it to the climactic confrontation in the Apocalypse before
the chaining of Satan, the poet at once reduced all the particular
historical and unhistorical conflicts in earlier prophecies to an

[26] See, for example, the Cambridge MS of *Tomas of Ersseldoune*, in *Ercildoune*,
ed. Murray, p. 36/560ff.

[27] Rawlinson C. 813, fos. 74^r-74^v. The Lansdowne version, which differs in
several minor respects, reads:

> here shalbe gladismore that shall glad vs all
> yt shalbe gladyng of oure glee
> yt shalbe gladmore wher euer yt fall
> but not gladmore by the see [fo. 76^v].

[28] Revelation 20:1-7; 21:4.

appropriately subordinate place in the overall design. They
were to be seen as manifestations of the tribulations that would
lead up to the final, climactic encounter. In 'The Prophisies of
Rymour, Beid, and Marlyng' this occurs when the poet asks a
dwarf who is standing nearby to elaborate further on 'What
shall ffalle or gladesmore be.'[29] As usual, he begins by 'predicting' recent English history, but whereas one might have
expected him to magnify the divisiveness of the Wars of the
Roses as the Tudor chroniclers did, the poet presents them as
merely the first in a sequence of conflicts extending right up to
Flodden and Henry VIII's battles in France at Thérouanne and
Tournai and, in unhistorical time, beyond. Personified moral
abstractions and images of discord and unnaturalness invest the
whole series with a quasi-supernatural significance:

> Charite shalbe laid awaye
> that Riffe in land hathe bene
> . . .
> The son ageynst the father shalbe
> right fercelye ffor to ffight
> then shall trouthe be baneshed ouer the See
> & faile bothe meane & might
> Then shall falshed & enuye
> blowe ther hornes on height.[30]

This is to last thirty-three years (from when the Duke of York
took up arms), after which 'A king shall reigne without righ-
twisnes' (Edward IV) and 'wrong warkes' prevail, until

> ther shall entre at milffort hauen
> uppon a horse off tree
> A banneshed buron that is boren
> off brutes blode . . .

This knight (transparently Henry Tudor) is to put the white
boar to death at Bosworth.[31] Working in many of the traditional

[29] Rawlinson C. 813, fo. 74^r.
[30] Ibid., fos. 74^v-75^r.
[31] Ibid., fos. 75^r-77^r.

Galfridian symbols (such as the red and white lions, the bull and
the bastard, the mole and the mermaid), the poet traces his way
past the plots involving Perkin Warbeck, the battle of Flodden,
and the taking of Thérouanne and Tournai, at which point the
'prophecies' cease to be historical. One can therefore presume
that this poem was composed soon after.

The writer has saved his big guns for last, however, for having
rid himself of historical events, he can combine all the most
horrible images from earlier prophecies with a few new ones of
his own to describe the battle of Gladesmoor. Altogether, they
evoke a fearsome vision of chaos and anarchy. England is to be
invaded by a king from Denmark and a king from Norway with
a black fleet, and 'Then shall the north Rise ageynst the southe,
/ & the Est ageynst the West.' Holy church will 'harnys hente'
and fight for three years 'euen as they seculers were'.[32] Most of
these motifs and the various symbolic animals that appear
derive from Geoffrey of Monmouth but, freed completely from
any topical meaning, they accrue an expressionistic luridness,
and their place in the total apocalyptic structure gives them
collectively a much greater force.

The Tudor poet's final innovation was to amplify the role of
the national deliverer by giving him a messianic mission. At
every point he enlarges upon the hints in his sources. In the *Vita
Merlini* Merlin prophesies that Conan and Cadwalader will
return from Brittany to create an alliance of Britons that will
throw off the Saxon yoke and restore the time of Brutus, a
prophecy repeated in the *Historia regum Britanniae*, where it is
revealed that this return will not take place until Cadwalader
has been to Rome to do penance and relics belonging to the
Britons have been transported back to Britain.[33] In the Tudor
prophecy deliverance is not to be deferred, but is to take place
before the king visits Rome. The young knight, who is to 'reigne
in welthe & Ryaltee / ffyve and ffyftee yere', will progressively
defeat his enemies so that in time 'the doble Roose shall laughe

[32] Ibid., fos. 81ʳ-81ᵛ.

[33] *Vita Merlini*, ed. Clarke, p. 105; *Geoffrey of Monmouth: the History of the Kings
of Britain*, tr. and ed. Lewis Thorpe (Harmondsworth, 1966), pp. 175, 282-3.

full right / & beire the gree ffor euer & aye.'[34] From this time 'all
warres is brought to an ende' and 'suche grace god shall send /
that exyled shalbe all syn'.[35] Only then will the king call a
parliament and appoint a protector so that he can lead a
crusade 'to ffeght ffor Jesu sake'.[36] The magnitude of this action
is vastly expanded from the modest prototype in the *British
History*. Not merely are British relics involved, but the relics of
Christendom itself; unlike Cadwalader, who is to do penance in
Rome, the king will receive homage there:

> The pope off Rome wythe processyon
> shall mete hym that same dey
> and all the cardinalles shalbe bowne
> In ther best arraye
> Ther shal knele iij kinges with crowne
> & homage make that dey.[37]

After winning seven mortal battles at Jerusalem and overcoming
the Turks, the conqueror will visit Sinai, where St Catherine is
buried, and win the holy cross, which he will send to Rome.
Then he will die in the Vale of Jehoshaphat and be buried with
the three wise kings who bore gifts to Christ at the nativity. Back
in England the Protector will be crowned,

> then shall ffalsehede be banisshed ffor aye
> And truthe shall redye be
> Trewe men bothe nyght & daye
> shall liffe jn Charyte.[38]

Far more than a merely national deliverer is suggested by all
this. Although the 'childe with a chaplet' is not identified with
Christ, he is Christ-like, and in his deeds one can trace the
shadowy outline of the Second Coming. The prophecy ends with
a prediction that all this will appear in the year 1531.[39]

[34] Rawlinson C. 813, fos. 83ᵛ-84ʳ.
[35] Ibid., fo. 84ʳ.
[36] Ibid., fo. 84ᵛ.
[37] Ibid., fo. 85ᵛ.
[38] Ibid., fo. 87ʳ.
[39] Ibid., fo. 88ʳ.

None of the pre-Tudor prophecies have such a strong apocalyptic outline as 'The Prophisies of Rymour, Beid, and Marlyng', but all other contemporary Tudor prophecies draw upon it to some degree. The same pattern is emphasized in the Lansdowne manuscript's version of 'The Cock in the North', with an even clearer parallel between the national deliverer and Christ:

> All grace and goodnes shall grow vs amonge
> and euery frute have his fusyon be londe and be see
> Than the spouse of Cryst with Joyfull songe
> Shall thanke god higly that is in Trinitie
>
> a dede man shall come and make them accorde
> When they here hym speke yt shalbe grete [w]vnder
> That he that was dede and buryed in sight
> Shall ryse ageyne and leve here in londe
> In strengh and in comforth of a yong knyght.[40]

Here, the poet has reinforced the old Celtic myth that a dead hero would return with suggestions of the resurrection of Christ. Consequently, the martial and messianic roles found fused in a single figure in 'The Prophisies of Rymour, Beid, and Marlyng' are here separated and assigned to two different figures. The resurrected dead man is to sustain a young knight who will win the holy cross and be buried in the Vale of Jehoshaphat. Typically, 'The Cock in the North' asserts the agreement of all the main prophets: 'This brydlyngton bede and banastour in þar bokes tellyth with Merlyn and many moo that thus do reherse.'[41]

A very interesting variant of this apocalyptic vision, 'The prophecy of Methodius', gives it a specifically ecclesiastical application. Churches throughout Christendom are to suffer in a general state of anarchy: 'ther shalbe noo comminalte butt partiality & singularite . . . wherfore almightye god shall take vengeance generally & spetiallye vppon all manner off people /

---

[40] Lansdowne MS 762, fo. 62ᵛ. The second of the passages quoted, concerning the resurrection of a dead man, is underlined in the manuscript.

[41] Ibid.

turkes & Infidels shall distroye manye landes provinces citiez & townes off cristendome.'[42] The church will be 'maculate & defiled', deprived of its tithes, nuns will forsake their convents, the flock will be without religion, and by 1535 all Christendom will weep for the sack of Rome. During this time there will exist neither pope, nor emperor, nor king of France, and all kinds of disturbances will afflict the elements so that 'the naturall course of thinges shalbe changed & turned vp soo doune'. At the height of this tribulation, which will be the worst since the world began, a young king shall come to the rescue who will return the crown of the lily and bear rule throughout the world. A new pope will be chosen who will reform the world by his holiness and good living, while a new emperor will deliver all Christian people from their enemies.[43] Thenceforth, there will be one faith and one law throughout the world, and unity and peace between all men for evermore 'vnto the cummynge off anticriste'.[44]

However extravagant and fanciful these Tudor prophecies may be, they all reproduce the same pattern: a descent into a condition of war, bondage, and division, followed by a recovery and renewal leading into a period of peace and unity. For this reason the prophecies may not be dismissed simply as the incoherent scribblings of a lunatic fringe: a Scottish writer could claim in 1549 that 'the inglishmen gifis ferme credit to diverse prophane prophesies of Merlyne, and til uthir corrupt vatici-naris, to quhais ymaginet verkis thai gyve mair faitht nor to the prophesie of Ysaye, Ezechiel, Ieremie, or to the evangel.'[45] Their enormous popularity during the reign of Henry VIII requires one to consider what their function may have been, and for whom.

As I suggested at the outset, the prophecies were an instrument whereby ordinary Englishmen could objectify their feelings

[42] Rawlinson MS C. 813, fo. 91^r.

[43] Ibid., fos. 91^v-94^r. On medieval prophetic literature concerning the *topos* of the Last World Emperor, see Reeves, *The Influence of Prophecy*, pp. 293-392.

[44] Ibid., fo. 94^r.

[45] *The Complaynt of Scotlande vyth ane Exortatione to the Thre Estaits to be vigilante in the Deffens of their Public veil*, ed. James A. H. Murray, Early English Text Society, extra series, nos 17-18 (London, 1872), p. 82.

about the course history was taking. Surviving records show that they circulated most widely among the relatively humble orders of society, not just in London, but also in the provinces. In December 1533 one John Broughton, monk, confessed that he had discussed changes to come in the world, should the king put away papistical power, with Sir Rob. Legate, friar; that he had shown his master prophecies; and that he had a bill of William Rawlinson of Colton containing prophecies.[46] On 20 May 1535 Sir Thomas Arundell reported to Cromwell that one of his father's tenants had heard prophecies from an old man called Payne dwelling three miles away (from Chydyoke), and that during an interrogation the old man had said that 'the white falcon should come out of the north-west and kill almost all the priests.'[47] In December 1538 a youth aged 17, Richard Oversole, got into trouble for interpreting what was, one can infer, a version of 'The Cock in the North'. He said that all the Percys were dead except one, and he would cause England to shine as bright as St George. Oversole is described as a 'tyllour', born in Northallerton, son of George Oversole, 'tyllour'. At the time of this event he had come to his aunt at Dover, described as a 'singlewoman, servant to Robert Welden, of Dover', after which he lodged at the house of Robert Kowe, palemaker, at Kay Street beside Chesynwoode, in the parish of Bobbyng, a mile from Sittingbourne.[48] Such details as these give us a fair idea of the stratum of society to whom the prophecies most readily, although not exclusively, appealed.[49] The prophecies undoubtedly gave form to their half acknowledged fears about the condition of England, as well as to their hopes for its future. A

[46] *LP*, VII, Appendix, 43.

[47] Ibid., VIII, no. 736.

[48] Ibid., XIII, ii, no. 996. For further cases, see Elton, *Policy and Police*, pp. 58-62, 71-2.

[49] No less a figure than the lord chancellor himself owned a compilation of prophecies. A manuscript in the Lambeth Palace Library (MS 527) containing the 'Prophecies of Merlin' amongst various genealogies, chronicles, and notes on the ecclesiastical system at Rome, has the following inscription: 'Ex dono amicissimi mei Thomae Mori generosi et honestissimi viri. Daniel Gray'(fo. 68ᵛ).

profitable analogy might be drawn with those who read horoscopes in modern newspapers: few but the most credulous readers would actually believe that what they read might be literally enacted, but they derive satisfaction from discovering patterns that answer to their desires or fears. In Henrician England this happened on a vast and communal scale, which is why we cannot afford to ignore the prophecies. People collected and listened to them because they knew that the condition of their country was sick. To see past and future political disturbances as part of an apocalyptic pattern with a happy outcome was to make them bearable. Moreover, the foreseen deliverance allowed people to invest their trust in the Tudor dynasty, and then when that dynasty seemed, to some, to be failing them after the break with Rome, to endure the dynasty in a hope that the real deliverance was yet to come.

At first, there seems to have been an ardent desire to identify Henry VIII with the young king who would secure a universal peace and conduct a crusade to the holy land. The Lansdowne manuscript, for example, at one point identifies Henry with the 'son of a man', and declares that 1524 is the year in which the crusade is to occur:

> Then shall manns son for crystis sake
> a mervelous thing vpon hym take
> And take his way to the lond of promission
> And thus god hath prouyded for kynge henrys
> Salvacion.[50]

Such hopes for the king are not surprising, given the enthusiastic fervour with which his accession was greeted in 1509, best summed up, perhaps, in Thomas More's epigram praising Henry as a king who would wipe the tears from every eye.[51] Without going so far, 'The Prophisies of Rymour, Beid, and Marlyng' encouraged a specific Tudor identification by referring

---

[50] Lansdowne MS 762, fo. 53ʳ. Another version occurs in Rawlinson MS C. 813, fos. 104ᵛ-105ʳ. See also V. J. Scattergood, *Politics and Poetry in the Fifteenth Century* (New York, 1971), pp. 77, 383-5.

[51] *The Latin Epigrams of Sir Thomas More*, tr. and ed. Leicester Bradner and C. A. Lynch (Chicago, 1953), pp. 16, 38.

to the rose as a Tudor emblem: 'the doble Roose shall laughe full
right / & beire the gree ffor euer & aye.'[52] No one, however,
could be entirely sure. In the Lansdowne manuscript we see the
compiler collating the statements of the 'sayntes and doctours
that speke of hym that shal wynne the holy crosse', but all his
collation produces is confusion: the writer notes that William of
Ambrose says 'he shalbe callyd H G or J'; that William the
Abbot of Ireland says G or J; that Mahomet says V or H; that St
Thomas of Canterbury says G or J; and that William of Silvester
says G or J.[53] Evidently, Englishmen grew increasingly uncertain as to whether their present king could possibly be the
promised deliverer, and after Henry's break with Rome, the
prophecies seem to have been used by those opposing the Reformation to focus discontent against the king and his administration. A document from 1538 reveals how volatile opinion could
be. One Thomas Gibson wrote to Cromwell that he had gathered certain prophecies of a king that should win the holy cross
and divers realms, and that as such things had been done to
advance the glory of the Emperor Charles, he, Gibson, has tried
to show that Henry VIII is the king meant, who would ultimately overthrow his enemies, the papists.[54] That Gibson was
forced into a figurative interpretation to reassert the identification with Henry reflects how insidiously dangerous the prophecies could be. They provided a mythic framework of expectation
which did not depend upon any particular historical figure. If
one historical figure disappointed, another could be substituted
with the change of an initial. Gibson goes on to give thirteen
'curious prophecies' by St Thomas, John Hermyte, Marlyn,
Silvester, and others. The sixth is that Ampho the patriarch of
Armonie 'calleth him the Weste beaste, the which shall put
down a part of the friar preachers and win a great part of the
world and make a free way unto the Holy Land, and in that time
shall be many marvels of Antichrist.' The thirteenth is that
'Macamyte' [Mohammed] said unto the pagans that he would

[52] Rawlinson C. 813, fo. 83[v].

[53] Lansdowne MS 762, fos. 48[v]-50[v].

[54] *LP*, XIII, ii, no. 1242. For further information on Gibson and his letter to
Cromwell, see Elton, *Reform and Renewal*, pp. 20-1.

be the very delicate rose of Britain. Gibson then concludes from
this that Henry must be the king meant, and that the prophecies
foreshadow that the king shall overthrow the Devil's minister,
the bishop of Rome.[55] Gibson's letter thus shows both sides in
1538 trying to allege the prophecies in their support. The fact
that the same thirteen prophecies, in the same order, occur as
part of a much longer list in the Lansdowne manuscript confirms that confusion and speculation concerning the national
hero had been rife at least from the early 1530s, if not earlier.[56]

Another manuscript collection of prophecies of about 1540
(now in the possession of the Folger Shakespeare Library) shows
the process continuing further. The same list of prophets is cited
(among others), but this time they are all made to agree that the
conqueror will be named Edward.[57] Ironically, once Henry's
son and heir was born, Englishmen could give up on Henry
himself, since hopes could be transferred to the new prince.
Furthermore, the speculation was far from harmless as far as
Henry's security was concerned. Madeleine Hope Dodds has
drawn attention to the way that during the Pilgrimage of Grace
monks and parish priests quoted prophecies to encourage men
to join the rebels.[58] Prophecies remained a potentially dangerous
weapon in the hands of the disaffected, so much so that by 1542
the administration felt moved to suppress them by proclamation
and statute.[59] Repression may not have been very effectual, as
the case of one Laynam proves. According to the confession of a
witness in 1546, Laynam, at that time in Wiltshire, had prophesied about 17 or 18 years earlier (i.e. about 1529-30) that there
should be a cock of the north who would 'busk' himself. Five or
six years later Laynam was in London, elaborating on this same
prophecy. In 1537-8 Cromwell had him committed to the Tower
for twelve months, but even this did not deter him, for in 1546

---

[55] Ibid.
[56] Lansdowne MS 762, fos. 48^v-50^v.
[57] Folger Shakespeare Library, Loseley MS L. b. 546.
[58] Dodds, 'Political prophecies', p. 281; see also *LP*, XII, ii, no. 1212.
[59] See *LP*, XVII, no. 28; XVIII, ii, no. 211. The Act of 1542 (33 Henry VIII,
c. 14) 'made it felony without benefit of clergy or sanctuary to erect tales and
prophecies of a political nature' (see Elton, *Policy and Police*, p. 82).

Laynam was again uttering prophecies, this time that Henry VIII would be the last of the six kings that Merlin had prophesied should follow King John: in other words, the hated Mouldwarp or Mole who would be driven from his own land.[60] These prophecies seem to have had a remarkably tenacious grip on the popular imagination.

The major political and literary figures during the reign of Henry VIII understandably attract most attention, but the prophecies were a startling phenomenon that should alert us to the existence of a very large substratum of opinion underlying the more visible outcrops of Tudor political thought. They reveal the political insights and expectations of many Englishmen who were not in the limelight, and, just as these days elections are won or lost according to the tide of such opinions, so, too, in the Henrician period, popular thought of this kind may not have been entirely negligible in influencing the outcome of events.

[60] *LP*, XXI, i, no. 1027. See also Dodds, 'Political prophecies', pp. 279-80; and Taylor, *The Political Prophecy*, p. 50.

5

Thomas More and Christopher St German: The Battle of the Books

John Guy

At 3 p.m. on Thursday 16 May, 1532, in the garden at York Place, Westminster, Thomas More handed back the white leather bag containing the great seal of England to Henry VIII, and thereby resigned the office of lord chancellor. It was the final, most awkward and most poignant moment of his career as a royal councillor and servant. It was an admission of public defeat; it was also an act of public defiance in face of the Submission of the Clergy that had taken place some hours before. The ironical inflexion of More's voice, the fierce gaze of his eyes, familiar to all who have stood before Holbein's great portrait, and the dignity of his composure all gave the lie to his excuse that he was 'not equal to the work'.[1] Yet, even on this most bitter occasion for both king and More, some of the warmth that had once characterized their relationship temporarily resurfaced. As More reminded Henry in March 1534, when that warmth had evaporated beyond all memory, 'Ye were so

---

[1] Guy, *Public Career*, pp. 200-1; Chapuys wrote to Charles V: 'The Chancellor has resigned, seeing that affairs were going on badly, and likely to be worse, and that if he retained his office he would be obliged to act against his conscience or incur the King's displeasure, as he had already begun to do, for refusing to take his part against the clergy. His excuse is that his entertainment (*traictement*) was too small, and he was not equal to the work (*il ne pouvoit la peyne*). Every one is concerned, for there never was a better man in the office.' (*LP*, V, no. 1046, p. 476). An earlier version of this paper appeared in *Moreana*, 21 (Nov. 1984), pp. 5-25.

good and graciouse vn to me, as at my pore humble suit to
discharge and disburden me, geving me licence with your graciouse favor to bestow the residew of my life in myn age now to
come, abowt the provision for my soule in the service of God,
and to be your Gracys bedisman and pray for you.'[2] More had
asked to withdraw entirely from public life, in order to fortify his
soul for the greater trials he knew must come, and to pray for the
king and his government – and Henry had replied kindly.

> It pleased your Highnes ferther to say vn to me, that for the
> service which I byfore had done you (which it than lyked
> your goodnes far aboue my deserving to commend) that in
> eny suit that I should after haue vn to your Highnes, which
> either should concerne myn honor (that word it lyked your
> Highnes to vse vn to me) or that should perteyne vn to my
> profit, I should fynd your Highnes good and graciouse lord
> vn to me.[3]

More brought that suit to Henry VIII in the spring of 1534,
when the king wished to include him, together with Bishop
Fisher, in an act of attainder as a misprisioner of the Nun of
Kent's alleged treason. Representations from the Council finally
obliged Henry to change his mind, for the evidence of More's
treasonable involvement was non-existent. More's escape, however, owed nothing to Henry's promises in the garden – quite the
reverse – and More soon learned the terrible extent of the king's
wrath and animus against a man who, as Henry believed, had
betrayed his former trust and friendship.

Why had Henry VIII turned against More in 1534, rather
than 1532? What had Sir Thomas been doing as a private
citizen in Chelsea? He had, of course, been writing books: at
Eastertide 1533 his *Apology* was published by William Rastell,
followed by *The Debellation of Salem and Bizance* in October the
same year.[4] And in December 1533 More put the finishing
touches to his *Answer to the Poisoned Book*, his confutation of

---

[2] *Correspondence*, ed. Rogers, pp. 488-9 (no. 198).
[3] Ibid., p. 489.
[4] The *Apology* is vol. IX of More, *CW*; *The Debellation of Salem and Bizance* is
forthcoming as vol. X.

George Joye's *Supper of the Lord*, which Rastell put out at Christmas time.[5] The *Apology* and *Debellation*, which comprised More's side of his polemical feud with Christopher St German, were printed because More meant them to be read, and the circumstances which surround them are of considerable interest. They illuminate some historical problems concerning More's later career; they mirror the clash of systems that characterized the Henrician Age.

The *Apology* and *Debellation* were components of a public controversy, the chronology of which must be explained. Towards the end of 1532, or at the beginning of 1533, Christopher St German wrote *A Treatise concerning the Division between the Spiritualty and Temporalty*, a tract printed at least five times between February 1533 and the end of 1537.[6] The book accused the clergy of undue harshness towards laymen and unfair partiality towards their fellows, the chief cause of St German's discontent being the methods used by the church courts in the detection, trial and punishment of heresy and heretics. More responded with his *Apology*, a blockbuster which left no stone unturned in the battle first to defend the traditional privileges of church and clergy, and secondly to discredit both St German's actual case and his motives for making it. In addition, More included in the work a defence of his own conduct in respect of the detection of heretics undertaken while he was lord chancellor, an area in which More had played an active role and for which he had reason to feel sensitive after his resignation. The *Apology* was, in turn, answered by St German's *Salem and Bizance*, published in September 1533.[7] Curiously enough, Salem and Bizance were Englishmen engaged in a dialogue on the subject of More's quarrel with St German. Quite why such characters had to be invented is far from plain, but Professor Trapp has offered two possible explanations. Either Bizance may be a punning reference to a patriarch of Constantinople, St Germanus (c.674-733), or the title *Salem and Bizance* may deplore the

---

[5] *Correspondence*, ed. Rogers, p. 468 (no. 194).

[6] *A Treatise concerning the Division* is reprinted as Appendix A in More, *CW*, IX.

[7] *Salem and Bizance* will be reprinted as Appendix A in More, *CW*, X.

fact that Christendom was rent by internal squabbles, as
between More and St German, while the two greatest Christian
shrines, Jerusalem and Constantinople, languished in the power
of the Turk.[8] Either way the work attacked More's *Apology* and
renewed St German's assault on what he still maintained were
the biased and unjust procedures of the heresy laws and church
courts. By way of rebuttal, More wrote *The Debellation of Salem
and Bizance*.[9] As he himself said, when *Salem and Bizance* came off
the press at Michaelmas 1533, 'I sodaynly went in hande ther-
wyth, and made it in a breyde.'[10] Elsewhere he said that he
composed the *Debellation* 'in few days'.[11]

St German answered *The Debellation of Salem and Bizance* with
The Additions of Salem and Bizance, published in mid-1534. Yet the
title of *The Additions* was something of a misnomer. For the
book's five chapters sidestepped the main theme of More's
Debellation, which had been the justification of inquisitorial procedures in church courts in cases of suspected heresy. St German's *Additions* instead continued his earlier attacks upon clerical greed and abuses, faults in liturgical observation, provincial
canons, pilgrimages, the law of tithes, and so on. *The Additions*
did introduce some new material: St German analysed the
technical limitations placed on ecclesiastical juridical process by
the Act of Appeals of 1533 (24 Henry VIII, c. 12). He fired, too,
an opening salvo in the campaign by which the history of St
Thomas of Canterbury would be rewritten. However, St German now had little to say upon heresy and heretics beyond

[8]These are J. B. Trapp's explanations, upon which I cannot improve (see
More, *CW*, IX, p. lii, n. 1). Professor Trapp prefers the second explanation
because *Salem and Bizance* expressly considers a crusade. The second explanation is reinforced by St German's appeal to English apocalyptic feeling in chs.
22 and 23 of *Salem and Bizance*: he calculates the number of the Beast and
prophesies the destruction of Islam. A regular feature of criticism of the clergy
was that they neglected their duty towards rescuing Jerusalem and Constantinople from infidel hands in favour of self-advancement. See P. A. Throop,
Criticism of the Crusade (forthcoming).

[9]More, *CW*, X will include an historical introduction by the present writer,
together with a textual introduction by Professor Clarence Miller.

[10]Quotations from More's preface to *The Debellation*, sig. a2^v (1533 edn).

[11] *The Debellation*, sig. a6^v (1533 edn).

repeating his claim that 'men wyll so lyghtly reporte as they do, that there be many heritikes', and noting with satisfaction that the newly-enacted heresy statute (25 Henry VIII, c. 14) had restored English law to the position reached immediately before Henry IV's statute *De heretico comburendo* (1401). In fact, it was Henry VIII's revised heresy law, which had received the royal assent on 30 March 1534, together with the First Act of Succession, that had vanquished More's defence of the *status quo* in his *Debellation*. Legislation had overtaken the debate: there was little more to be said. The details of the new heresy law were not identical to St German's arguments in *Salem and Bizance*, but we have reason to suspect that St German's writings and the Commons' campaign to change the law of heresy since 1532 were connected.[12]

Regarding the participants in this literary conflict, we know well enough who More was, but who was Christopher St German?[13] St German was a Warwickshire man, from Shilton, near Coventry. Born in 1460, he was aged seventy-two when his feud with More commenced. St German, like More, was an English common lawyer; he was of the Middle Temple, a barrister intimately acquainted with the doctrines and procedures of English law who had practised, among other places, in the courts of Star Chamber and Requests. He had retired from active legal practice in 1512 or thereabouts; he had not married and had no immediate family. When he died, aged over eighty, in 1541, his estate was valued mainly in books, and he directed that these be sold in order to provide benefactions to his nephews and nieces. In particular, though, St German was the author of the most famous legal treatise composed between the time of Fortescue and that of Sir Edward Coke. He wrote the two dialogues on English law collectively known as *Doctor and Student*, the first dialogue being first published in 1528 and the second in 1530.[14] *Doctor and Student* went through numerous editions; it was on sale in rival commercial editions within

---

[12] *STC*[2], no. 21585, sig. B7[v]. See J. A. Guy, 'The legal context of the controversy: the law of heresy', in More, *CW*, X (forthcoming).

[13] For St German's biography, see Guy, *St German*, pp. 3-10.

[14] *Doctor and Student*, ed. Plucknett and Barton.

twelve months of initial publication; it was a standard law text
for English legal students in the sixteenth century. By writing in
Latin and English, moreover, rather than in Law French, St
German revealed that it was his intention to address a broader
constituency than that within the Inns of Court.

St German's collision with More stemmed unquestionably
from the ideas he first mooted in the second dialogue of *Doctor
and Student*, and I shall examine those ideas shortly. Meanwhile,
it should be noted that St German played a role in the politics of
the 1530s and the making of the English Reformation; for a
special reason, he was a valuable asset during the divorce crisis;
circumstantial evidence suggests he was in touch with Henry
VIII and his policy advisers on the divorce. And in 1531 St
German published an appendix to *Doctor and Student* entitled *New
Additions*: that tract was important because it was linked to a
draft for parliamentary legislation which St German was permitted simultaneously to prepare. We should pause for a
moment to survey the contents of *New Additions*, for these comprised a blistering review of the issues disputed between church
and state in 1531.[15] The subjects included the efficacy and legal
validity of the statute of mortuaries, which had been enacted in
1529; the question of lay property passing into mortmain; the
extent of Parliament's jurisdiction over appropriated benefices
and sanctuaries; the rights disputed between church and state
regarding trees and grass in churchyards; the issues of clerical
apparel and dilapidations; the matter of Parliament's right on
behalf of Englishmen to validate the 'true' incumbent of the
papacy in case of schism; Parliament's right to enforce strict
observation of Catholic liturgical worship on idle or slovenly
priests, together with its power to demand mutual respect and
good relations between clergy and laity; Parliament's power to
regulate admissions to the priesthood and religious life; its right
to control shrines, pilgrimages and the investigation of miracles
in order to eliminate clerical rackets, profiteering and supersti-
tion; its power to dictate the assignment of tithes and to oversee
the conduct of ecclesiastical visitations, and so on. Debating the

[15] *New Additions* is reprinted as an appendix to *Doctor and Student*, ed. Plucknett and Barton, pp. 315-40.

pros and cons in *New Additions*, St German was distinctly in favour of unilateral reforming action on the part of the state against the church in the name of efficiency and good government. Furthermore, almost all the issues raised in *New Additions* were constructively tackled in St German's parliamentary draft along identical unilateral lines: there can be no shadow of doubt that Christopher St German was at work in 1531 on a programme of parliamentary reform and propaganda designed to purchase peace between church and state at the expense of the clergy's traditional privileges and jurisdictional independence, and for the benefit of the Crown and laity, who were now to control virtually the whole gamut of ecclesiastical functions save the purely sacramental life of the Roman Church.

St German had more than a foot on the greasy pole in 1531, because the special reason that made him such an asset to Henry VIII and his advisers was that he had shed light upon the most intractable problem of the day, namely the divorce issue. For *New Additions* did not only promote the cause of those unilateral reforms which St German desired by statute; it also addressed itself to the fundamental question of statutory competence in the situation of 1530 to 1532, the question that alone blocked immediate action on the divorce at that time. For until May 1532 the schemes of Henry VIII's men were directed to a divorce pronounced by an archbishop or committee of bishops, and enforced throughout the realm by Act of Parliament.[16] The one obstacle was, could Parliament lawfully legislate in defiance of papal anathema and Roman custom? What were the boundaries of Parliament's power? In *New Additions* St German formulated a succession of arguments for the power of parliamentary statute, the most robust of which was that the king-in-parliament was 'the hyghe soueraygne ouer the people / whiche hath not onely charge on the bodies, but also on the soules of his subiectes'.[17] Despite claims for the revolutionary mind and thought of Thomas Cromwell, it was Christopher St German who, two years before the Act of Appeals, and three before the Supremacy Act, started to articulate the sovereignty of the king-

[16] See Guy, *Public Career*, chs. 7-9.
[17] See below, p. 169.

in-parliament – the theory that erected the English Reformation and that which subsequently prevailed, save during the eleven years of the English Republic and Protectorate.

Yet the most devastating aspect of St German's work, from the point of view of the English Church, sprang from the *general* theory enshrined in the dialogues known as *Doctor and Student*. Any man could argue, assert or propose, but could such views prevail against centuries of Roman tradition or English custom? St German was a dangerous man, because between 1528 and 1530 he had, in *Doctor and Student*, constructed a brilliant, comprehensive and *systematic* theory of law within an English context, something far ahead of a mere amalgam of separate theories or proposals. In short, St German did for English law what, a generation or so later, John Jewel and Richard Hooker did for the Anglican Church. Within St German's framework, the universal laws of God and Nature were shown to be rationally antecedent to, and harmoniously co-existent with, native English common law (the law of man) and good conscience (equity), despite the fact that conscience, as derived from natural reason and moral calculation, might nevertheless speak directly contrary to individual rules of common law in specific instances. The key to St German's theory was that equitable interventions in the name of good conscience, which were sometimes necessary to mitigate the rigour of common law, were designed to reinforce, not to contradict, existing legal principles. General rules of law could not be expected automatically to take cognizance of every particular human situation, but since positive human law had always *originated* from the laws of God and Nature, it could never be discarded or discounted, but must, in difficult cases, be interpreted in accordance with the presumed intention of the legislator. Normally, this added element of flexibility, when applied to such difficult cases, could avert any obvious injustice to particular individuals, although (at worst) St German conceded that equity must never be allowed to overrule or nullify an accepted maxim of law, even if manifest injustice might result.

The effect of St German's theory was twofold. It created the impression that English law was an homogeneous *corpus*, the pervasive logic of which was to produce similar results in similar situations or types of case, and it enhanced vastly the status of English common law with regard to other species of law, especially canon and papal law. It was a radical feature of St German's thought that it showed no greater, nor less, favour to clergy or laity under the law, a position bolstered by St German's ancillary account of the historical origins of property rights. According to the first dialogue of *Doctor and Student*, private property was an institution of human convenience, probably introduced by Nimrod at a time when the world's population had increased to the point where common possession was no longer practicable. It followed that property *was not a divine institution*, and property rights were firmly vested by St German within the temporal sphere of jurisdiction, where they were subject to regulation by the law of man. In his second dialogue, St German led his doctor of divinity and student of common law into debate upon a series of test cases, the purpose of which was to demonstrate that there were few, if any, areas of ecclesiastical activity, beyond the exercise of purely sacramental functions, which did not in some sense touch property rights. Yet property rights in St German's thought were subject to *human positive law*, the law of the state. For example, it pertained to the church to have the probate and execution of wills, but the church was barred from deciding such issues as the lawful age of majority for the purposes of inheritance. The goods of convicted heretics were temporal property, as St German claimed, and 'belonge to the iugement of the kyngs courte'.[18] Thirdly, covenants made upon gifts of property to churches should be strictly enforceable in both law and conscience; general rules of property law were involved, and such points 'muste of necessytye be iuged after the rules & groundes of the lawe of the realme [that is, common law] and after no other lawe'.[19] Whenever the church made laws pertaining to men's goods or property, men were not obliged to observe those laws, for two reasons: first, the ecclesiastical arm in such cases was no better than another human legislator who had exceeded his authority; and secondly because, where property rights were at stake, the church 'may erre and be deceyuyd and deceyue other eyther for syngularytye or for couetyce or for

[18] *Doctor and Student*, ed. Plucknett and Barton, p. 243.
[19] Ibid., p. 254.

some other cause'.[20] St German exhorted common lawyers to
prepare systematic studies of the ecclesiastical laws and Roman
canons, to know 'whan the lawe of the chyrche must be folowyd
and when the lawe of the realme'.[21] But such inquiries, if
undertaken on the basis of St German's terms of reference,
nudged English common law inexorably towards the apex of the
jurisprudential pyramid, because St German had resolved the
sixteenth-century conflict of laws in favour of English common
law and statute, and had simultaneously erected common law
as the species of law which should properly govern the consciences of Englishmen in matters of equity.[22]

The issues debated by More and St German between 1532
and 1534 sprang from St German's general proposition in *Doctor
and Student* that no greater, nor less, favour should be shown to
clergy or laity under the law. St German's *Treatise concerning the
Division* set out to show why grudges and division had arisen
between clergy and laity over the years, and what reforms were
required to restore unity and harmonious relations between
church and state.[23] More's *Apology*, in fact, disputed the existence of widespread division between church and state, and
depicted St German as an *agent provocateur*; the main point,
though, was More's categorical rejection of the *Division*'s
premise that the law under which clergy and laity were to be
equal was English common law and statute except where the
clergy could prove that an ecclesiastical law rested expressly on
the law of God. The validity of that premise was witnessed by
the following arguments from the *Division*: that the church had
historically made laws in its own interests which exceeded its
powers; that these laws were in the nature of a conspiracy
against the laity; that the clergy had exempted themselves from
trial in the English courts of common law, to the detriment of
clerical discipline; that *ex officio* proceedings in church courts in
cases of alleged heresy were unfair, vexatious and contrary to

[20] Ibid., p. 309.
[21] Ibid.
[22] See below, pp. 179–98.
[23] See More, *CW*, IX, Appendix A.

natural justice, because accused persons were denied their normal common-law rights; and, finally, that the clergy used church
courts to enforce clerical obligations on the laity in the matters of
offerings, tithes, mortuaries, probate fees, etc., when they had no
lawful authority to touch rights of property, which were temporal matters subject to the exclusive jurisdiction of the state
and royal courts.

More cast his *Apology* as an attack on Protestant theology and
its assumptions, a justification of his own campaign against
Protestant writers and books as lord chancellor, and as 'a
defence of the very good olde and longe approued lawes, bothe of
thys realme and of the whole corps of chrystendome',[24] which
laws the author of the *Division*, as More claimed, 'to thencora-
gynge of heretyques and parrell of the catholyque faythe, wyth
warme wordes & colde reasons oppugneth'.[25] I shall focus here
on the last of More's declared aims. He tackled first St German's
accusation that the clergy adhered to canon law above the law
of the realm, notably in proprietal and disciplinary matters.
More thought that this charge simply reflected St German's bad
faith. He pointed out that canon law was the common law of
Christendom: the specific laws which St German had singled out
for criticism were, in fact, obeyed and observed, without resistance or objection, throughout Europe, and the heresy laws, in
particular, had been ratified by temporal and spiritual arms
alike for generations. It was the heretics who feared those laws.
The ecclesiastical laws had been made in councils and synods
with the guidance of the Holy Spirit, who, according to Christ's
own promise, was as much present and assistant as in the time
of the Apostles. More held that Christians ought to receive laws
made by such authority without grudge or arguments. And if a
provincial council erred, there were ways to make amends.
Furthermore, if the clergy occasionally interpreted canon law
partially against the laity, did not laymen also sometimes pursue their own interests in executing common law? The discovery
of one black sheep did not entitle St German to condemn the

[24] *The Debellation*, sig. bl^v (1533 edn).
[25] Ibid.

entire English clergy as corrupt or vainglorious. When there had been one traitor even among the twelve Apostles, why did St German expect a perfect clergy? The English clergy were, in More's opinion, as effective and well-disciplined as any in Europe – a finding certainly endorsed by modern ecclesiastical historians. Far from St German's goals being the right ones, then, the real reforming need in the English Church, and the most efficacious route to peace, unity and harmony between temporalty and spiritualty, was for the two estates to forge an alliance to extirpate Protestants and heretics from church, state and society. The true faith, as practised for over a thousand years, would thus be liberated from such controversies and disputes as those currently being engineered by St German.

Concerning *ex officio* procedure in heresy cases in spiritual courts, More branded heresy as a crime *simpliciter*; heretics were traitors to God. If the existing ecclesiastical system was altered to permit the admission of common law rules of accusation and evidence, the streets 'were lykely to swarme full of heretykes before that ryght fewe were accused, or peraduenture any one eyther'.[26] Hearsay evidence was necessarily admissible, and More asserted that in practice it was admissible, too, in the royal courts in cases of felony and corruption of justice; this, said the ex-chancellor, had been his personal experience. Admittedly the canon law permitted trial of heresy on suspicion without any witnesses at all, in which case a man might be put to his purgation and to penance without clear proof one way or the other, as had sometimes happened. But that law, noted More, had been made by a general council of the church; did St German deny the authority of general councils? In an extended treatment, More next subjected canon and common law to a precise investigation in order to prove that, if St German's opinion of natural justice was to be given full credence, English common law and statute would have to be revised as much as, or more than, ecclesiastical law. Yet More's ultimate argument was the one founded on enforcement. He concluded this section of his *Apology*, as he had begun, by observing that in every session of gaol delivery and in every court leet throughout the

[26]More, *CW*, IX, p. 130/29-31.

realm, the first charge given to the jury was to enquire of heresy. And despite this, a mere five or so presentments for heresy had resulted in a fifteen-year period. If *ex officio* procedure was to be disrupted, even marginally, heresy would increase and multiply. The Catholic faith would be subverted, with the result that mankind would be faced with the vicissitudes and misfortunes that sprang from God's vengeance.[27]

Finally, More attacked St German's propositions that ecclesiastical law was in the nature of a clerical conspiracy against the laity, and that the English clergy had exempted themselves deliberately from due process in the courts of common law. He re-emphasized that the main body of ecclesiastical law was not English provincial law, but the common law of Christendom, the making of which might not easily be laid at the door of the English clergy, so that it was even more unfair to blame English clerics for the substance of canon law than it was to criticize them for obeying and executing it. In any case, provincial canons, even supposing that these were numerous, were not made at 'confederacies' of clergy. More reminded St German that provincial legislation had been the business of synods lawfully instituted and recognized throughout Christendom since the time of the late Roman emperors. In England, moreover, convocations were invariably summoned by royal writ, hence it was untrue to claim, as St German did, that they and their membership formed a law unto themselves. More ended this passage on a note of comprehensible humour. Provincial assemblies, as he had heard, were committees to be avoided at all costs by prospective members: 'For I could neuer wyt theym yet assemble for any great wynnynge but come vppe to theyr trauayl, labour, coste, & payn, & tary and talke, &cetera, & so gete them home agayne.'[28]

But it was More's tendency in his *Apology* to dismiss his opponent's arguments humorously, or with a quibble, that helped St German construct the counter-offensive which was *Salem and Bizance*. It is, too, a tribute to the intellectual achievement of *Doctor and Student* that More's case that canon law was

[27] More repeated these arguments in his *Debellation*.
[28] More, *CW*, IX, p. 145/9-12.

the common law of Christendom no longer carried immediate
conviction in this dispute. For St German had *already* condi-
tioned his readers, and More's, to the *a priori* notion, as it would
have appeared to More, that similar sorts of situations and types
of legal case should result in similar solutions, whether these
matters were adjudicated before royal or ecclesiastical courts.
One law or the other had to give, and in St German's system
that was canon law. Yet *Salem and Bizance* pressed home with
greatest force St German's arguments on heresy and heresy
trials in England.[29] After a preliminary sortie against More's
use of terminology and definitions, St German noted that previous discussion had admitted the possibility that heresy trials
could take place without the benefit of witnesses. But how could
such trials ever have begun, if a man's heresy was a secret in his
own breast? The supposed 'heretic' must have been denounced
or accused by someone, and if that accuser would not appear in
court, then the original accusation was probably malicious. St
German had already proposed that accusations of heresy should
be channelled centrally through the King's Council, which
would supervize the initial investigations before passing cases
back to the bishops for judgement. His idea was in the interests
of natural justice, uniformity of practice, and fairness to accused
persons as against malicious accusers, but More rejected reform
out of hand. Indeed, he had rejected it twice, once when
proposed in St German's *Treatise concerning the Division*, and once
when St German had reiterated almost identical ideas in chapter
14 of *Salem and Bizance*.[30] St German was adamant that it was
necessary to protect defendants from spiteful, vexatious and
unsubstantiated charges; he believed More's stand to the contrary to be irrational, unreasonable, and illegal, designed to prop
up an ailing ecclesiastical procedure that overtly incited rumour,
rancour, and malice in society.

Turning to More's comparison of the admissibility of evidence
in heresy cases in church courts with that in cases of felony and
corruption of justice in common-law courts, St German now

---

[29] See especially chs. 15 and 16 of *Salem and Bizance*.

[30] Guy, *St German*, pp. 127-8; More, *CW*, IX, pp. 151/33–155/22; *Salem and
Bizance*, sig. F6; *The Debellation*, sigs. l8–m4ᵛ (1533 edn).

claimed to have found flaws in More's knowledge of legal practice at grass-roots level. Persons arrested for felony on suspicion,
were never arraigned on that arrest prior to proclamation made
that evidence be laid, and if no evidence was forthcoming, the
prisoner was delivered out of prison without fine or other punishment, even if he were bound over. By contrast, persons accused
of heresy were obliged to make purgation on suspicion, and they
were not permitted oath-helpers. The worst that could happen
to suspects at common law, or even in Star Chamber, was thus
far less than under canonical procedure, namely that they would
be temporarily imprisoned, bound over and then released,
unless public accusation was made. St German noted that,
where More had alleged that accusers upon juries of present-
ment at common-law sessions were not accustomed to reveal the
names of their sources of information, this was because jurors
could not be bound to help the party to his writ of conspiracy.
Furthermore, the accusers themselves appeared in public, and
judges did not proceed *ex officio* at common law. More had
quipped that he would rather trust the truth of one judge than of
two juries, but that was skating on excessively thin ice, as St
German thought: 'it is not the maner of the iuges to ley vntruth
vpon a iurie, ne yet to commende them that do it, but it be
proued afore them of recorde after the order of the lawe.'[31] As a
former lord chancellor More should have known better.

In the second part of his *Debellation of Salem and Bizance*, More
focused the full intensity of his intellectual searchlight on St
German's case against *ex officio* proceedings in church courts.[32]
He had truly perceived that St German laboured, as More
claimed, 'to brynge the spyrytuall iudges in[to] suspycyon and
obloquy, and make the people wene yᵗ they meruelousely dyd
with mych wronge & cruelty myssehandle men for heresye'.[33] To
rebut the first of St German's points, More argued that a man

---

[31] *Salem and Bizance*, sig. G6.

[32] The most impressive chapter of *The Debellation* is the fifteenth, the first
chapter in part two of the book, and that which refuted ch. 15 of *Salem and
Bizance*. This is the passage that defends *ex officio* proceedings in church courts
in cases of suspected heresy. One does not have to agree with More's case to be
struck by the power of his argument.

[33] *The Debellation*, sig. A1-A1ᵛ (1533 edn).

might be a witness of heresy, but not a denouncer. For several persons might have relevant knowledge of heresy which could be combined to effect proof, when each individual's knowledge was insufficient in itself to convict. *Ex officio* accusation made provision for that situation, which, if it were not covered, would expose souls to the teaching of perilous heretics. Second, it was mere conjecture on St German's part that evidence obtained secretly was malicious; if it was indeed secret, the extent of its malicious ingredient could not adequately be calculated by outsiders. Moving on to St German's proposal for centrally based heresy investigations co-ordinated by the King's Council, More announced, thirdly, that his position had been misunderstood by his opponent: it was quite right that the Council should do all in its power to assail heresy, to which end the law officers from the lord chancellor downwards were bound by their oaths of office; More's point was that this conciliar-based procedure should not be enacted as law, either to supplement or replace the due process of the bishops. The reason was that canonical procedure, based on the law of the church, which was the common law of Christendom, had been carefully devised with reference to countries other than England. Was there a King's Council in all the territories of Christendom? Not so, especially in Germany, applied to which St German's idea would be singularly inappropriate.[34]

More tackled next St German's example of the person accused of heresy *ex officio* without witnesses, who was driven to his purgation and penance without a clear-cut case being proved one way or the other against him. According to More, such a man was well, not harshly, treated, because if he could not clear his name when given the opportunity, but seemed to observers so like a heretic that they could not positively reject the possibility that he was indeed such, then his conviction for heresy was good enough justice for Sir Thomas More. Finally, More returned to the comparison between the respective procedures of canon law and common law with regard to arrests on suspicion, accusations and rules of evidence. He noted that St

[34] Ibid., sigs. A1-B6 (1533 edn).

German's purported vindication of common-law procedure was actually irrelevant to the controversy, because St German had not addressed the true point at issue, which was whether or not more people were wrongly convicted on suspicion of heresy than on suspicion of felony. Whether or not people were delivered from gaol by proclamation, or whether those indicted knew the names of their accusers – these were questions far removed from the key issue of conviction of innocents. Yet taking St German's arguments on their merits, More held that, in any case, canonical purgation and common-law accusatory procedures gave the accused person who was subsequently discharged equal warning and, what More called, 'a good lesson at hys departynge'. (We should observe that More's automatic assumption was 'No smoke without fire!')[35]

This survey has provided a mere outline of More's *Apology* and *Debellation*, but the time has come to begin stocktaking. More's literary battle with St German was a *cause célèbre*, a public conflict waged by intellectual titans; it was akin to a major political confrontation in a national daily newspaper. Above all Christopher St German had been within Henry VIII's counsels in 1531 when he wrote *New Additions* and drafted his parliamentary programme of reform in the same year. He was the first exponent of the Henrician theory of sovereignty of the king-in-parliament. It is true that his star waned after 1532, when the decision was taken not to seek an annulment of the king's marriage to Catherine of Aragon under the direct authority of an Act of Parliament. It is equally plain that St German was no intellectual puppet, no sordid slave of the propaganda machine of Henry VIII and Thomas Cromwell. I have argued elsewhere that his status in the 1530s was that of an independent scholar in touch with, but not a pensioner of, the government of Henry

[35] Ibid., sig. F6 (1533 edn). Cf. sig. D7^v, where More wrote thus of the person accused of heresy upon suspicion alone: 'I say that he doth a great offence, & well wurthy were to be dreuen to his purgacyon & to do penaunce to, if he be not able to purge hym selfe/ but haue vsed hym selfe so lyke an heretyke in all good folkes opinion, y^t he can fynd no good folke y^t dare in theyr conscience swere that they thynke other wyse. This saye I is a great offence and worthy to dryue hym to this poynte.'

VIII; there is a considerable weight of evidence in favour of that view.[36] Nevertheless, it is important to notice one indisputable fact. St German's books from *New Additions* to *The Additions of Salem and Bizance*, in other words his entire literary output of the period 1531-4, were published by the king's printer, Thomas Berthelet. We know that the bulk of Berthelet's work as king's printer at this time was material passed to his press by the government, and the suspicion is overwhelming that St German's *New Additions*, his *Treatise concerning the Division, Salem and Bizance* and its *Additions* had been adopted as part of the secondary line of official propaganda justifying and exploring the nature of the Henrician revolution that the king and his advisers put out in the 1530s. Despite one recent assertion that none of St German's books was published by Berthelet,[37] and that his writings thus have no relevance to a discussion of official propaganda, Berthelet, in fact, printed three editions of *New Additions*, four of the *Treatise concerning the Division*, and one each of *Salem and Bizance* and its *Additions*.[38] The evidence of such extensive contacts with the king's printer cannot be ignored or discounted. In attacking St German with relentless zeal, Thomas More was not merely nourishing his soul as a private citizen in prayer and meditation at Chelsea – he was confuting the king's secondary propaganda.

To support this opinion, I propose a brief excursion into the details of my case. It may be asked, first, why did More wait for the *Treatise concerning the Division* in order publicly to assail St German, when he might already have replied to *New Additions*, which, as I have described it, was a truly subversive tract from More's point of view? Secondly, why did More pretend, as he did, in his *Apology* and *Debellation* not to know the identity of his opponent, devising an elaborate charade by which that anonymous writer was characterized as an obscure country priest dubbed by More 'The Pacifier' and 'Sir John Some-say'. It

[36] See Guy, *St German*, pp. 19-55.

[37] Elton, *Policy and Police*, p. 174.

[38] *STC²*, nos 21563-4, 21586-7.7, 21584, 21585. E. G. Duff, *A Century of the English Book Trade* (London, 1905), p. 11.

should be said immediately that St German always wrote anony-
mously, a habit which has led modern scholars into difficulties. But this anonymity created no problems for St German's
contemporaries. It was common knowledge in Chancery Lane
and at the Inns of Court that St German had written *Doctor and
Student* and the *Treatise concerning the Division*. And *New Additions*
was published by Berthelet as an appendix to *Doctor and Student*,
as its title page made clear. Next, the *Treatise concerning the
Division* manifestly shared a common origin with *New Additions*:
the ideas, assumptions, definitions, and proposals, the list of
clerical abuses and purported quotations from 'John Gerson',
the hypothetical cases and examples, even the prose style and
sentence structure, all these are the same in the two books, for St
German was a repetitious man. Moreover, we know that *Salem
and Bizance* and its *Additions* were by the same author as the
Division, for all these books were St German's side of the controversy with More. Yet *New Additions* and the *Division* were also
linked to St German's parliamentary reform programme of 1531
– his comprehensive scheme for the entire progress of the Henrician Reformation prior to the Submission of the Clergy.[39] St
German's programme included the preparation of an English
New Testament, the reform of procedures for the investigation of
heresy, the rigorous enforcement of Catholic liturgical worship,
the abolition of clerical abuses and alleged profiteering, and the
amelioration of poverty and social distress by secularized
schemes of state roadworks, wage and price regulation, and
local taxation.[40] The parliamentary draft is extant in the Public
Record Office, where it is corrected by St German after the
fashion of an author in full charge of his text. St German's
handwriting has been identified, in turn, by comparison with his
holograph letter of 1539 to Thomas Cromwell and the original
manuscript of his *A Little Treatise concerning Writs of Subpoena*.[41] It
is clear that the 'St German' who wrote these papers is one and
the same man, because his letter to Cromwell takes up family

[39] The text is printed by Guy, *St German*, pp. 127–35.
[40] Ibid., pp. 25-33.
[41] Ibid., pp. 8-9, 56.

matters residual both to other legal documents concerning St German, and to his will, while *A Little Treatise concerning Writs of Subpoena* was another tract supplementary to *Doctor and Student*.

If, however, St German wrote the parliamentary draft and the related *New Additions* and *Treatise concerning the Division*, we can no longer continue to suppose that More was ignorant of his opponent's true identity when he composed his *Apology* and *Debellation*. For More had been lord chancellor and chairman of Henry VIII's Council in Star Chamber when St German published *New Additions* and prepared his parliamentary draft. The King's Council was responsible for managing government policy in Parliament. It stretches credulity too far to assume that anyone could seriously have drafted parliamentary legislation in 1531 without the knowledge, though not necessarily with the personal approval, of the lord chancellor. But the man who prepared the parliamentary draft wrote *New Additions*, the *Treatise concerning the Division*, *Salem* and its *Additions*. More knew his opponent's identity. And there may be further evidence that he did. At the opening of the *Debellation*, More described one of his adversaries as by reputation 'one greate cunnynge man' whose handwriting was 'nere to gyther and with a smale hande'. It is not established from the passage in question that the 'greate cunnynge man' was St German – More mentioned 'dyuerse' men who were his opponents.[42] It may be that the 'greate cunnynge man' confined himself to an attack on that part of More's *Apology* that had confuted 'certayne sermons'.[43] The fact remains, however, that More's account of the man's handwriting perfectly describes the compact lines and minute characters that were St German's.

Manifestly, however, More could not have refuted St German in 1531 while he remained lord chancellor. As a king's councillor and officer of state, he was bound on oath not to subvert government policy, however much he might have disliked that policy personally. In fact, none of St German's actual proposals was translated into official government measures before May

---

[42] Quotations from More's preface to *The Debellation*, sig. a3^v (1533 edn).
[43] More, *CW*, IX, pp. 12-18.

1532, which may even testify to More's activity behind the scenes before the Submission of the Clergy. Yet St German's initial lack of impact cannot alter the fact that he had enjoyed Henry VIII's confidence when his parliamentary draft was conceived, and when his books were passed to Berthelet for printing. When More resigned in May 1532, his promise was not to meddle in affairs of state, but to fortify his soul, and to pray for king and realm. His personal safety depended on that resolution. However, when the *Treatise concerning the Division* was published, More dared to intervene. St German was a dangerous man; More held it to be his Catholic (and public) duty to refute the *Division*'s arguments. Thus the controversy began. In political exile, More believed he might answer St German provided he was circumspect. But discretion demanded that he should profess ignorance of his 'anonymous' adversary's identity in his *Apology* and *Debellation*. By this method, More could conscientiously maintain ignorance of the fact, too, that the *Division* and *Salem* were published with government approval. In short, More could defend himself from a charge of meddling in politics after his resignation, while his depiction of St German as a misguided, rustic cleric in the *Apology* and *Debellation* added a note of irreverent humour that enhanced More's polemical position.

On its merits, More's device was indeed legally watertight; his profession of ignorance as to St German's true identity was justified by the strict rules of English law. In law, a man could only 'know' what had been certified to him directly, either verbally before witnesses or in writing. He 'knew' no more nor less. Since More had left the Council and withdrawn to Chelsea in May 1532, he could 'know' thereafter only rumours or conjectures concerning St German's role in government policy, or regarding Berthelet's printing work. London gossip was not legal 'knowledge'; More's technical position was strong in 1533. Yet politics and coercion sometimes overtook law and morality in the revolutionary situation of the 1530s. In particular, Henry VIII's emotional fear of Catholic counter-offensive against his government's propaganda on divorce and schism in mid-1533 is well documented by the quest for intelligence. Thomas Cromwell sent his servant Stephen Vaughan to Antwerp in early

August 1533 to gain news of the underground press.[44] Vaughan's report confirmed previous suspicions that at least one of Bishop Fisher's seven tracts against the divorce had reached Antwerp via Friars Peto and Elstow, 'beyng the only men that have and do take upon them to be conveyers of the same bookes into Englond, and conveyers of all other thinges into and out of Englond'. Vaughan urged that, 'If pryvey serche be made and shortly, peradventure in the howse of the same Busshop shalbe founde his first copie.' With reference to More, he continued: 'Maister More hathe sent often tymes, and lately, bookes unto Peto in Andwerp, as his book of the confutacion of Tyndale, and Frythe his opynyon of the sacrament, with dyvers other bookes. I can no further lern of More his practises, but if yow consider this well, yow may perchance espye his crafte.' Although More had committed no offence in his literary defence of the Catholic cause, he was suddenly under investigation.

Cromwell knew well enough that his servant had axes to grind. Nevertheless, Vaughan's report was only marginally edited by Cromwell upon receipt in England. The editor of the *State Papers* thought that a copy was prepared for Henry's eyes, and it certainly looks from Cromwell's amendments to Vaughan's original as if such a copy was made for the king or Council. If so, a misleading impression was given. For Vaughan's principal informant was none other than George Joye, Protestant author of *The Supper of the Lord* – hardly an impartial observer of the Catholic underground. Joye's name was deleted by Cromwell throughout the report in favour of the words 'oon whoo'. Otherwise, Vaughan's 'intelligence' was communicated virtually intact.

Since Vaughan had so exaggerated the danger in mid-1533, it was hardly surprising that fears were aroused of active Catholic conspiracy. In January 1534, Cromwell personally interviewed William Rastell, More's publisher, to investigate a rumour that More had written a reply to the *Articles devised by the Whole Consent of the King's Most Honourable Council*, published by Berthelet in

[44] *SP*, part 5, no. 372.

late December 1533 and distributed at court two days after Christmas.[45] The *Articles* were a piece of front-line official propaganda, probably devised at a Council meeting on 2 December. They defended the divorce, denounced Clement VII's excommunication of Henry VIII, asserted that the pope had no more authority than any other bishop *extra provinciam* (that is, outside his own diocese), and accused him of heresy for denying the decree *Sacrosancta* of the Council of Constance (1415). Copies were quickly nailed up in London and throughout the realm: it was the most extensive exercise in public persuasion since Henry's marriage to Catherine of Aragon had been annulled by Cranmer at Dunstable. The harvest had been abundant in 1533, and the threat of popular disorder was thereby reduced; but even so the Council was taking no chances, for its greatest worry since at least the beginning of 1532 had been that England would be subjected to papal interdict, and that this would fuel co-ordinated Catholic resistance.

Hearing of Cromwell's visit to Rastell, More sent the minister a letter on 1 February 1534, informing him that rumour spoke false and that he had written nothing since the *Articles* appeared in print. His latest work was his *Answer to the Poisoned Book*, which was already on sale. Yet More had read the *Articles*, 'ones ouer, and neuer more'. In some matters he knew not the law, in others the facts, thus he would not presume to answer the tract, whoever had written it. More continued:

And then while the matter parteined vnto the Kinges Highnes, and the boke professeth openly that it was made by hys honorable Counsail, and by them put in print with his Graces licens obteined therunto, I verely trust in good faith that of your good mind toward me, though I neuer wrote you worde thereof, your selfe will both think and say so much for me, that it were a thing far vnlikely, that an answer shold be made therunto bi me . . . Yet suerly if it shold happen any boke to come abrode in the name of hys

[45] *Correspondence*, ed. Rogers, pp. 467-8 (no. 194); *LP*, VI, no. 1571; the *Articles* is reprinted in *Records of the Reformation: The Divorce, 1527-1533*, ed. Nicholas Pocock, 2 vols (Oxford, 1870), vol. II, pp. 524-31.

Grace or hys honorable Counsail, if the boke to me semed
such as my selfe would not haue giuen mine owne aduise to
the making, yet I know my bounden duety, to bere more
honour to my prince, and more reuerence to his honorable
Counsaile, than that it coulde become me for many causes,
to make an aunswere vnto such a boke, or to counsail and
aduise any man els to do it.[46]

Here More offered a statement of principle. He affirmed the
distinction between books published 'openly' in the name of king
or Council and other literature. His duty as a subject precluded
his making answer to the former.

The trouble was that by answering the *Treatise concerning the
Division* and *Salem and Bizance*, More had already rebutted
Henry's propaganda in the eyes of the regime. More and the
government were now applying different definitions. Whether its
propaganda was 'openly' declared as such on its title page was
plainly irrelevant to the Council in the wake of the schism. More
relied, too, on the 'anonymity' of St German and his lack of strict
legal 'knowledge' of what the Council passed to Berthelet's press
at a time when Henry VIII had started to feel haunted by the
Catholic underground. Some form of collision was inevitable.

On 21 February 1534, the bill of attainder against Elizabeth
Barton, the so-called Holy Maid or Nun of Kent, was laid before
the House of Lords. Fisher and More, the latter at Henry VIII's
own insistence, were named among those who 'by the act shalbe
atteynted of mysprision and have imprisonament at the kynges
will and lose all their goodes'.[47] More's name was eventually
deleted; the accusation was a sham. Yet why had Henry's
affection for his former chancellor – visible even at York Place in
May 1532 – turned to malice and hatred a month before the
First Act of Succession was on the statute book? The reason was
in part that More had refused to attend Anne Boleyn's coronation the previous June. But it must in part, too, have reflected
Henry's current mental association of More and Fisher as equal

[46] *Correspondence*, ed. Rogers, pp. 468-9 (no. 194).

[47] S. E. Lehmberg, *The Reformation Parliament, 1529-1536* (Cambridge, 1970),
p. 194.

partners in the Catholic press campaign against 'his' jurisdictional revolution. Nowhere was the juridical aspect of the Henrician schism better defended than in those books of Christopher St German which were printed by Berthelet. Since we must evaluate the *Division* and *Salem* as components of the king's secondary line of propaganda, More's *Apology* and *Debellation* gain political significance. However More perceived his position in law and morality during 1533, Henry VIII believed that his ex-chancellor had broken his trust. Within the volcanic recesses of the king's consciousness, Thomas More's mere existence came to pose an intolerable threat.

What was the significance of the 'battle of the books'? I think the debate did not make history, but it marked it. Before the Henrician Reformation England was powerfully exposed to dualism and interchange: despite the later contrary protestations of seventeenth-century lawyers, Roman-canon law had influenced the development of English law and particularly its procedures. What were Chancery and Star Chamber oaths and interrogatories if not ecclesiastical in origin? Litigants' oaths were modelled on those of calumny and speaking the truth; examinations had shared origins.[48] And the English law of uses, contract, and defamation owed substantive content to the church. Both More and St German respected the thought of Sir John Fortescue, the fifteenth-century exponent of mixed monarchy and representative institutions, yet Fortescue's constitutional paradigm was a subtle blend of religious and secular ideas. In the 1530s historic links were broken – but in a manner displeasing to both disputants in the battle of the books. More believed duality to have been replaced by Henry VIII's extreme theocratic pretensions; St German too viewed pure theocracy with revulsion, for his goal was an ecclesiastical structure headed by the king-in-parliament, not the king alone.

Brilliant and incisive as was St German's mind, his intellectual position became untenable as soon as the Act of Supremacy

[48] Ecclesiastical procedure is outlined by N. Adams and C. Donahue (eds), *Select Cases from the Ecclesiastical Courts of the Province of Canterbury*, Selden Society (London, 1981), pp. 43–52.

reached the statute book. In 1537 he unsuccessfully urged Thomas Cromwell, the king's vicegerent in spirituals, to propose an internationally conceived reforming church council to resolve issues of controversy.[49] The question of Parliament's role in the supremacy was not settled until the events of 1549, 1559, and 1662 had been played out. Yet if St German's laurels shrivelled before the furnace of real-life politics, More's moral victory could only be posthumous. As to their quarrel over the respective merits of jury trials and *ex officio* judicial procedures – given the modern debate in England begun by lawyers who suggest that common-law jury trials are too time consuming, expensive, and ineffective to survive the twentieth century in certain types of case, one may but remark *plus ça change, plus c'est la même chose.*

[49] See below, pp. 217–19.

6

The King's Council
and Political Participation

John Guy

During the Pilgrimage of Grace a remarkable 'book of advice' was laid before the rebel council at Pontefract. The document was prepared in all probability by Sir Thomas Tempest, whose 'old diseases of colic, stone, and strangurion' obliged him to address the Pilgrims on paper through his cousin Robert Bowes.[1] But Tempest's authorship of the advice book is less important than its contents, which considered political participation, in particular the vexed issue of membership of the King's Council. The document is not so badly mutilated that it cannot be quoted:

> Firste, where yt is a[l]legyd that we schulde not tayke upon us to assy[g]ne his Gr[ace's Council] yt ys ne[ce]ssary that vertuus men that luffythe the communwelthe schulde be of his [Counci]l . . . [if] he wyl have a Cunsell for his person at hys pleasur, then yt ys ne[ce]ssary that a [Council] be had for the cummunwelthe as the cunsell off Parys ys in France, for princys schuld [choose] susche vertus men as woylde regarde the communwelthe abuffe their princys lo[ve] . . .

Tempest next developed the theme of deposition of rulers. If Henry VIII preferred such favourites as the upstart 'traitor'

[1] *LP*, XI, nos 1211, 1244. See also *LP*, XII, i, no. 901, p. 404. M. H. and R. Dodds, *The Pilgrimage of Grace 1536-1537 and the Exeter Conspiracy 1538*, 2 vols (Cambridge, 1915), vol. I, pp. 345-6, 357-8.

Thomas Cromwell to more experienced councillors, he would come to a miserable end like Rehoboam who provoked political schism by heeding 'yonge folyshe cunselle'. Tempest continued:

> And in thys nobyll rey[l]m who reydes the crownakylls of Edwarde the ij. what juperdy he was in for Peres de G[ave]stun, Spenseres, and susche lyke cunsellars and . . . Rycharde the ij. was deposyd for folowing the cunsell of susche lyke.[2]

The references to Rehoboam, Edward II, and Richard II are significant. Rehoboam, however, was already a platitude. Christine de Pisan, France's first professional woman writer, herself drawing upon the *Facta et dicta memorabilia* by Valerius Maximus, had used his *exemplum* to illustrate the value of 'old wise men' as councillors.[3] The young upstarts had offered Rehoboam evil counsel: the prince should therefore listen to senior persons 'good and expert' in counsel. Christine's book was translated into English in the 1470s and printed in a slightly revised version by John Skot in 1521.[4] In the English translation the passage, which also draws upon Aristotle's *Rhetoric* and Cicero's *De Senectute*, culminates thus: 'For aftir the wyse werkyng and counceilles of the olde wyse men be well susteyned and gouerned the royall magestes, the citees, and the policies, and the comon wele, whiche oftyn tyme be caste down by the yong men.'[5] But it is with Edward II that we move expressly to the theme of political participation.

Edward II's reign witnessed serious friction between militant nobles and the king's favourites: the lords attacked Piers Gaveston, Hugh Despenser, Nicholas Segrave and others, and condemned 'unworthy and evil counsel'.[6] Matters were complicated by military failure, but the mistrust Edward engendered

---

[2] *LP*, XI, no. 1244, p. 504.

[3] D. Bornstein (ed.), *The Middle English Translation of Christine de Pisan's* Livre du corps de policie (Heidelberg, 1977), pp. 86-8.

[4] *STC*, no. 7270.

[5] Livre du corps de policie, p. 87.

[6] M. V. Clarke, *Medieval Representation and Consent* (London, 1936), pp. 154-95, 230-347; J. F. Baldwin, *The King's Council in England during the Middle Ages* (Oxford, 1913), pp. 69-102.

brought about his deposition. During these conflicts the constable, earl marshal and high steward emerged as pre-eminent among the baronage. Thomas of Lancaster as high steward and Humphrey de Bohun, earl of Hereford, as constable led the resistance to Edward II, and Lancaster was perhaps thinking of Simon de Montfort when he projected himself as a guardian of the public interest. A tract was drafted, 'the Treatise on the Steward', which described his function as 'to supervise and to regulate, under and immediately after the king, the whole realm of England and all the officers of the law within the realm in times of peace and of war'. He was to ensure that grievances were heard in Parliament and that official malfeasance was corrected. Especially, he was charged to punish evil counsellors.[7]

Less tendentious ideas were incorporated into the *Modus tenendi parliamentum*:

> And if there is discord between the King and some magnates, or perhaps between the magnates themselves, whereby the King's peace is undermined, and the people as well as the land is afflicted . . . then the earl steward, the earl constable, and the earl marshal, or two of them shall elect twenty-five persons from all the peers of the kingdom, that is to say two bishops and three proctors for all the clergy, two earls and three barons, five knights of the shire, five citizens and five burgesses, which make twenty-five, and these twenty-five can elect twelve from among themselves if they wish and reduce into them, and these twelve can reduce into six, and these six into three and reduce into them, but these three cannot reduce themselves further unless they obtain leave from the Lord King . . .[8]

The deputation sent by Parliament to inform Edward II at Kenilworth of his deposition may have been such a committee of delegates, but whatever view is taken of this, the *Modus*, which

[7] Clarke, *Medieval Representation*, pp. 241-3, 358-60. The text of the tract is printed in Vernon Harcourt, *His Grace the Steward* (London, 1907), pp. 164-7.

[8] N. Pronay and J. Taylor (eds), *Parliamentary Texts of the Later Middle Ages* (Oxford, 1980), pp. 74-5, 87-8.

became a minor legal treatise, validated the idea of participation by subjects in resolving political crises.[9] Early modern England thus inherited the formal notion of ascending as well as descending power – ascending power vested in the communities of the realm represented by the 'grades' in Parliament. Edward I had summarized this theory as early as 1301: 'It is the custom of the realm of England that in all things touching the state of the same realm there should be asked the counsel of all whom the matter concerns.'[10] The convening of an assembly of 'estates and people' in 1399 at Westminster Hall when Richard II was over-thrown reinforced the validity of this reasoning.[11]

The representative ideal which resonates through Tempest's 'advice' and through the writings of Sir John Fortescue, Christo-pher St German and Thomas Starkey, is the chief focus of this chapter,[12] although other authors also discussed the King's Council, in particular Edmund Dudley, Sir Thomas More, and Sir Thomas Elyot.[13] By the time of Fortescue, however, tradi-tional political language had been enriched by newly adapted

[9] Clarke, *Medieval Representation*, pp. 188-93; B. Wilkinson, *Constitutional History of Medieval England*, 3 vols (London, 1948-58), vol. II, p. 161. See also G. T. Lapsley, 'The parliamentary title of Henry IV', *English Historical Review*, 49 (1934), pp. 423-49, 577-606; B. Wilkinson, 'The deposition of Richard II and the accession of Henry IV', *English Historical Review*, 54 (1939), pp. 215-39. The legal importance of the *Modus* is stressed by N. Pronay and J. Taylor, 'The use of the *Modus tenendi parliamentum* in the Middle Ages', *Bulletin of the Institute of Historical Research*, 47 (1974), pp. 11-23. The tract 'was used for business purposes and remained in use until at least the reign of Henry VIII' (p. 14). For some other views, see M. Prestwich, 'The *Modus tenendi parliamentum*', *Parliamentary History*, 1 (1982), pp. 221-5; G. O. Sayles, '*Modus tenendi parliamentum*: Irish or English?', in J. F. Lydon (ed.), *England and Ireland in the Later Middle Ages* (Dublin, 1981), pp. 122-52.

[10] Clarke, *Medieval Representation*, pp. 245-6.

[11] E. F. Jacob, *The Fifteenth Century 1399-1485* (Oxford, 1961), pp. 10-17.

[12] C. Plummer (ed.), *The Governance of England* (Oxford, 1885); S. B. Chrimes (ed.), *De laudibus legum Anglie* (Cambridge, 1942); T. Fortescue [Lord Cler-mont] (ed.), *The Works of Sir John Fortescue, Knight, Chief Justice of England and Lord Chancellor to King Henry the Sixth*, privately printed, 2 vols (London, 1869); Guy, *St German*; K. M. Burton (ed.), *A Dialogue between Reginald Pole and Thomas Lupset* (London, 1948); *Starkey*, ed. Herrtage, pt. 1.

[13] D. M. Brodie (ed.), *The Tree of Commonwealth* (Cambridge, 1948); More, *CW*, IV; *The Governour*, ed. Croft; *Pasquil the Playne* (London, 1533); *STC*, no. 7672.

concepts of 'common weal'. This mode of address was first used
in Henry VI's England during the crisis of 1449-50: it appeared
in the Commons' allegations against the Duke of Suffolk, and
according to *Gregory's Chronicle* it was in the mouths of Cade's
rebels, who advanced into London 'as they sayde, for the comyn
wele of the realme of Ingelonde'.[14] 'Common weal' or 'commonwealth' then reappeared in debates of the 1450s, to culminate in
the claim by the Yorkist magnates *en route* for Ludford Bridge in
1459 that their intent was the augmentation of Henry VI's royal
estate and 'the common weal of this realm'.[15] Applied in this
way 'common weal' was a rhetorical device, or slogan, whereby
embattled men appealed to altruism over dynasty. Claude de
Seyssel later made this point through the medium of Roman
history: 'for men unable to get the management of great affairs
... by merit, beneficence, and authority of the senate found
chances to win the favour of the people by persuading them to
self-indulgent courses on the pretext of the common weal.'[16] He
may have been thinking of the French War of the Public Weal in
1465. Warwick, Clarence, and Archbishop Neville, rebels during Edward IV's first reign, invoked 'commonwealth' in this
spirit when in 1469 they enumerated 'the occasions and true
causes of the great inconveniences and mischiefs that befell in
this land in the days of King Edward II, King Richard II, and
King Henry VI, to the destruction of them, and to the great hurt
and impoverishment of this land':

> First, where the said kings estranged the great lords of their
> blood from their secret council, and were not advised by
> them, and taking about them others not of their blood, and
> inclining only to their counsel, rule and advice, which
> persons took no respect or consideration to the welfare of
> the said princes, nor to the commonwealth of this land, but
> only to their singular honour and enriching of themselves

[14] D. R. Starkey, 'Which Age of Reform?', in *Revolution Reassessed*; J. Gairdner
(ed.), *The Historical Collections of a Citizen of London in the Fifteenth Century*,
Camden Society, new series, 17 [4] (London, 1876), p. 191.

[15] Starkey, 'Which Age of Reform?'. For the background see R. A. Griffiths,
The Reign of King Henry VI (London, 1981), pp. 817-25.

[16] D. R. Kelley (ed.), *The Monarchy of France* (New Haven, 1981), p. 41.

and their blood . . . by which the said princes were so impoverished that they had not sufficient livelihood or goods whereby they might keep and maintain their honourable estate and ordinary charges within this realm.[17]

Fortescue, author of *De natura legis naturae, De laudibus legum Anglie* and *The Governance of England*, prepared a cautionary memorandum addressed to Warwick 'for the good publique of the Reaume'. Written in late 1470 or early 1471 after the readeption of Henry VI but before the battle of Barnet, it was his own version of ideas first mooted in Parliament during the 1450s. He highlighted the inefficiency, corruption, and malfeasance in matters of patronage that accompanied the 'myscounceling' of the king. The 'olde counsell' in England 'was mooste of grete lordis that more attended to their owne matieres thanne to the good universall profute, and therfore procured [t]hemselfe to be of the counsell . . .'. Fortescue proposed a council of thirty-two persons selected entirely on account of their capacity for business: twelve clerics and twelve laymen, to whom were conjoined four bishops and four peers chosen annually. The officers of state might attend, but Fortescue maintained the principle of a working council equipped to foster the public good:

> It is thoughte good that it shulde please the king testablysshe a counseill of Spirituel men xij, and of temporel men xij, of the mooste wise and indifferente that can be chosen in alle the londe. And that ther be chosen to theime yerly iiij. lordis spirituelx, and iiij. lordis temporelx, or in lasse numbre. And that the king do no grete thing towching the rewle of his reaume, nor geve lande, ffee, office, or benefice, but that firste his intente therinne be communed and disputed in that counseill, and that he haue herde their advises ther upon; whiche may in no thing restreyne his power, libertee, or prerogatiff. And thanne shall the king not be counseled by menn of his Chambre, of his housholde, nor other which can not counsele hym; but the good publique shal by wise men be condute to the prosperite and

[17] A. R. Myers (ed.), *English Historical Documents 1327-1485* (London, 1969), pp. 300-1.

honoure of the land, to the suretie and welfare of the kyng, and to the suretie of alle theyme that shal be aboute his persone, whome the peopull haue oftyn tymes slayne for the myscounceling of theire Soueraigne lorde . . . Neverthelesse it is thoughte that the grete officeres, as Chaunceller, Thresorer, and prive seale, the Juges, baron[s] of the eschequer, and the Clerke of the Rolles, may be of this counseill whanne they wil come therto, or whan the seyde xxiiij^{ti} and viij^{te} lordis will desire them to be with theyme.[18]

Since Richard II's minority, Parliament had several times attempted to appoint named persons from the different estates to membership of the King's Council together with the great officers.[19] Fortescue's scheme of 1470 was not parliamentary, but it was firmly within the representative tradition because his council was public not private. It aimed to prevent the king listening to the counsel of 'menn of his Chambre' on matters of patronage and finance. But Fortescue was antagonistic to the role of the aristocracy, unlike Warwick: he did not complain about the dearth of noble blood in the Council and the magnates were to be outnumbered by three to one in his overall plan. It goes too far to say that Fortescue was anti-aristocratic, but such a slant characterizes *The Governance of England*, the tract Fortescue either wrote for Edward IV or more probably revised for presentation after 1471. *The Governance* advocated the same council of thirty-two that appeared in the memorandum to Warwick: the twenty-four established councillors were to be 'off the wysest and best disposed men that can be ffounde in all the parties off this lande'. They were to be sworn in, something the magnates considered *infra dignitatem*. Thereafter they were to serve as continual councillors unless 'ther be any defaute ffounde in [t]hem, or that hit lyst the kynge, be the advise off the more parte off [t]hem, chaunge any off [t]hem'. As before, minority representation only was provided for the magnates: the eight councillors appointed annually were to be *consiliarii nati* but were so styled 'be reason off ther baronyes and estates', not by blood.

[18] Plummer, *The Governance of England*, Appendix B, pp. 348-53.
[19] Baldwin, *The King's Council*, pp. 115-208. Factionalism underpinned these schemes.

Furthermore, these lords were to be constitutionally restricted: none could serve as presiding officer in council, a role reserved for one of the twenty-four or the lord chancellor.[20]

The idea of a representative council of thirty-two persons reappeared in the 1530s at the time of the break with Rome. It was a parliamentary version of Fortescue's arrangement that Christopher St German advocated in his parliamentary draft of 1531. Called 'the great standing council', it was to comprise bishops, peers, and other members of Parliament, both clerical and lay, together with other persons chosen by the king who were not already in Parliament. The councillors were to be 'named' by Henry VIII but 'authorized' by Parliament; they were to report on the need for an English New Testament, to investigate the spread of heresy, and to reform canon law and the church courts. In addition, they were to organize a national programme of public works on the highways in an effort to ameliorate poverty and unemployment. They were also to regulate wages and prices, and to inquire into enclosures and rural depopulation.[21] St German's motive in proposing a representative council in 1531 was, however, somewhat different from Fortescue's earlier objective of controlling Crown patronage and finance. St German wanted an authorized public committee to be created chiefly so that it could usurp the *ex officio* jurisdiction of the bishops in cases of suspected heresy. His representative scheme was really another aspect of his strident anticlericalism, best articulated in his books *New Additions*, *A Treatise concerning the Division between Spiritualty and Temporalty*, and *Salem and Bizance* and its *Additions*.[22] There is no explicit evidence that St German's ideas were implemented, but the very next year, under the terms of the Submission of the Clergy, a committee of thirty-two persons, half clergy, half from Parliament, was called upon to revise canon law. There is again no sign that such a body was appointed or actually met, but the representative ideal underpins the plan. Further demands for this committee of revision received statutory expression in 1534, 1536 and 1544, but the

[20] Plummer, *The Governance of England*, pp. 145-9.
[21] See above, p. 113.
[22] See above, pp. 95–120.

collection of depapalized canons that apparently resulted from this initiative was prepared by four canonists not by a committee of thirty-two. Nor did the canons come into force, since royal approval was never given to the new collection.[23]

The variant emphases of Fortescue and St German reflect the different political conditions under which they wrote. In 1531-2 the constitutional initiative lay with Parliament as much as with the Council. The theory of the king-in-parliament as 'hyghe souerayne ouer the people' had been adduced by St German in *New Additions*, and the legislation of the 1530s established the partnership between Crown and Parliament that enabled Henry VIII to validate Tudor claims to autonomous sovereignty.[24] In *The Governance of England*, by contrast, Fortescue referred to the Council thirty-eight times and to Parliament only six times. His scheme mirrored Edward IV's conscious development of his Council as a ruling institution more important to daily government than Parliament or the Great Council. Likewise his weighting of the scales against the magnates arose from his concern to eliminate private vested interests from behind the throne. But Fortescue was not explicitly anti-aristocratic, and this is entirely consistent with Edward IV's policy. Although the relative proportions of magnates on the King's Council diminished after 1471 as Edward's security increased, there was no attempt at deliberate exclusion. Between 1461 and 1470 the Council comprised twenty magnates, twenty-five clerics, eleven lay administrators and four others. Between 1471 and 1483 it contained twenty-one nobles, thirty-five clerics, twenty-three lay officials and nine others. However, the notion that the nobles were the king's natural councillors underwent a reverse under Edward IV, which squares with Fortescue's position.[25] Loyalty to the Crown and ability were the sole criteria of Council

[23] *LP*, VI, no. 276; 25 Henry VIII, c. 19; 27 Henry VIII, cc. 15, 20; 35 Henry VIII, c. 16; F. D. Logan, 'The Henrician canons', *Bulletin of the Institute of Historical Research*, 47 (1974), pp. 99-103.

[24] See below, p. 169.

[25] J. R. Lander, 'Council, administration and councillors, 1461 to 1485', *Bulletin of the Institute of Historical Research*, 32 (1959), pp. 138-80; 'The Yorkist Council and administration', *English Historical Review*, 73 (1958), pp. 27-46.

membership under Edward IV: this principle he shared with
Henry VII and Henry VIII.

Aristocratic representation in the Council is more likely to
have been an issue in Henry VII's reign, when magnate participation was low.[26] Henry VII's Council comprised forty-three
peers, forty-five courtiers, sixty-one clerics, twenty-seven lawyers
and forty-nine lay officials, but the most important councillors
were the king's officers and intimates, who were knights, gentry,
clerics, and lawyers.[27] Magnate decline was partly due to
natural causes. The old nobility's stock had withered in the
fifteenth century through infertility and extinction, while
attainders, forfeitures and the battle of Bosworth exacted further
tolls. The Wars of the Roses and events of 1483-5 may actually
have demoralized the nobility: we recall the advice of John, third
Lord Mountjoy, to his sons, 'to leve rightwisley and never to
take the state of baron upon them if they may leye it from them,
nor to desire to be grete about princes, for it is daungeros'.[28] Of
the magnates who did sit in Council under Henry VII, the most
prominent were the earls of Ormond, Derby and Arundel, Viscount Wells and Lord Burgavenny. Ormond attended twenty-
nine Council meetings, Arundel sixteen, Derby twenty, Wells

[26] For the King's Council under the Tudors see Elton, *Tudor Revolution*, pp.
60-5, 316-69; *The Tudor Constitution: Documents and Commentary*, 2nd edn (Cambridge, 1982), pp. 88-116, 163-99; 'Henry VII's Council', 'Why the history of
the Early Tudor Council remains unwritten', and 'Tudor government: the
points of contact, the Council', in *Studies*, vol. I, pp. 294-9, 308-38, vol. III, pp.
21-38. J. A. Guy, *The Cardinal's Court* (Hassocks, 1977); *Star Chamber*; 'Wolsey,
the Council and the Council courts', *English Historical Review*, 91 (1976), pp.
481-505; 'The Privy Council: revolution or evolution?', in Coleman and Starkey (eds), *Revolution Reassessed*; A. F. Pollard, 'Council, Star Chamber, and
Privy Council under the Tudors', *English Historical Review*, 37 (1922), pp. 337-
60, 516-39, 38 (1923), pp. 42-60; C. G. Bayne and W. H. Dunham (eds), *Select
Cases in the Council of Henry VII*, Selden Society (London, 1958); L. M. Hill (ed.),
*The Ancient State, Authoritie, and Proceedings of the Court of Requests by Sir Julius
Caesar* (Cambridge, 1975); D. E. Hoak, *The King's Council in the Reign of Edward
VI* (Cambridge, 1976).

[27] Bayne and Dunham, *Select Cases*, pp. xix-xxiv, xxix-xlviii.

[28] K. B. McFarlane, *England in the Fifteenth Century: Collected Essays* (London,
1981), p. 260.

sixteen, and Burgavenny twelve. Derby, Wells, and Arundel were Henry VII's kinsmen, Ormond was a Lancastrian loyalist and queen's chamberlain. Burgavenny, a member of the Neville family, by contrast lived his political life under a cloud. Beyond these individuals two-thirds at least of the peerage attended the Council once or twice during Henry VII's reign, but their role was consultative and ceremonial rather than executive: they added dignity but little else.

Some oblique commentary upon Henry VII's Council was tendered by Edmund Dudley in *The Tree of Commonwealth*, a work written during his imprisonment in the Tower of London. Dudley's remarks, however, were surprisingly narrow. His specific ideas were cast in an antique mould, particularly his social and economic proposals. On the Council itself his observation that the king should 'take counsell of good and wise men, for thei y^t drede not god syldome gyve good counsell, and syldome it profiteth a prince to gyve confydence to young counsell' might have come straight from Christine de Pisan.[29] But More's *Utopia*, the product of humanist rather than commonwealth debate, offered some new perspectives.

In Book I of *Utopia* the relationship between good counsel and public welfare is symbiotic. The crucial point is that the interests of the ruler potentially conflict with those of the ruled, hence councillors cannot equate the *res privata* of the prince with the common profit.[30] Councillors also confuse political stability with the wealth and power of the ruler. They veer towards territorial aggrandizement and outright warfare, which wastes resources and bankrupts the people. Conventional policy is flawed, too, by the assumption that the ruler's security is enhanced by the people's poverty.

> Picture the councillors of some king or other debating with
> him and devising by what schemes they may heap up
> treasure for him. One advises crying up the value of money
> when he has to pay any and crying down its value below

[29] Brodie, *The Tree of Commonwealth*, pp. 3, 4, 5, 9, 13, 22, 27-8, 35-7, 49.

[30] M. Fleisher, *Radical Reform and Political Persuasion in the Life and Writings of Thomas More* (Geneva, 1973), pp. 35-44.

the just rate when he has to receive any. . . Another
suggests a make-believe war under pretext of which he
would raise money and then, when he saw fit, make peace
with solemn ceremonies to throw dust in his simple people's
eyes. . . Another councillor reminds him of certain old and
moth-eaten laws, annulled by long non-enforcement, which
no one remembers being made and therefore everyone has
transgressed. The king should exact fines for their trans-
gression. . . All the councillors agree and consent to the
famous statement of Crassus: no amount of gold is enough
for the ruler who has to keep an army.[31]

Hythlodaeus maintains such counsels to be dishonourable and
dangerous. The safety of the ruler, not merely his honour, rests
upon the people's resources, not his own. Proverbial wisdom is
invoked: 'it is the duty of a shepherd . . . to feed his sheep rather
than himself', 'he is an incompetent physician who cannot cure
one disease except by creating another.'[32]

The response of Morus to Hythlodaeus is well known. Good
counsel is a matter of time and place: 'If you cannot pluck up
wrongheaded opinions by the root, if you cannot cure according
to your heart's desire vices of long standing, yet you must not on
that account desert the commonwealth. You must not abandon
the ship in a storm because you cannot control the winds.' Yet
Hythlodaeus held his ground and developed his case:

Yet surely, my dear More . . . it appears to me that
wherever you have private property and all men measure
all things by cash values, there it is scarcely possible for a
commonwealth to have justice or prosperity – unless you
think justice exists where all the best things flow into the
hands of the worst citizens or prosperity prevails where all
is divided among very few – and even they are not altogether well off, while the rest are downright wretched.[33]

This passage is often read as a criticism of the account just given
in the dialogue by Morus of a 'practical philosophy' that knows

[31] More, *CW*, IV, pp. 87-93.
[32] Ibid., pp. 95-7.
[33] Ibid., pp. 99-103.

instinctively the limitations of good counsel. I do not, however, accept this reading, because what Hythlodaeus says can be taken not to contradict, but to complement the position advanced by Morus. It was Fortescue's *Governance of England* which had most powerfully put the case for the English monarchy to regain stability by financial re-endowment, and Edward IV and Henry VII had taken the necessary practical steps, not all of them agreeable, as Dudley had confessed.[34] More as author of *Utopia* is saying in Book I that power must be exercised responsibly and with reference to the ideal of social justice. The 'stability' of a government cannot be measured simply by its bank balance but the moral issues are not confined to governments, they affect everyone. The motor of human misery is *meum et teum*. Private property and social inequality are linked: the theoretical answer is community of goods. This paved the way for Book II where Hythlodaeus expounded More's Platonic vision. Yet it was not the counsel of senators that guaranteed the welfare of Utopian citizens but inherent constitutional safeguards that removed the human element and so reduced the risks of tyranny and evil counsels. More took a pessimistic view of human nature. Utopian government was representative to a degree but genuine political participation he deemed impolitic. Indeed *Utopia* was not of this world, which denied it any value as a constitutional manual. Fortescue's parameters remained of greater practical relevance in 1516, but More had highlighted with novel force the antithesis between *res publica* and *res privata*. He thus discussed participation through the medium of philosophy rather than a manifesto.

Yet the dynamic political context of Henry VIII's reign was the issue of conciliar reform raised by Thomas Wolsey. The great cardinal of York, legate *a latere* and lord chancellor from Christmas 1515 until his overthrow in 1529, complicated inherited structures because his expansion of conciliar justice and

---

[34] Plummer, *The Governance of England*, pp. 120-40, 142-4, 154-7; C. J. Harrison, 'The petition of Edmund Dudley', *English Historical Review*, 87 (1972), pp. 82-99. Fortescue did, however, warn of the danger of impoverishing the commons, adding 'hit is the kingis honour, and also [h]is office, to make [h]is reaume riche' (Plummer, *The Governance of England*, pp. 137-40).

tendency to personal aggrandizement effectively divided the
Council in Star Chamber, where he presided, from the council-
lors attendant on Henry VIII at his itinerant court.[35] In fact,
Wolsey virtually extinguished the king's 'continual' council. In
April 1518 it comprised the Dukes of Buckingham and Suffolk,
Sir Thomas Lovell, and Sir Henry Marney, knight of the body.
It met at court after supper, when the king discussed Wolsey's
letters just brought from London by John Clerk. But the atmosphere was charged: Henry VIII told Clerk 'that in no wise he
should make mention of London matters before his lords'. The
king wished Clerk to report, too, that Wolsey would be at court
in five or six days. 'It may like your grace', Clerk wrote to
Wolsey, 'the King's grace was not only well contented with such
order as you have taken in all matters, with the advice of his
Council there, but . . . gave unto you openly, before all his
Council, great lauds, commendations and right hearty thanks
for the same, saying these words: "That there is no man living
that pondereth more the surety of his person and the common
wealth of this his realm."'[36] Such sentiments would have gone
down like lead with the attendant councillors, who by 1522 had
been pruned by Wolsey to two: Sir Thomas More and Sir
Thomas Neville, men acting as little more than spare secretaries
and masters of requests sorting petitions. For Wolsey feared
competition from those with access to the king and his attention
focused after 1518 upon reducing the political influence of both
Privy Chamber and Council attendant in favour of his own
monopoly of power.[37]

In Star Chamber the position was better defined: one hundred
and twenty councillors served Henry VIII under Wolsey, thirty-
two of whom attended meetings at least once a week during the
law terms. These thirty-two chiefly comprised officers of state
and household, clerics, knights, justices, and king's serjeants,
but the nobility were represented by the Dukes of Norfolk and
Suffolk, the Marquis of Dorset, the Earls of Shrewsbury and

[35] Guy, *Cardinal's Court*, pp. 23-50; 'Privy Council'.

[36] *LP*, II, ii, no. 4124.

[37] D. R. Starkey, 'The King's Privy Chamber, 1485-1547' (unpublished
Ph.D. dissertation, Cambridge, 1973).

Surrey, and Lord Burgavenny. Peers who attended Star Chamber less frequently were the Duke of Buckingham (executed in 1521), the Earls of Arundel, Cumberland, Derby, Essex, Kent, Northumberland, Oxford, Rutland, Wiltshire, and Worcester, Viscounts Fitzwalter, Lisle, and Rochford, Lords Berners, Dacre of Graystock, Darcy, Hastings, and Mountjoy, and Thomas Docwra prior of the Order of St John of Jerusalem.[38]

Before 1525 there was no real collision between Wolsey and the nobility over political participation, but the treaty of The More, which achieved the diplomatic revolution of an Anglo-French alliance and ended significant warfare for England until the Scottish campaign of 1542, resulted in the return of the magnates to domestic routine at a time when Wolsey was weakened by the uproar over the Amicable Grant. The idea that Wolsey and the aristocracy were in active political opposition in 1525 is far too sweeping, but the Eltham Ordinance of January 1526 was a deliberate attempt by Wolsey to thwart both the magnates' return to politics and Henry VIII's own wish for a rejuvenated Council attendant. Under the cover of wider household reform mainly directed against the Privy Chamber, Wolsey proposed the reconstruction of the Council upon new lines. A reduced council of twenty from within the larger body was to attend the king and perform the administrative and judicial work of the old 'secret' or 'continual' Council.[39] Peers among these twenty 'virtuous, sadd, wise, experte, and discreete persons' were the Dukes of Norfolk and Suffolk, the Marquises of Dorset and Exeter, the Earls of Oxford, Shrewsbury and Worcester, and Lord Sandes, but this list was essentially compiled *ex officio*. It represented the offices of lord treasurer, earl

[38] Guy, 'Privy Council'; 'The Court of Star Chamber during Wolsey's Ascendancy' (unpublished Ph.D. dissertation, Cambridge, 1973), Appendices 1-2. I have updated my figures in the light of my latest research.

[39] Wolsey's parchment 'original' of the Eltham Ordinance is Bodleian Library, Oxford, MS Laud Misc. 597. The Council proposals appear there on fos. 30-1. The best printed text is in *A Collection of Ordinances and Regulations for the Government of the Royal Household* , Society of Antiquaries (London, 1790), pp. 159-60. Another text is calendared in *LP*, IV, i, no. 1939, but some misprints have crept in.

marshal, lord great chamberlain, admiral, lord steward of the household, and chamberlain of the household.

This new council would, of course, have exercised immense power had it ever met, but Wolsey contrived that it did not. By permitting the absence in London of the important office-holders, especially in term time, Wolsey reduced the twenty councillors for practical purposes to a committee of ten and then to a subcommittee of four, it being finally provided that two councillors from among those resident in the household should always be present to advise Henry VIII and dispatch matters of justice unless he otherwise gave them leave. Nevertheless, the Eltham Ordinance commanded the attendant councillors to meet each day in the king's dining chamber at 10 a.m. and 2 p.m. Those who may have done so were John Clerk, Thomas More, Richard Sampson, and William Knight.[40] What Wolsey did in 1526, then, was to offer wide political participation on paper to a representative group of *consiliarii nati*, leading officers of state and household, and experts in conciliar justice; but he ensured in reality that the Council attendant remained virtually in abeyance except for daily routine arising from the complaints of poor suitors. In other words, he preserved the *status quo* established since 1518 but with a fanfare of trumpets.

Wolsey had another scheme for re-organizing Council business, but his fall intervened and his system based on personal networks of authority in Chancery and Star Chamber was eroded. In response to the immense workload generated by his popularization of conciliar justice, Star Chamber continued as a permanent court of law. But political consultation, executive policy and decision-making became concentrated in the hands of an 'inner ring' of 'secret' or 'close' councillors at court. The reason was Henry VIII's first divorce, which split the Council into supporters and opponents, thus raising the thorniest questions of confidentiality and management. During the break with Rome and Henry's promulgation of royal supremacy, the need to manage the Council and Parliament was paramount. It was in this situation that Thomas Cromwell rose to power as Henry's business manager.[41]

[40] *LP*, IV, i, no. 1939, p. 864.
[41] Guy, 'Privy Council'.

Yet the rise of an 'inner' or 'secret' Council which met at court after 1530 raised the very same questions that had reverberated through the Middle Ages: to paraphrase Fortescue, Henry VIII was being counselled 'by menn of his Chambre, [and] of his housholde' in a private, rather than a public, Council. The *res privata* and *res publica* were in conflict. In particular, Henry turned to trusted servants and supporters in preference to *consiliarii nati* and those like Thomas More who were sceptical of the 'private law' governing his conscience on the divorce. In short Henry VIII looked to Cromwell as Edward II had looked to the Despensers, or so it seemed. For theorists the Roman model had always been the weightiest. Fortescue wrote:

> So as at Cristis birthe themperour commaunded the hoole worlde . . . Whiche lordship and monarchie themperour kepte all the while thei were reuled bi the counsele of the Senate. But after that, whan themperour lafte the counseill of the Senate, and somme of theime, as Nero, Dommacion, and other, had slayne grette partey of the Senatours, and were reuled by their privat counsellours, thastate of themperour fill in dekeye, and their lordship woxe alwey sythen lasse and lasse . . . We also Englishemen, whos kinges som tyme were counseled by sadde and wele chosen counseilloures, bete the mightieste kinges of the worlde. But sithen our kinges have been reuled by private Counselloures, such as have offered their seruice and counseile and were not chosen therto, we haue not be able to kepe our owne lyvelode, nor to wiren hem that have take it from us . . . And our Reaume is fallen thereby in dekeye and povertie, as was the Empire whanne themperour lafte the counsell of the Senate.[42]

Tacitus wrote of Augustus: his influence was 'edging ahead step by step, drawing into his own hands the functions of senate, magistrates and the law'.[43] Measured against Roman experience, Henry VIII's inner Council was conspicuously 'private' in the 1530s. Wolsey's senatorial Star Chamber was eroded after 1529 but was not formally superseded, since it continued to meet

[42] Plummer, *The Governance of England*, Appendix A, pp. 347–8.
[43] R. J. A. Talbert, *The Senate of Imperial Rome* (Princeton, 1984), p. 488.

regularly under Thomas More as lord chancellor.[44] But More's Star Chamber did not take decisions or counsel the king; it was reduced to the status of a law court, as was obvious to everyone. There was, of course, provision in the Roman scheme for private counsel: it was an honour to sit on the emperor's private *consilium*, membership of which was extended to a small nucleus of senators if rarely to anyone else. But the ideal council of state remained the well-attended senate, because it played an independent role in government.[45] In Tudor terms the best comparison was with the French Parlement, the magistrates of which liked to compare themselves to Roman senators and who acted, with varying success, as a constitutional check upon royal authority.[46] It is no coincidence that Tempest's 'advice' in 1536 urged the creation of a council for the commonwealth 'as the cunsell off Parys ys in France'. But in England during the 1530s the repository of counsel was exclusively Henry VIII's private *consilium*. Furthermore, Henry took advice from men who were not senators – that is, he listened to Thomas Cranmer and Edward Foxe, perhaps to Cromwell and Thomas Audley, too, before they were sworn in as councillors.[47] In short, he took counsel outside his formal council. If the Roman model was to be taken seriously, this was a retrograde step. The writings of Sir Thomas Elyot and Thomas Starkey show that the matter was noticed.

In *Pasquil the Playne*, printed by Berthelet in 1533, Elyot declared:

> In olde tyme men used to occupie the mornynge in deepe and subtile studies and in counsailes concernynge the comune weale, and other matters of great importaunce. In like wise than to here controversies, and gyve judgement. And if

[44] Guy, 'Privy Council'. Sir Thomas Elyot used the word *senatus* for Star Chamber; see his endorsement on the parchment bill of complaint in *Staunton* v. *Maunde*, filed among loose documents in the Public Record Office, STAC 10/4, pt. 2.

[45] Talbert, *Senate of Imperial Rome*, pp. 73-4.

[46] J. H. Shennan, *The Parlement of Paris* (London, 1968), pp. 192-202.

[47] Guy, *Public Career*, pp. 129-44.

they had any causes of theyr owne, than to treate of them, and that dydde they not without a great consyderation, procedynge bothe of naturall rayson, and also counsayle of phisike. And after diner they refreshed their wittes, eyther with instrumentes of musike, or with redynge or heringe some pleasant storie, or beholdinge some thynge delectable and honest. And after theyr diner was digested, than eyther they exercysed them selfes in rydynge, runnynge on fote, shoting, or other like pastime, or were with theyr haukes to se a flighte at the ryver, or wolde se theyr grehoundes course the hare, or the dere: whiche they dydde as well to recreate theyr wyttes, as also to gette them good appetite. But now all this is tourned into an other fascion, god helpe us, the worlde is almost at an ende: For after noone is tourned to fore noone, vertue into vice, vice into vertue, devocion into hypocrisie, and in some places men saye, faythe is tourned to herisye.[48]

Elyot had served Wolsey as an assistant clerk of Star Chamber and had witnessed the pre-1529 system at its height.[49] After Wolsey's fall he had lost his post: personal frustration is therefore an aspect of his complaint, but his message is unusually direct. Ambition and private causes rather than love for the commonwealth have turned the world upside down. Virtue has become vice, vice virtue, faith is turned to heresy, but top of Elyot's list 'after noone is tourned to fore noone'. This observation is capable of two readings. Either Elyot meant that pleasure-seeking had almost completely displaced counselling after Wolsey's fall: there was no 'counsel' any more since pleasures proper to the afternoon were being enjoyed in the mornings too, which was to repudiate public responsibility. Or he meant that business proper to the morning was being dealt with after dinner. The wisdom of the senatorial council that had met at 9 a.m. in Star Chamber under Wolsey had been usurped by a private *consilium* of time-servers gathered about the king at supper time. Whichever of these readings is correct, Elyot's

---

[48] *STC,* no. 7672, sigs. B4^v-B5.
[49] Guy, *Star Chamber,* pp. 11-13.

conviction that 'good counsel' had recently become debased is evident.

Thomas Starkey tackled the same issue from a broader perspective in his *Dialogue between Reginald Pole and Thomas Lupset*, a work compiled in England, France, and Italy between 1529 and 1533. Starkey approached counsel in an hereditary monarchy from the perspective of public authority as enshrined in Parliament:

> Forasmuch as the great parliament should never be called but only at the election of our prince, or else for some other great urgent cause concerning the common state and policy, I would think it well if that at London should ever be remaining . . . the authority of the parliament, which ever there should be ready to remedy all such causes, and repress seditions, and defend the liberty of the whole body of the people at all such time as they king or his counsel tended to anything hurtful and prejudicial to the same. This counsel and authority of parliament should rest in these persons: first, in four of the greatest and ancient lords of the temporalty; two bishops, as of London and Canterbury; four of the chief judges; and four of the most wise citizens of London. These men jointly togidder should have authority of the whole parliament in such time as the parliament were dissolved.[50]

This council of fourteen persons was 'to see that the king and his proper counsel should do nothing again the ordinance of his laws and good policy'. They should have power, too, 'to call the great parliament whensoever to them it should seem necessary for the reformation of the whole state of the commonalty. By this counsel also should pass all acts of leagues, confederation, peace and war'.[51] All these ideas were proposed in the *Dialogue* by Reginald Pole, who added: 'Our old ance[s]tors, the institutors of our laws and order of our rea[l]m . . . ordained a Constable of

[50] *A Dialogue*, ed. Burton, p. 155. The authoritative account of the context and date of composition of the *Dialogue* is by Mayer, 'Faction and ideology', pp. 1-25.

[51] *A Dialogue*, ed. Burton, pp. 155-6.

England, to counterpaise the authority of the prince and temper the same – giving him authority to call a parliament in such case as the prince would run into any tyranny of his own heady judgement.'[52] It is not clear from this what Starkey had been reading: his *Dialogue* blends Italian civic humanism with English constitutional traditions in a manner verging on the idiosyncratic, but either he, or much more likely his patron at the time, the real-life Pole, might have known the *Modus tenendi parliamentum* or an associated text. The four lords temporal who were to head the representative council in the *Dialogue* were the constable, earl marshal, high steward, and lord great chamberlain.[53] In fact, the office of constable (or hereditary viceroy) had been dormant in England since Edward Stafford, Duke of Buckingham, claimed it by inheritance from Humphrey de Bohun at the beginning of Henry VIII's reign. Stafford had been rebuffed, and his claim reverted to the Crown on his attainder in 1521.[54] The constable, earl marshal, and high steward, or two of them, were authorized, however, according to the *Modus* to intervene when political friction afflicted the land: they were to elect twenty-five persons from the estates of the realm, who in Starkey's words of his council of fourteen were to 'represent the whole body of the people . . . to see unto the liberty of the whole body of the rea[l]m, and to resist all tyranny which by any manner may grow upon the whole commonalty'.[55]

Yet Starkey took his ideal further. Not only was political power to ascend as well as descend, but the representative council was to elect the king's private counsel:

For this may in no case be committed to the arbitrament of the prince – to choose his own counsel – for that were all one and to commit all to his affects, liberty and rule.

This therefore should be the second thing pertaining to this counsel (and as a little parliament): to elect and choose

[52] Ibid., p. 165.
[53] Ibid., p. 166. That the *Modus* may have been Starkey's source was suggested to me by Dr D. R. Starkey.
[54] British Library, Lansdowne MS 639, fos. 34ᵛ-5ᵛ.
[55] *A Dialogue*, ed. Burton, p. 166.

ever such men as they should judge meet to be about a prince, and to be very counsellors of the common wealth, and not to be corrupt by fear or affection. This counsel I would have to be of ten persons: two doctors learned in divinity, and two in the law civil, and two of the common law . . . and four of the nobility, expert and wise men in matters of policy. And by this counsel all things pertaining to the princely state should be governed and ruled; of the which the king should be the head and president ever when he might or would be among them. By them all bishoprics and all high office of dignity should be distributed. The rest the king should dispose, of his own proper liberty, when it should please him.[56]

Five themes thus pervade the writings of Fortescue, St German, More, Elyot, and Starkey upon the King's Council. There is the representative ideal as exemplified in the *Modus*, there is the idea of the estates as guardian of the public good, the theory of counsel as mediated through Roman history, the concern that the king should not be counselled 'by menn of his Chambre' but within some acceptable public forum, and there is the recognition of conflict between the *res privata* of the ruler and the *res publica*. But this framework raises a fascinating dichotomy between Tudor comprehension of Thomas Cromwell's management of the Council and modern interpretations. Historians agree that Cromwell's chief administrative goal in the 1530s was to reform permanently the traditional King's Council so that the loose 'inner ring' of nineteen or so members operating at court during the break with Rome became organized into a new-style executive Privy Council.[57] The streamlined body existed by August 1540, when it declared its hand, appointed a clerk and instructed him to keep 'a leger aswell for the discardge of the sayde Counsaillors touching such thinges as they shuld passe from tyme to tyme, as alsoo for a memoriall unto them of their owne procedinges'.[58] A professional secretariat and its own

[56] Ibid.

[57] Guy, 'Privy Council'.

[58] Public Record Office, PC 2/1, p. 1; N. H. Nicolas (ed.), *Proceedings and Ordinances of the Privy Council of England, 1368-1542*, 7 vols (London, 1834-7), vol. VII, p. 4.

registers gave the new body organized bureaucracy and institutional veracity. The Privy Council excluded former second-rank councillors, the judges, and king's serjeants from membership: these persons retained honorific status as 'ordinary councillors' or councillors 'at large' for life, and continued to work as judges in Star Chamber or as masters of requests at court, sifting petitions on behalf of the Privy Council. In fact, the reformed Privy Council resembled Wolsey's council as proposed by the Eltham Ordinance but with one essential difference. The new privy councillors were chosen by the Crown for exclusively political services: they were not there because they were magnates, because they 'represented' anything, or because they held great offices of state. Many obviously did hold offices, but that is different from *ex officio* membership. In late medieval terms, then, Cromwell's executive Privy Council stood for bureaucracy as against aristocracy: that is, he asserted the king's right to call to counsel his own nominees on the basis of experience, opinion, education, or potential. Henry's right under Cromwell's system was absolute: he chose councillors on the basis of discretion, not because of birth, blood or landownership. Hence *consiliarii nati* became fossils: they had no automatic right to participate in politics, and it is easy to see why changes of this type provoked resentment and confusion. Elyot's dismay and the argument of Starkey's *Dialogue* that the right to choose counsel 'may in no case be committed to the arbitrament of the prince' for fear of tyranny become comprehensible. After Wolsey's fall, Henry VIII was cast in an absolutist posture by men who were shunted into the political wilderness.[59]

In view of Cromwell's known affection for Parliament, his belief in the supremacy of statute and common law over other species of law, and his repeated efforts to achieve a parliamentary dimension to Henry VIII's royal supremacy, the idea that he was 'absolutist' is strange. But the grievances of the rebels in 1536 gain coherence in that light, and so do Henry VIII's replies to them. The rebels made thoroughly consistent demands concerning the Council. They claimed that Henry chose as councillors persons of base birth and evil reputation who manipulated

[59] This point was made in a Folger Institute seminar by Dr D. R. Starkey.

business for their own private advantage. Cromwell, Cranmer, Thomas Audley, and Sir Richard Riche were singled out as 'subverters of the good laws of this realm and maynteners of the false sect of those heretiques and the first inventors and bryngands in of them'.[60] In addition, Tempest urged that if Henry were to insist on retaining his 'private' Council, then it would be necessary to have a commonwealth council after the manner of the parlement of Paris.

To the men of Lincolnshire Henry VIII retorted; 'I never have redde, harde, nor knowen that Prynces Counsailours and Prelates shoulde be apoynted by rude and ignorant common people.'[61] To the Pilgrims he answered:

> Now, touching the comon welth . . . where ye say so many noble men were Counsaillours; who were then Counsaillours . . . but 2, worthie calling noble; the one Treasourer of Englonde, the other High Stewarde of our House; others, as the Lorde Marney, and Darcye, but scant well borne gentilmen; and yet of no grete landes, till they were promoted by Us, and so made Knightes, and Lordes: the rest were lawyers and preestes, save 2 Bisshoppes, which were Caunterbury and Wynchester. Yf . . . ye semed then to be content withall, whye then, now, be ye not moche better content with Us; which have now so many nobles, in dede, both of byrth and condicyon? For first of the Temporaltee; in our Pryvey Counsell We have the Duke of Norfolke, the Duke of Suffolke, the Marques of Excester, the Lorde Stewarde (when he may com), the Erle of Oxforde, the Erle of Sussex, the Lord Sandes our Chamberleyn, the Lorde Admyrall Tresourer of our House, Sir Willyam Poulet Comptroller of our House: and of the Spiritualtee; the Bisshop of Hereford, the Bisshop of Chichester, and Bisshop of Wynchester.[62]

[60] *LP*, XI, no. 705 (1, 2, 4); XI, no. 714, p. 276; XI, no. 902 (2); XI, no. 1246; XII, i, no. 900, p. 401; XII, i, no. 1022, p. 466; *SP*, I, pp. 466-7; A. Fletcher, *Tudor Rebellions*, 2nd edn (London, 1979), pp. 128-30.
[61] *SP*, I, p. 463.
[62] Ibid., I, pp. 507-8.

The king ended by reminding the Pilgrims that he 'hathe as good discression to electe and chose his Counsaillours, as those . . . that hathe put this in your heddes'.

Yet Henry VIII was disingenuous. The persons he listed by name were of the Privy Council in 1536, but some qualifications must be made. First, the Earls of Oxford and Shrewsbury were senior men of uncertain activity as councillors. Shrewsbury was important as a leader of the forces that suppressed the rebels, but it is not clear how often he attended the Council. The evidence for the 1530s is too thin to be relied on, but under Wolsey he attended only one-fifth of the possible meetings.[63] By contrast Oxford attended only three meetings in fourteen years.[64] Next, Cromwell, Cranmer and Audley were missing from Henry's list, which may have been prudent in the circumstances but was hardly honest. Third, Sir William Paulet and Bishop Sampson were excluded from the Privy Council established in 1540 in favour of Richard Riche, Thomas Wriothesley, and Ralph Sadler, three of Cromwell's men.[65] In fact, Henry's list was fashioned so as to make a convincing reply to the rebels' complaints: it merged the surviving nobility with the offices of lord treasurer, earl marshal, lord great chamberlain, admiral, lord steward, comptroller, and chamberlain of the household. The mix was almost identical to that of Wolsey's Council in the Eltham Ordinance, and it probably meant as little. It was in accordance with legitimate expectations, but it is hard to conclude other than that Henry VIII in 1536 was very much on the defensive.

Henry's victory over the rebels retrieved his security and concluded the medieval debate on participation. The 'upstarts' were vindicated; Prometheus languished in chains. Henry VIII was not to be like Rehoboam or Edward II; representation was henceforth to be confined within Parliaments summoned and dissolved by the Crown; the 'consent of the realm' was to be restricted to the theory of statute. The apparatus whereby the estates participated in resolving crises became redundant:

[63] Guy, 'The Court of Star Chamber', Appendices 1-2.
[64] Ibid.
[65] Guy, 'Privy Council'.

except during the crisis of 1584 there were no further plans under the Tudors for Great Councils, for deputations of the estates, for standing councils representing the whole realm, or for committees of public safety. The streamlined Privy Council forged ahead after 1540 as the executive arm of government: it made and enforced policy under the Crown, it supervised the law courts, managed Exchequer finance and co-ordinated the localities. Proceeding by state paper rather than by royal writ it became a partner of the Crown as much as a corporate servant. But if medieval debate was dead, the representative ideal only slumbered. In his 'Discourse of the Laws and Government of England', Nathaniel Bacon wrote: 'And albeit that by the Resignation of Richard the Second, the Parliament might seem in strict construction of Law, to be expired . . . yet did not that Parliament so apprehend the matter, but proceeded not onely to definitive Sentence of deposing him, but declared themselves by their Commissaries, to be the Three States, and Representative of the People of England.'[66] Bacon drew upon manuscript notes by John Selden, and his tract was printed in 1689, which suggests that it was as relevant to the status of the Convention Parliament as to the reign of Charles I.

In general, however, seventeenth-century debates were conducted on changed lines: the antiquity of Parliament, its practice and procedures, and the role of the Commons in the Ancient Constitution were dominant themes. The issue in relation to the Privy Council was less that of representation than of accountability to Parliament. But the second of the Nineteen Propositions of 1642 has a familiar ring:

> That the great affairs of the kingdom may not be concluded or transacted by the advice of private men, or by any unknown or unsworn councillors, but that such matters as concern the public, and are proper for the High Court of Parliament, which is your Majesty's great and supreme council, may be debated, resolved and transacted only in Parliament . . . and such other matters of state as are proper for your Majesty's Privy Council shall be debated and concluded by such of the nobility and others as shall,

[66] Clarke, *Medieval Representation*, p. 319.

from time to time, be chosen for that place, by approbation of both Houses of Parliament: and that no public act concerning the affairs of the kingdom, which are proper for your Privy Council, may be esteemed of any validity, as proceeding from the royal authority, unless it be done by the advice and consent of the major part of your council, attested under their hands: and that your council may be limited to a certain number, not exceeding twenty-five, nor under fifteen: and if any councillor's place happen to be void in the intervals of Parliament, it shall not be supplied without the assent of the major part of the council, which choice shall be confirmed at the next sitting of Parliament, or else be void.[67]

We are far removed from the Henrician age, but Thomas Tempest would have felt at home.

[67] J. P. Kenyon, *The Stuart Constitution* (Cambridge, 1966), pp. 244-5.

PART THREE

Reform

7

Thomas Cromwell and the Intellectual Origins of the Henrician Revolution

John Guy

The field of Henrician studies is at present more active than ever before. New books and articles roll off the presses at a formidable pace. Yet among the familiar scholarship and revisionist new learning, one topic remains relatively underexplored: the intellectual origins of the 'political' revolution itself.[1] The view is too often uncritically repeated that one man, Thomas Cromwell, 'made' or 'was the architect of' these events. 'Wherever one touches him, one finds originality and the unconventional,' writes Professor G. R. Elton.[2] Regarding the Act of Appeals (1533) we are told:

> The critical term is 'empire'. Kings of England had before this claimed to be emperors – the title occurs in Anglo-Saxon times and was taken by Edward I, Richard II, and Henry V – but the meaning here is different. Those earlier 'emperors' had so called themselves because they ruled, or claimed to rule, more than one kingdom, as Edward I claimed Scotland and Henry V France. In the act of

[1] For the literature on this question, the following works are essential: Elton, *Tudor Revolution*; *The Tudor Constitution*; *England under the Tudors*; *Reform and Reformation*; *Policy and Police*; *Studies*, vol. I, pp. 173-88, vol. II, pp. 82-154, 215-58; P. Williams and G. L. Harriss, 'A revolution in Tudor history', *Past and Present*, no. 25 (1963), pp. 3-58, and no. 31 (1965), pp. 87-96; Coleman and Starkey, *Revolution Reassessed*.

[2] Elton, *Reform and Reformation*, p. 169. See also his *Reform and Renewal*; 'Thomas Cromwell Redivivus', pp. 192-208; *Studies*, vol. I, pp. 173-88.

appeals, on the other hand, England by herself is described as an empire, and it is clear both from the passage cited and from what follows that the word here denoted a political unit, a self-governing state free from (as they put it) 'the authority of any foreign potentates'. We call this sort of thing a sovereign national state.[3]

In this chapter I propose to look more closely at the Henrician concept of 'empire' – to examine its meaning and native intellectual origins. In doing this, the ideas that underpin the Act of Appeals must be considered, and an attempt made to locate in contemporary debate the definition attributed to 'empire' by Henricians themselves. It then becomes possible to make a case for tracing the origins of the Tudor political revolution back to 1485, and to put forward the necessary arguments to reinforce that position as the basis of an alternative approach.

The political creed of Thomas Cromwell, it is said, was most fully declared and expounded in the preamble to the Act in Restraint of Appeals to Rome, passed in April 1533.

Where by divers sundry old authentic histories and chronicles it is manifestly declared and expressed that this realm of England is an empire, and so hath been accepted in the world, governed by one supreme head and king having the dignity and royal estate of the imperial crown of the same, unto whom a body politic, compact of all sorts and degrees of people divided in terms and by names of spiritualty and temporalty, be bounden and owe to bear next to God a natural and humble obedience; he [the king] being also institute and furnished by the goodness and sufferance of Almighty God with plenary, whole and entire power, preeminence, authority, prerogative and jurisdiction to render and yield justice and final determination to all manner of folk resiants or subjects within this realm, in all causes, matters, debates and contentions happening to occur,

---

[3] Elton, *England under the Tudors*, p. 161.

insurge or begin within the limits thereof, without restraint
or provocation to any foreign princes or potentates of the
world . . . [4]

Cromwell, it is said, here announced a novel theory of empire.
He proclaimed the radical notion that the territorial realm of
England was a sovereign national state, because all aspects of
law and legislation, both temporal and spiritual, were henceforward within the exclusive competence of England's properly
constituted courts which, in turn, derived their authority from
the king. Since the highest court of England was that of Parliament, an explicit feature of the Cromwellian revolution was also
that the human positive law of the realm as enacted by king,
lords spiritual and temporal, and commons in Parliament
assembled, now enjoyed an omnicompetent supremacy over the
amalgam of diverse central and local jurisdictions, both ecclesiastical and lay, which formed the Tudor constitution.

The questions to ask are, how accurate is this concept of
England's imperial status, and to what extent was it an original
exercise in statecraft inspired by Thomas Cromwell? To
approach the answers, it is necessary to look at two letters.
Writing to Cromwell in 1535 John Stokesley, bishop of London,
explained how some points he had made in an *extempore* sermon
were those set out in the 'king's book' made before 'my going
over sea in embassy'.[5] Stokesley had left England in October
1529 as an ambassador to France and Italy, and did not return
until October 1530. He described how the 'king's book' had been
written by Edward Foxe, Nicholas de Burgo, and himself, being
translated afterwards into English with changes and additions
by Thomas Cranmer. The 'king's book' was thought by Profes-
sors H. A. Kelly and Edward Surtz to be the tract *Gravissimae
censurae*, a work dated April 1530 in the printer's colophon but
demonstrably not printed until the spring of 1531. Dr Virginia
Murphy has now, however, established that the 'king's book'
was an earlier tract, one that lay behind the *Gravissimae censurae*,

[4] Elton, *The Tudor Constitution*, pp. 353-8.
[5] *LP*, VIII, no. 1054.

so that Stokesley's comment is explicable, but which was itself a manuscript version of the king's own *libellus* submitted to Wolsey's and Campeggio's legatine court at Blackfriars in 1529. The earlier tract is the 'Henricus Octavus', the authoritative text of which has been found in a binding from the shop known as 'King Henry's binder'.[6]

Stokesley's letter was written in 1535: it perhaps needs some corroboration. And there is, in fact, a second letter. Sir Thomas More, writing to Cromwell in 1534, reported in some detail how, shortly after he became lord chancellor in October 1529, Henry VIII referred him to a team which was working out details of the royal divorce strategy. The team consisted of Thomas Cranmer, Edward Foxe, Edward Lee, and Nicholas de Burgo – the very same persons mentioned by Stokesley save Stokesley himself, who was, of course, away in Europe at the time. More was required to 'confer with' these scholars and to inform his conscience: he was unconvinced by their materials. 'Wheruppon the Kyngis Highnes being ferther advertised both by theym and my selfe of my pore opinion in the mater . . . his Highnes graciousely takyng in gre my good mynd in that byhalfe vsed . . . in the prosecuting of his great mater onely those . . . whose conscience his Grace perceived well and fully persuaded vppon that parte.'[7] More was excused on the issue, though Henry's 'great matter' became More's 'matter' too in 1534, when the king decided to test allegiance to his proceedings by means of oaths.

It is thus established that an identifiable team of royal scholars was engaged on the divorce issue in 1529 and 1530; Cranmer, Foxe, Lee, de Burgo, and Stokesley (to whom Dr Murphy would add Stephen Gardiner, because some drafts related to 'Henricus Octavus' seem to be in his handwriting), were busily raiding the libraries of London and Europe and

[6] The 'Henricus Octavus' is named after its incipit, which was the salutation from Henry VIII to the cardinal legates at Blackfriars. See Virginia Murphy, 'The debate over Henry VIII's first divorce: an analysis of the contemporary treatises' (unpublished Ph.D. dissertation, Cambridge, 1984), pp. 66-80. Her findings on the 'Henricus Octavus', the *Gravissimae censurae*, and *Determinations* supersede those of H. A. Kelly, *The Matrimonial Trials of Henry VIII* (Stanford, 1976), pp. 180-1.

[7] *Correspondence*, ed. Rogers, no. 199 (p. 496).

preparing papers on current policies with the characteristic enthusiasm of intellectuals eager to display the relevance of learning to government in the interests of self-advancement. The petulant king had been dismayed by the decision of the legatine court of Cardinals Wolsey and Campeggio to adjourn his case in July 1529, and was angry at the greater humiliation of the advocation of his suit to Rome by Pope Clement VII. He had decided to turn for support to other authorities, especially to the universities of the continent. He continued to rely on his coterie of scholars, who prepared for the printing press the 'king's book'.[8] The pages of the main body of this work were probably ready for printing in October 1529 when Stokesley went abroad. However, printing was delayed until the opinions of seven leading French and Italian universities, those of Orléans, Paris, Angers, Bourges, Toulouse, Bologna, and Padua, could be included by way of a preface to the whole work. The *Gravissimae censurae* was finally issued in Latin in April 1531, and an English translation by Cranmer *The Determinations of the . . . Universities* was printed the following November.[9]

Henry's literary enterprises in 1529 and 1530 introduced him to important sources of knowledge: the councils of the church, the Fathers Greek and Latin, the writings of the popes, the schoolmen, and so on. The *Censurae* and *Determinations* make plain the purpose to which this learning was applied by the king. The Levitical law that forbade a man to marry his brother's wife was divine, not human. Such incestuous relationships were also forbidden by the law of nature. If Pope Julius II had granted a dispensation to Henry VII contrary to divine and natural law, upon the strength of which Henry VIII had married Catherine of Aragon, widow of Prince Arthur, Henry VIII's elder brother, that dispensation was invalid and the pope was

[8] Murphy, 'The debate over Henry VIII's first divorce', pp. 164-218.

[9] The printed tracts are *Gravissimae atque exactissimae illustrissimarum totius Italiae et Galliae Academiarum censurae . . .* (London, c.1531), and *The determinations of the moste famous and mooste excellent vniuersities of Italy and Fraunce, that it is so vnlefull for a man to marie his brothers wyfe, that the pope hath no power to dispence therwith* (London, 1531). A critical edition of both works is in preparation. *STC*[2], nos 14286, 14287.

no better than another human legislator who had exceeded his authority. Indeed should the pope grant a dispensation against the divine and natural law, any Christian might lawfully resist and condemn him – for this the authorities were no less than St Augustine and St Ambrose. If the pope erred, he was to be corrected or resisted.[10]

The *Censurae* and *Determinations* encapsulated ideas of 1529 and early 1530, not those preparatory to the Act of Appeals. Yet it was out of the endeavours of Henry's research team in 1530 that remarkable ideas evolved. Henry VIII probably sat back while the *Gravissimae censurae* and *Determinations* were in the press, though his interest in the finished product of the *Determinations* has been questioned, but not formally proposed, on the basis of some marginal notes in the British Library copy.[11] Henry's scholars, however, continued to work while the king reclined. In particular, they explored anew the sources used for the *libellus* of 1529 and the *Censurae* of 1531, and turned them gradually about to serve a new and revolutionary purpose. Under the direction, perhaps, of Edward Foxe, the author of the *De vera differentia* of 1534, and a member of the group since at least 1529, the king's scholars addressed an issue bigger even than that of the divorce – the 'true difference' between regal and ecclesiastical power.[12] It is possible that the Boleyn faction provided the momentum whereby the royal scholars changed the direction of their research; if so, Thomas Cromwell may have played some part in the shift, though his involvement in Henrician policy-making at any level above that of parliamentary draftsman between 1531 and 1533 remains speculative. Cranmer is a better candidate than Cromwell as agent of this new direction: already part of the team when More was obliged to 'confer', firmly attached to the Boleyn interest, and, with Foxe, one of the compilers of the *Collectanea satis copiosa*. We may suspect some truth lies behind

[10] Cf. *A Glasse of the truthe*, ready in 1532, which is more emphatic. *STC*, nos 11918-19. A modern edition is by Pocock, *Records of the Reformation*, vol. II, pp. 385-421.

[11] Elton, *Policy and Police*, p. 177 n.2.

[12] Guy, *Public Career*, pp. 131-51. The authoritative account is by G. D. Nicholson, 'The nature and function of historical argument in the Henrician Reformation' (unpublished Ph.D. dissertation, Cambridge, 1977), pp. 74-156.

the traditions that tell of Henry VIII's meeting with his future archbishop at Waltham.[13]

It was the inquiry into regal and ecclesiastical power that paved the way for the Act of Appeals and break with Rome. During and after 1530, Henry's scholars compiled a new source collection inspired by but distinct from that upon which 'Henricus Octavus' and *Gravissimae censurae* were based. The new compilation was the *Collectanea satis copiosa* which, by September 1530, was indeed literally 'satis copiosa': it was adequate both in quality and quantity to be shown to the king, possibly by Edward Foxe. The *Collectanea* exists only in manuscript in the British Library, but the text there is an original, from which it is clear that Henry VIII himself studied the work closely. Thus Henry's own hand is to be found in forty-six places on the manuscript, variously signifying his notes and queries, agreements or disagreements, pleasure or perplexity.[14] The *Collectanea* was discovered and identified by Dr Graham Nicholson, who demonstrated, too, the document's links with the Act of Appeals, the *Glasse of Truthe*, and Foxe's *De vera differentia*.[15]

In fact, Henry applauded the work of his scholars, because Foxe and the others, beginning from the scriptural premises previously invoked to prove the case for Henry's annulment of his marriage, had now validated the king's regal power in such circumstances – not from the viewpoint of immediate need but from general theological and historical perception. Many of the sources used in the *Collectanea* were the same as in *Gravissimae censurae* but slanted differently: the Old and New Testaments, the Fathers, church councils, learned 'authors', and English texts and chronicles. However, councils, Matthew Paris, William of Malmesbury, Bede, Geoffrey of Monmouth, and Anglo-Saxon laws were prominent in the *Collectanea*. The reason was the change in emphasis. Not only did the royal scholars aim to

---

[13] W. F. Hook, *The Lives of the Archbishops of Canterbury*, 12 vols (London, 1860-76), vol. VI, pp. 435-40.

[14] Nicholson, 'Nature and function of historical argument', pp. 111-13. The *Collectanea* is British Library, Cotton MS Cleopatra E. vi, fos. 16-135.

[15] Nicholson, 'Nature and function of historical argument', pp. 74-214.

verify the right of the English bishops to pronounce Henry's divorce unilaterally in England and without reference, if possible, to Rome, the policy advocated in the *Glasse of Truthe* in 1532;[16] but they had also conceived a revolutionary theory of English regal power, showing how kings in general, and the kings of England in particular, had exercised that power historically in handling the clergy. In short, the *Collectanea* imbued Henry with an imperial sovereignty, part of which had been 'lent' to the priesthood by previous English monarchs. It was this thinking that underpinned the Act of Appeals.[17]

For instance, the authors of the *Collectanea* used the ancient *Leges Anglorum* to show that King Lucius I had in 187 A.D. become the first Christian ruler of Britain. In reality, the *Leges Anglorüm* was a source less authoritative than it seemed, being a thirteenth-century interpolation of the so-called *Leges Edwardi Confessoris*. But it was a most pregnant source. It showed that the mythical Lucius had endowed the British Church with all its liberties and possessions, and then written to Pope Eleutherius asking him to transmit the Roman laws. However, the pope's reply explained that Lucius did not need either Roman or imperial law, because he already had scripture from which he might legislate as king of Britain for both *regnum* and *sacerdotium*. The papal letter is twice quoted in full in the *Collectanea*, the second time immediately beneath the heading 'Institutio officium et potestas Regum Anglie':

> You seek from us the Roman and imperial laws to be sent
> to you, which you wish to use in the kingdom of Britain.
> The Roman and imperial laws we may always reprove, but
> the law of God we may not. You have received recently by
> divine mercy the law and faith of Christ in the kingdom of
> Britain. You have with you in the kingdom both books of

[16] Cleopatra E. vi, fos. 16-42, 64, 76, 84, 92ᵛ, 94-119, 134-5. Cf. Pocock, *Records of the Reformation*, vol. II, pp. 385-421.

[17] Nicholson, 'Nature and function of historical argument', pp. 179-214; W. Ullmann, 'This realm of England is an empire', *Journal of Ecclesiastical History*, 30 (1979), pp. 175-203.

scripture, from which by God's grace with the counsel of
your realm take a law, and by that law through God's
sufferance rule your kingdom of Britain. For you are vicar
of God [vicarius dei] in your kingdom . . . A king is named
by virtue of ruling and not for having a realm. You shall be
king while you rule well, but if you do otherwise the name
of king shall not remain upon you, and you will lose it. The
omnipotent God grant you so to rule the kingdom of Britain
that you may reign with him eternally, whose vicar you are
in the said realm.[18]

In other words, Cranmer and Foxe were not merely justifying
Henry VIII's divorce in *Collectanea satis copiosa*; they were simultaneously announcing doctrines of royal supremacy and empire.
The result was that Henry, as he read the *Collectanea*, became
more convinced than ever before of the rights of his position. But
not only should his suit for annulment of his marriage be dealt
with promptly and in England, as he had thought previously,
but he must now reassert, too, the imperial status of which
English kings had been deprived by the machinations of popes.
For England was an empire; it had been one in the ancient
British past, and English imperial jurisdiction was a theological
truth which no pope could conscionably disregard.

What exactly was meant by 'empire' in this context? Despite
undoubted complexity, it seems that the authors of the *Collectanea* were seeking to establish three basic principles of English
regal power: secular *imperium*, spiritual supremacy and the right
of the English Church to provincial self-determination, i.e. national independence from Rome and the papacy. Therefore, the
Collectanea cited the passage of Bracton that makes the king the
true sovereign because he has neither equal nor superior and is
vicar of God. A phrase was, however, slanted to increase royal
power.[19] Next, extracts were made from chronicles in defence of
Edward I's claim to suzerainty over Scotland and Wales. Their

[18] Cleopatra E. vi, fos. 27, 35. The letter is dated 169 A.D. in the *Collectanea*.
[19] '[Rex debet esse] sub Deo et sub lege, quia lex facit regem' appears as 'sub
Deo. Non sub lege, quia Rex legem facit'! Ibid., fo. 28ᵛ. Were Cranmer and
Foxe using a royalist text or were they vetting Bracton?

purpose was. to show that the authority of the English crown
extended over other realms, and that the sum of the king's feudal
rights amounted to a right of empire. On the question of spiritual
supremacy, Cranmer and Foxe relied on the spurious letter of
Pope Eleutherius already quoted, describing King Lucius as
'vicarius dei', a position strengthened by the fact that Lucius, it
was alleged, had single-handedly endowed the English Church,
with the result that the clergy's jurisdiction and standing were
vindicated solely by a royal grant of lands and liberties. The
implication, as with the theory of Edward I's *imperium*, was that
what had been granted remained inalienably in the king's
possession, and might be resumed at will by Henry VIII.[20] By
way of confirmation, Henry VIII, himself no mean scholar,
invoked Justinian in 1531, perceiving a distinct spiritual estate
comprising an emperor and his clergy, which took decisions on
spiritual matters in church councils and promulgated them by
the emperor's authority alone.[21] The Donation of Constantine,
revealed to be a forgery in 1440, was also (perversely) used in
Collectanea satis copiosa to show, after Marsilius of Padua, that if
the Emperor Constantine had granted the Roman Church its
pre-eminent jurisdiction and temporal powers, such powers
plainly could not have been granted by God and the papacy
could not be a divinely ordained institution.

The third and most radical principle of English power, provincial self-determination, necessarily earned the most learned
treatment at the hands of Cranmer and Foxe. By provincial self-
determination was meant the right of the English Church to
settle its affairs unilaterally in national synods and without
reference to Rome. If this right could be satisfactorily asserted,
the annulment of Henry VIII's marriage might be pronounced
by the archbishop of Canterbury or the English Church in
Convocation, declared nationally by letters placard or parliamentary statute, and enforced by new treason laws drawn
(plausibly enough) to prevent malcontents dividing the realm

[20] W. Ullmann, *Principles of Government and Politics in the Middle Ages*, 2nd edn
(London, 1966), pp. 178-81, 204.

[21] D. Wilkins (ed.), *Concilia Magnae Britanniae et Hiberniae*, 4 vols (London,
1737), vol. III, pp. 762-5.

over Henry VIII's private life.[22] Needless to say, the authors of the *Collectanea* discovered England's right to ecclesiastical independence in the sixth canon of the Council of Nicaea (A.D. 325), when the precedence due to metropolitan churches was recognized. Likewise they drew Henry VIII's attention to the Council of Toledo (589), where the bishops assembled at the command of Wambar, king of the Visigoths. Cranmer and Foxe headlined such canons as that of the sixth Council of Carthage (419), which enacted that no bishop, not even the *Romanus Pontifex*, shall be called 'universal bishop'. On the same theme, *Collectanea satis copiosa* included predictable but invaluable material from Gallican sources, Anglo-Saxon pseudo-history and conciliar theory, notably the view expressed at the Council of Constance (1414-18) that a future pope should reform the 'abuses' of appeals to Rome.

No wonder that Bishop John Fisher and Thomas More found the work of the king's scholars unpersuasive. Yet that is aside from the present analysis. No recorded role in the making of the divorce tracts or *Collectanea* can be assigned to Thomas Cromwell; he was not a member of Henry's coterie of scholars, although he had established himself as a man of business at court by the spring of 1530, and was a member of the Council by the end of that year. By the middle of 1531 and in early 1532, Cromwell and his assistant Thomas Audley had established themselves as Henry VIII's parliamentary draftsmen working at the king's immediate behest.[23] Indeed in early 1533 it was Cromwell who was chiefly responsible for drafting the Act of Appeals, the principal legislative instrument of the break with Rome.[24] But the draftsman of a legal document need not be the true author or architect of its content. In short, if Thomas Cranmer and Edward Foxe had attributed secular *imperium*, spiritual supremacy and provincial self-determination to Henry VIII and England in and after 1530, is this not perhaps the allegedly Cromwellian 'national sovereignty' of the Act of Appeals itself?

[22] Guy, *Public Career*, pp. 181-3.
[23] Ibid., pp. 176-99. Much of the paperwork is, however, filed in Cromwell's archive.
[24] Elton, *Studies*, vol. II, pp. 82-106.

It thus becomes a possibility that the concept of Henry VIII's sovereignty erected by Cranmer and Foxe in 1530 is in fact the source of that 'revolutionary' theory of the unitary state attributed to Thomas Cromwell and 1533. Perhaps the key that unlocks the secret is actually buried in the Act of Appeals itself, not in the text as passed, but in its preparatory drafts. In draft form, the opening passage of the Act with which this discussion commenced contained an additional section:

In confirmation wheroff dyvers of the kinges most royall pro-genytours kinges of this realme and Impier by the epistoles from the See of Rome have ben named, called and reputed the vicars of god within the same, and in their tymes have made and devised ordenaunces, rules and statutes conso-nant unto the lawes of god by their pryncelie power, auc-torytee and prerogatif royall aswell for the due observing and executing of thinges spirituall as temporall within the lymytes of thimperiall crowne of this realme. So that no worldelie lawes, ordenaunces, iurisdictions or auctoritee of any person at the begynnyng of the catholike faith nor long after was practised, experymented or put in execucion within this realme but onelie such as was ordeyned, made, deryved and depended of thimperyall Crowne of the same, for when any cause of the law devyne happened to cum in question or of lerning then was it declared, interpret and shewed by that parte of the saide bodie poletike called the spiritualtie, now being usuallie called the Englisshe churche, which alweyes hathe ben reputed and also founde of that sorte that both for knowlege, integryte and sufficien-cie of nomber it hathe ben always thought, and is also at this hower sufficient and mete of it self without the inter-medling of any *exterior* person or persons to declare and deter-myn all suche doubtes, and to administer all suche offices and dueties as to their rowme doth apperteyn, for the due administracion whereof and to kepe them from corrupcion and synyster affection, the kinges most noble progenitours and antecessours of the Nobles of this realme hath suffi-cientlie indowed the sayde churche both with honor and possessions . . .

The words in italics were added in one draft by Henry VIII himself, who also wrote that any foreign jurisdiction over English affairs permitted in the past was 'but wonly by necligence or usurpation as we take it and estime'.[25]

It seems that the language of this passage is inherently that of secular *imperium*, spiritual supremacy, and provincial self-determination, and that the basic historical manual referred to, with oblique allusion in passing to the laws of the Anglo-Saxon kings, is quite specifically the passage on King Lucius and Pope Eleutherius from the *Leges Anglorum* as expounded in *Collectanea satis copiosa*. No wonder, then, that the early drafts were hastily abandoned in favour of the more arresting respectability of the preamble to the Act of Appeals as passed. To have left King Lucius unexpurgated would have been to proclaim to the world the poverty of the Henrician political alphabet – a schism which rested on pro-baronial propaganda cooked in the reign of King John. It was a sign of weakness and Henry VIII's desperation that the Act of Appeals as passed defined the king's sovereignty in terms of 'divers sundry old authentic histories and chronicles' alone. Henry VIII became *rex imperator*; England became an empire. But a theological and political revolution was made through necessity – Anne Boleyn's pregnancy – to rest on an assumption that could not be made good by an agreed definition of an imperial constitution.[26]

Yet was the theory of 'empire' in the Act of Appeals in any sense novel? Was it more than the sum of the parts of secular *imperium*, spiritual supremacy and provincial self-determination? Was it tantamount to national sovereignty and the idea of statutory omnicompetence? Or have such modernist concepts merely been attributed to the mid-1530s by later historians and legal commentators? Certainly the issue of statutory competence aroused perceptible agony in the 1530s. Thomas More knew well enough the efforts made by the draftsmen of the Act of Supremacy (1534) to avoid stating that Parliament had made

[25] Cleopatra E. vi, fos. 180-4.
[26] Cf. R. Koebner, 'The imperial crown of this realm', *Bulletin of the Institute of Historical Research*, 26 (1953), p. 30; Nicholson, 'Nature and function of historical argument', pp. 182-91.

Henry VIII supreme head of the Church of England, but that, rather, the king had always been supreme head and that Parliament was simply declaring an historic truth. Naturally More knew also that these efforts were futile, a point he proved definitively by being executed, not for denying the supremacy *per se*, but for refusing to be convinced that Parliament could do what Christendom said it could not. We have the record of More's own words on the subject, spoken to Richard Riche in the Tower on 12 June 1535:

> 'A Kyng [ma]y be made by parlyament and a Kyng depryved by Parlyament to whiche act any [of his] Sybyettes beyng of the parlyment may gyve his concent, but to the case . . . [in question] a Subyett can not be bound by cause he cannot gyve his consent . . . [in] Parliament Saying further that although the Kyng were acceptyd in Ingland yet moste Utter [i.e. foreign] partes doo not affirme the same.' Whereunto the sayd Ryche sayd, 'Well Sir, God comfort you for I see your mynd wyll not change, which I fere wyll be very daungerous to you . . .'.[27]

Of course, Henry VIII did not regard the break with Rome as a revolution: that was the ultimate measure of the genius, ingenuity, and ingenuousness of the authors of the *Collectanea satis copiosa*. Indeed the Dispensations Act of 1534 positively affirmed England's commitment to the Catholic faith.[28] For England's political theory until 1536, when the last vestiges of the pope's authority as pastor, teacher, and interpreter of scripture were cast off,[29] was less that of statutory omnicompetence than that which assumed that conflicts between ecclesiastical and secular jurisdiction should properly be resolved in favour of

---

[27] E. E. Reynolds, *The Life and Death of St Thomas More* (London, 1968), pp. 385-6. I have checked Riche's manuscript (Public Record Office, SP 2/R, fos. 24-5) under ultra-violet light, and am satisfied that the reading 'consent' (Reynolds, p. 368, line 11) is correct. It is a pity that this document is so badly mutilated.

[28] 25 Henry VIII, c. 21.

[29] By 28 Henry VIII, c. 10.

the state and imperial crown, save in cases where the enabling legislation was directly contrary to divine law.

The fascinating thing is that this last idea was much older than *Collectanea satis copiosa* and the Act of Appeals. Dr John Baker's researches into Tudor law have demonstrated that a belief in the supremacy of common and statute law over canon law and ecclesiastical custom was a shared attitude or cultural assumption among many common lawyers by 1485.[30] For example, Chief Justice Hussey asserted in 1485 that the king of England was answerable directly to God, and was therefore superior to the pope within his realm. Thomas Kebell, an Inner Temple barrister, said in the same year that 'if all the prelates should make a provincial constitution, it would be void, because they cannot change the law of the land.' He meant that provincial constitutions were invalid if they contradicted prevailing English law, and the jurisdiction of the church courts in cases of debt and contract had already been attacked by writs of prohibition awarded by King's Bench. John Hales, another barrister, in a Gray's Inn reading of 1514, expounded his objections to the problems of dual authority caused by parallel jurisdictions exercised by church and state. He thought it inconvenient that similar questions should be decided differently in different courts, an argument that became the hallmark of the royal cause in the 1530s.[31] In 1512 a law and order statute removed the privilege of benefit of clergy from persons not ordained in the three higher orders of clergy in cases of murder, and robbery in churches, highways or dwelling houses.[32] This Act was the beginning of the abolition of clerical immunity from the effects of

---

[30] J. H. Baker (ed.), *The Reports of Sir John Spelman*, 2 vols, Selden Society (London, 1977-8), vol. II, pp. *64-70*. The chief legislation of the Middle Ages regulating ecclesiastical jurisdiction was the Statutes of Provisors and *Praemunire*: 35 Edward I, st. 1; 25 Edward III, st. 5, c. 22; and st. 6, c. 2; 27 Edward III, st. 1, c. 1; 38 Edward III, st. 1, c. 4; and st. 2, cc. 1-4; 3 Richard II, c. 3; 7 Richard II, c. 12; 12 Richard II, c. 15; 13 Richard II, st. 2, cc. 2-3; 16 Richard II, c. 5; 2 Henry IV, cc. 3-4; 6 Henry IV, c. 1; 7 Henry IV, c. 8; 9 Henry IV, c. 8; 3 Henry V, c. 4.

[31] *Reports of Sir John Spelman*, ed. Baker, vol. II, p. *65*.

[32] 4 Henry VIII, c. 2.

secular law in cases of felony, the privilege won posthumously by
Thomas Becket in the Compromise of Avranches, confirmed by
the *Concessimus Deo* clause of Magna Carta and many times
since. That statute of 1512 was, in turn, contradicted in May
1514 by Pope Leo X's pronouncement during the Fifth Lateran
Council that laymen had no jurisdiction over criminous clerks,
and was denounced in a sermon preached at Paul's Cross in
February 1515 by Richard Kidderminster, abbot of Winch-
combe. Kidderminster said that the statute was against the law
of God and the liberties of the church; that it was void and sinful
to put into effect; and that those who had made it, spiritual as
well as lay (and including Henry VIII) were subject to ecclesiastical censure, and thus excommunication, if they remained
obdurate.[33] This sermon caused a furore: as Hughes aptly
remarks, Wolsey 'began his career as a cardinal as he was to
end it, kneeling before the king and begging his mercy from the
pains and penalties of praemunire'.[34] For Henry VIII himself
joined the debates in the wake of Kidderminster's sermon.
Ending the affair in November 1515 at Baynard's Castle, he
declared: 'By the ordinance and sufferance of God we are king of
England, and the kings of England in time past have never had
any superior but God alone. Wherefore know you well that we
shall maintain the right of our crown and of our temporal
jurisdiction as well in this point as in all others.'[35] Henry in 1515
had already studied the maxim that a king who does not recognize a superior is free from outside jurisdiction. Furthermore, he
spoke in the context of a judges' opinion that the writ of *praemunire facias* ran against all members of convocation who appealed
to Roman canon law not demonstrably based on divine law or
approved in advance by the king. In other words, Henry, fifteen
years before *Collectanea satis copiosa*, defined his regal power in

[33] J. Duncan M. Derrett, 'The affairs of Richard Hunne and Friar Standish',
in More, *CW*, IX, p. 226.

[34] P. Hughes, *The Reformation in England*, 3 vols (London, 1950-4), vol. I, p.
153.

[35] J. A. Guy, 'Henry VIII and the praemunire manoeuvres of 1530-1531',
English Historical Review, 97 (1982), p. 497.

terms of his right to monitor the reception of canon law, in which case his 'superiority' was already deemed to embrace denial of the pope's right to infringe his territorial sovereignty on the basis of the Petrine commission.[36]

Another clash occurred in 1519-20 over the ecclesiastical privilege of sanctuary. Matters had come to a head in the wake of a local feud in 1516 when John Pauncefote, a Gloucester justice, was shot and mutilated on his way to the sessions at Cirencester. The murderers, and their supporters, took sanctuary. Once again the matter was argued in the King's Council and before the judges, and ended by a pronouncement from Henry VIII himself:

> I do not suppose that St Edward, King Edgar, and the other kings and holy fathers who made the sanctuary ever intended the sanctuary to serve for voluntary murder and larceny done outside the sanctuary in hope of returning, and such like, and I believe the sanctuary was not so used in the beginning. And so I will have that reformed which is encroached by abuse, and have the matter reduced to the true intent of the making thereof in the beginning.[37]

Chief Justice Fyneux welcomed this statement, and made it the basis of a judgement in Hilary term 1520 reversing accepted law upon ecclesiastical sanctuary: the notion of permanent sanctuary, he declared, 'is a thing so derogatory to Justice and contrary to the common good of the Realm that it is not sufferable by the law' unless usage time out of mind, that is, before 1189, had been recognized at a general eyre. Nor should this allowance be regarded as meaning much, since Fyneux observed that no one had ever found such a recognition in the records of the eyres. This amounted to saying that the only possibility of watertight sanctuary after 1520 was when the privilege had stemmed from a royal grant with papal confirmation and use before legal memory, supported by royal confirmation and use

[36] Ibid.
[37] *Reports of Sir John Spelman*, ed. Baker, vol. II, pp. *342-3*.

since. Mere papal grants were in breach of the statute of *praemunire*, even if the statute annulled them retrospectively; furthermore subsequent royal confirmations did not mend the defect.[38]

No doubt all this sounds technical, legal and dense. But it may point towards an intellectual shift in attitudes to Rome and canon law in the forty-five years between 1485 and 1530. When John Colet preached his Convocation sermon in 1512, he appealed to the leaders of the English Church not only to reform the church but to defend it against lay encroachments.[39] The same line was epitomized by the career of Sir Thomas More, whose ultimate defences of historic attitudes are best read in his *Apology* and *Debellation of Salem and Bizance*, rather than in the records of his trial and execution.[40] The *Apology* and *Debellation* were More's replies to books by the learned Middle Temple lawyer, Christopher St German, author of *Doctor and Student* (1528 and 1530), *New Additions* (1531), *A Treatise concerning the Division between the Spiritualty and Temporalty* (1532), *Salem and Bizance* (1533) and numerous other works.[41] In these books, St German made quite categorical statements on the supremacy of English common and statute law over canon and papal law. For instance, he held that the law of the state, not the church, governed all matters touching property, which taken to its logical conclusion meant that the church retained jurisdiction only over its sacramental life and ceremonies. Discussing one of the anti-clerical Acts passed in the 1529 session of Parliament, which Bishops Fisher, West and Clerk had asked the pope to condemn as invalid on the grounds that it touched clerical immunity,[42] St German said that this legislation was made 'by the assente of the kynge, and of all the lordes spirituall and

[38] E. W. Ives, 'Crime, sanctuary, and royal authority under Henry VIII: the exemplary sufferings of the Savage family', in M. S. Arnold, T. A. Green, S. A. Scully and S. D. White (eds), *Of the Laws and Customs of England* (Chapel Hill, NC, 1981), pp. 298-9.

[39] J. H. Lupton, *A Life of John Colet, D.D.* (London, 1909), pp. 293-304. For the date, see J. B. Trapp, 'John Colet and the *Hierarchies* of the Ps-Dionysius', *Studies in Church History*, 17 (1981), pp. 130-3.

[40] More, *CW*, IX, pp. 1-172; the *Debellation* is *STC²*, no. 18081.

[41] See above, pp. 95–120.

temporall of the realme, and of all the commons: and I holde it
nat best to reason or to make argumentes / whether they had
auctoritie to do that they dydde or nat. For I suppose / that no
man wolde thynke, that they wolde do any thynge, that they
hadde nat power to do.'[43] Yet St German went further. In his
New Additions, he observed that the king-in-parliament was 'the
hyghe soueraygne ouer the people / whiche hath not onely
charge on the bodies, but also on the soules of his subiectes'.[44] A
revolutionary proposition – or was it? In fact, St German's
intellectual mentors turn out to be Sir John Fortescue, Jean
Gerson the Parisian conciliarist, and Marsilius of Padua.[45] He
had read and digested their writings before producing his own
books. His 'revolutionary statement' may therefore really mean
that he wanted the king to share with Parliament the *regimen
animarum* – the tutorial 'care' or 'charge' of souls already
entrusted to princes. Although St German was the first writer to
emphasize Parliament as the legislative (and consultative)
instrument for achieving the victory of the common over the
canon law, it is, however, questionable how far statutory
omnicompetence in the modern sense is what he had in mind
when he spoke of the king-in-parliament as 'hyghe soueraygne
ouer the people'. We are left wondering where medieval concepts
end and modern thought begins – if indeed the transition was
ever clear cut, which seems unlikely.

If, however, this reading is correct, Cromwell becomes the man
who, if he did not 'invent' St German's theory, nevertheless
translated it into action between 1534 and his fall, since he
succeeded in neutralizing the essentially absolutist characteristics of Henry VIII's 'imperial' kingship.[46]

Yet if 'assimilation' rather than 'revolution' was the keynote
of juristic thought in the 1520s and 1530s, the work of St
German, notably the twin dialogues of his *Doctor and Student*,

---

[42] 21 Henry VIII, c. 6; Guy, *Public Career*, p. 139.

[43] *Doctor and Student*, ed. Plucknett and Barton, p. 317.

[44] Ibid., p. 327.

[45] Guy, *St German*, pp. 35-6, 40, 43-4, 51, 72-3, 87.

[46] Elton, *Reform and Reformation*, pp. 197–200.

testifies to a change since the time of Sir John Fortescue – a shift of either mentality or modes of expression. If a change of mentality occurred it was inspired, I think, by juristic ideas at the Inns of Court. Thomas Cromwell might have been influenced, with others, but such a change of mentality would have been partial, or partisan, since Thomas More was a common lawyer too. If a shift in modes of expression lies at the heart of changed emphasis, it was signalled by St German's desire to circulate *Doctor and Student* in printed form, particularly by his decision to write and print in Latin and English rather than Law French, for this reveals his conscious wish to appeal to a constituency much broader than that of the Inns of Court.[47]

Another scholar, one directly concerned with the gestation of official Henrician ideology and the concept of 'empire', also wrote a Latin treatise for the press. Edward Foxe's *De vera differentia* (1534) must be regarded as an acid test of the extent to which Henrician dogma might be revealed to a learned international audience during the year of the Act of Supremacy. (Foxe's book was in 1548 translated into English and printed in black letter, the preferred typeface of the literate people.)[48]

Foxe had four self-conscious aims in the *De vera*: (1) to establish that ecclesiastical jurisdiction had no foundation in divine law save in respect of the sacramental life of the church, and that provinces of the universal church were largely self-governing; (2) that the contents of canon law had validity only as 'informations', 'rules', or 'traditions' for the guidance of Christian men, but not as laws that commanded obedience; (3) that holy bishops and church councils repudiated the dominion of one man, favouring limited episcopal authority in the church, and that holy bishops had sometimes rightfully resisted papal encroachments when guided by 'conscience' or 'private law' as written in

---

[47] *Doctor and Student*, ed. Plucknett and Barton, pp. lxix-lxxvi, 176-7. See below, p. 156.

[48] *Opus eximium. De vera differentia regiae potestatis et ecclesiasticae, et quae sit ipsa veritas ac virtus utriusque* (London, 1534); *STC*, no. 11218. The translation by Henry, Lord Stafford, *The true dyffere[nce]s betwen ye regall power and the ecclesiasticall power*, is competent but marred by misprints and Protestant influences; *STC*, no. 11220. Cotton MS Cleopatra E. vi, fos. 1-15, is a manuscript of the latter part of the Latin text of *De vera differentia* headed 'De potestate regia'.

their hearts by the Holy Spirit; (4) that the power of kings in general, and kings of England in particular, vouchsafed them undisputed rights of ecclesiastical government over both their churches and clergy. Both scripture (mainly the Old Testament) and the law of Nature validated royal power – it was for kings to govern and judge. Kings were superior to bishops and bishops subject to kings. The clergy were only to administer the sacraments and to guide Christians by the holiness of their examples. Romans 13 was the key New Testament text, as expounded by Fathers and learned 'authors': the text gave authority to kings over bishops and clergy as much as over lay people. The thesis here may be summarized thus: all power is of God and must be so obeyed; the distinction is between lawful power entrusted to kings, and ecclesiastical tyranny permitted by God in order that men might be scourged for their transgressions.

The emperors Constantine and Justinian, together with the Anglo-Saxon kings, and William I and Edward I, were the historical models erected by Foxe. Yet the concept of 'empire' as announced in the Act of Appeals, at any rate in relation to the specific issue of ecclesiastical appeals, is almost overlooked in *De vera differentia*. The issue of appeals is mentioned, but briefly. Following a passage on Justinian, who enacted laws *De episcopis et clericis*, many 'laws' of England were cited to establish that kings there had maintained their historic authority over the church. The matter of appeals is tucked away in this section between Justinian's laws and the regalian rights of Henry I's reign. Foxe quotes chapter 8 of the Constitutions of Clarendon, which had also appeared in the *Collectanea satis copiosa* in a version taken from William of Malmesbury.[49] The Constitutions of Clarendon were, however, a weak authority for the king's oversight of appeals: it is plain that an attempt is being made to give the legislation of 1533 spurious historical force. Otherwise the Anglo-Saxon kings predominate: the 'laws' of Cnut, Edgar, Aethelstan, Ine, Ethelred and others are listed. King Lucius

---

[49] *De vera differentia*, sigs. M3^v-4; Cleopatra E. vi, fo. 40 (annotated 'de appellationibus' by Henry VIII); W. Stubbs, *Select Charters*, ed. H. W. C. Davis, 9th edn (Oxford, repr. 1962), p. 165; Nicholson, 'Nature and function of historical argument', p. 194.

turns up again, as ever the joker in the pack. Likewise King Edgar's speech to his clergy, the Acts of the Bishops of Durham, the Battle Abbey charter, William I's letter to the pope, and Edward I's claim to overlordship of Scotland appear. The last issue is represented by long documentary quotation: Edward's royal dignity and customary law demand papal recognition of his right and title to Scotland, which the king must assert as an inalienable function of the English crown, one that could not be granted away even if an individual English king were willing to do so. The argument is familiar, but Foxe's *De vera* adds nothing to the episode. One senses, above all, no awareness in the work that England's 'imperial' status was perceived as anything beyond what was actually maintained by the Lincoln Parliament in the political context of 1301. If national sovereignty and statutory omnicompetence in the modern sense were at stake in 1533 and 1534, Edward Foxe, one of the minds behind 'Henricus Octavus', *Gravissimae censurae*, the *Collectanea, Glasse of Truthe* and the rest, prefers not to say so.

Before we abandon the vexed question of statutory omnicompetence, it does seem bizarre that the supposedly cohesive policy which manufactured the Act of Appeals under the guiding hand of Thomas Cromwell contained so dramatic an internal contradiction as between the notion of the supremacy of statute and that of the caesaropapist supreme head, Henry VIII. If Henry VIII was henceforward to manage the English Church and clergy directly after the manner of a late Roman emperor, it would appear that Parliament was no more sovereign than it had been when the English Church owed allegiance to Rome that the papacy. The reason for this contradiction was perhaps that the Act of Appeals was itself a compromise document, partly between Henry VIII and Cromwell, partly between Henry VIII and the clergy. It is plain that the king could only achieve the declaration of the English Reformation by parliamentary statute with the co-operation of the lords spiritual in the House of Lords, who, if not in the majority there, were nevertheless in a substantial minority, namely fifty or so as against fifty-seven temporal peers. Since there were conservative lords temporal as well as spiritual, everything depended on politics and parliamentary management. Of course, Henry coerced some of his clerical opponents into submission by threats, *praemunire* and punitive taxation, but most bishops actually supported the king, and a vital truth lies behind this capitulation. It is beginning to look as if Henry VIII had decided from the beginning of his reign that he meant to control and manage the English Church; for fourteen years he ran the church and clergy through Wolsey, and the clergy connived, because it was better to be ruled by a churchman, however abrasive, than more directly by the king – and Wolsey certainly protected the clergy from the full force of Tudor policy between 1515 and 1529. Then Wolsey was destroyed by *praemunire*; the anticlerical laity and common lawyers were given their heads as an integral aspect of the king's divorce policy; by 1532 it looked as if the Tudor supremacy would be a parliamentary one, not a purely royal instrument of control. The king, who disliked representative assemblies out of 'imperialism' and emulation of the French, wished to cut back Parliament's contribution to the mechanical, but still revolutionary task of enacting the requisite legislation. He found among the clergy some unexpected allies, because it was plain to all but the most ultramontane papalists in the years 1532 to 1536 that a parliamentary supremacy would have exposed the clergy directly to the pent-up fury, and hatred, of the anticlerical laity and common lawyers. Thus to politically alert bishops royal supremacy was the better of two evils: the clergy would not have to counter the approaching anticlerical backlash without the necessary filter of royal mediation.

I have already hinted that the intellectual origins of the Henrician revolution must be traced back before the Act of Appeals, and that the principles of equality before the law, laicization, and rationalization as espoused by some English common lawyers reflected perhaps some sort of union of the juristic specifics of the English situation with the citizen-centred philosophy of the Renaissance that developed without direct regard to England or the Tudors. Of course, we must recognize the obvious: the 1530s saw dramatic changes; the break with Rome was in this sense a revolution. The triumph by 1580 of Protestantism and the Anglican Church was an even greater

revolution. Yet we should return, finally, to the suggestion that a
case might be made for 1485 as a date of some significance. In
addition to the arguments of the judges and common lawyers in
the courts, in their Inns, and as members of the King's Council –
all of which had a cumulative effect, though they had all been
fundamental to the English scene for hundreds of years – we
must face some harsh political realities. It was the first of the
Tudors, Henry VII, who transformed the relationship between
civil and church authorities. The Tudors could not tolerate
vested interests incompatible with their secular aims: thus fran-
chises were attacked, liberties suppressed, actions of *praemunire*
and *quo warranto* begun in the royal courts against church and
churchmen; appeals to Rome were monitored and suffered
decline; requests for secular aid against excommunicates
dropped to the lowest level since 1250.[50] All this was happening
between 1485 and 1509, and every available method was used:
an Act of Parliament of 1489 curtailed benefit of clergy; Archbishop Morton, Henry VII's lord chancellor, secured bulls from
Rome modifying the privileges of sanctuaries which had become
refuges for criminals, and to conduct visitations of religious
houses hitherto exempt from royal jurisdiction.[51] We have seen
that such policies were continued by Henry VIII.[52] Furthermore, Henry VII changed the character of the bench of bishops
to the extent that it has been suggested that in the long term,
secularization of the bench may have enervated its religious
leadership.[53] First, Henry VII's appointments to bishoprics
favoured lawyers at the expense of theologians. The king's first
consideration was always that of service to the Crown, thus of
twenty-seven episcopal preferments during his reign, sixteen

[50] R. L. Storey, *Diocesan Administration in Fifteenth-Century England*, Borthwick
Papers no. 16, 2nd edn (York, 1972), pp. 29-33; *Reports of Sir John Spelman*, ed.
Baker, vol. II, pp. *66-8*; Henry E. Huntington Library, San Marino, California,
Ellesmere MS. 2652, fo. 6.

[51] Storey, *Diocesan Administration*, pp. 29-30; *Reports of Sir John Spelman*, ed.
Baker, vol. II, pp. *332-40*.

[52] Ibid., vol. II, pp. *64-70, 326-46*.

[53] R. J. Knecht, 'The episcopate and the Wars of the Roses', *University of
Birmingham Historical Journal*, 6 (1957-8), pp. 108-31.

were of lawyers, and only six of theologians. Most of his theologians, too, were administrators.[54] Second, service to the state to the detriment of the church was exacted as a conscious act of policy under Henry VII: thus William Smith, petitioned in vain to be allowed to leave the Marches of Wales in order to pay attention to his neglected see, and Richard Redman, had to fine with the king for permission to reside in his diocese.[55] The status of bishops in the King's Council declined, and Henry showed a ruthlessness to them typical of his treatment of other peers. Even Richard Fox paid £2,000 for a pardon, while all were subject to fiscal feudalism and the quest for revenue.

Under Henry VIII, though, the clergy were subjected to the harshest and most extensive taxation in previous English history. In addition to normal contributions in other years when general taxation was exacted, in 1523 and 1531 the English provinces were obliged to offer £118,000 the first time as the triumph of Wolsey's legatine ingenuity, and the second in exchange for the ominous Pardon of 1531.[56] Each of these donations was equivalent in value to the yield of a parliamentary lay subsidy of 2s. 8d. in the pound; thus the clergy were paying above traditionally accepted proportions of general taxation as between them and the laity. In short, a systematic attack on ecclesiastical revenues had begun. Henry VIII's attacks on benefit of clergy and sanctuary have already been mentioned; so too has his study in 1515 of the maxim that a king who does not recognize a superior is free from outside jurisdiction. Yet surely such study was not undertaken in isolation. For Henry's imperial ambitions, though they came to new and ripe fruition with *Collectanea satis copiosa* and the Act of Appeals, had more obvious origins even than the pronouncements of 1515. Henry had briefly sought the imperial crown of Germany in 1519. He hoped, too, to conquer the throne of France, and alongside that ambition, first given military expression in 1512, went the propaganda war in which the French and English monarchies vied

[54] M. M. Condon, 'Ruling elites in the reign of Henry VII', in *Patronage, Pedigree and Power*, ed. C. Ross (Gloucester, 1979), pp. 110-11.

[55] Ibid., pp. 111-12.

[56] Guy, 'Henry VIII and the praemunire manoeuvres', pp. 481-503.

with each other for primacy in sacerdotal sovereignty. For instance, the French in 1515 republished the fifteenth-century dialogue known as the *Debate of the Heralds*. The French herald in that exchange praises the independence of his king from all overlordship, whereas, he jibes, the English king holds from the see of Rome. Moreover, the Frenchman boasts that his king can outshow the English in symbolic emblems of regal pre-eminence.[57] In reply, the English exhumed and embellished the ideology of the Hundred Years War. The exchange ended with an English vernacular edition of the *Debate*, printed in 1550, in which the English herald answered that his king was emperor within his own realm and 'holdeth of no man', that he is supreme head of the churches of England and Ireland, wears an imperial diadem, holds in his left hand an orb representing his empire, and in his right hand carries a sword to minister and defend justice.[58]

The *Debate of the Heralds* has recently been addressed by Professor McKenna; it would be interesting to discover more concerning the transfer of any similar English materials from manuscript to print between 1513 and 1550.[59] Yet such enquiry should be widely extended. Henry VIII, we know, had placed the arched or imperial crown as a decorative motif on his gold and purple pavilion at the tournament of 1511;[60] in 1513 the arched crown was struck on a special issue of coinage during the English occupation of Tournai, that emblem having first appeared on the coinage in 1489, when Henry VII minted his new gold sovereign.[61] When in 1517 Henry VIII was musing on the idea of aspiring to succeed the Emperor Maximilian, who

[57] *Le debat des heraulx darmes de Fra[n]ce et de[n]gleterre* (Rouen, [1515]), British Library, C.32.g.4; L. Pannier (ed.), *Le Débat des Hérauts d'Armes de France et d'Angleterre* (Paris, 1877). See J. W. McKenna, 'How God became an Englishman', in *Tudor Rule and Revolution: Essays for G. R. Elton from his American Friends* ed. D. J. Guth and J. W. McKenna (Cambridge, 1982), p. 29.

[58] *The Debate betwene the heraldes of Englande and Fraunce, compyled by Jhon Coke, clarke of the kynges recognysaunce, or vulgerly, called clarke of the Statutes of the staple of Westmynster, and fynyshed the yere of our Lorde.* M.D.L.; *STC*, no. 5530.

[59] Cf. 'How God became an Englishman', pp. 27-31, 35-43.

[60] C. Whibley (ed.), *Henry VIII* [an edition of Edward Hall's *Chronicle*], 2 vols (London, 1904), vol. I, p. 24.

[61] C. E. Challis, *The Tudor Coinage* (Manchester, 1978), pp. 49-51, 65-6.

had purported to be willing to resign in favour of Henry in order to gain a subsidy, Cuthbert Tunstall informed him:

> Oon of the cheffe points in the Election off th'emperor is that he which shal be electyd must be off Germanie subgiet to [the] Empire; wheras your Grace is not, nor never sithen the Cristen faith the Kings of Englond wer subgiet to th'empire. But the Crown of Englond is an Empire off hitselff mych bettyr then now the Empire of Rome: for which cause your Grace werith a close Crown. And.therfor yff ye wer chosen, sens your Grace is not off th'empire the Election wer voide. And iff your Grace shuld accepte the said Election therby ye must confesse your realme to be under subjection off th'empire to the perpetual prejudice off your successor . . .[62]

All these matters require further research. Yet one thing is perhaps apparent. Politics, ideology and the divorce issue provided an explosive mixture in the wake of the fall of Wolsey. But the ensuing fusion was of formidable complexity. The opportunities that the political situation created were considerable, but policy could be ambiguous and was not fully coordinated. Many minds were at work; decisions had to be taken under pressure in response to royal requirements and immediate needs. There was no overall blueprint. Furthermore, unexpected traps beset the unwary. One awaited Edward Foxe, whose exposition of 'private law' or 'conscience' in *De vera differentia* justified Thomas More's defensive stand against Henry VIII far better than Robert Grosseteste's against Innocent IV. Finally, the cultural and mental background since 1485 may be significant: we need to know more about the Inns of Court, who was active there, whether readings and moots reflect discernible patterns of opinion, how widespread were St German's attitudes, how far juristic thought mirrored royal policy or vice versa, and so on.

---

[62] H. Ellis (ed.), *Original Letters Illustrative of English History*, 1st series, 3 vols, 2nd edn (London, 1825), vol. I, p. 136 (*LP*, II, no. 2911). For further evidence of the intellectual origins of Henry VIII's 'imperial' sovereignty, see Ullmann, 'This Realm of England is an Empire', pp. 175-203; D. B. Quinn, 'Henry VIII and Ireland', *Irish Historical Studies*, 12 (1960-1), pp. 325-6.

The search for the intellectual origins of Henrician 'imperial' kingship will thus extend far beyond the achievements, and lifetime, of Thomas Cromwell. It will reach beyond England and the sixteenth century, too, since the theme of imperial *renovatio* was European: Charles V, Francis I, and Henry VIII stood in a tradition that sprang from Augustus, Marcus Aurelius, and Charlemagne. The theme of 'imperialism' in the Renaissance had been articulated by Ariosto in the *Orlando furioso* and was consummated for England by Spenser in *The Faerie Queene*. It is unlikely that Henry VII and Henry VIII were much influenced by this universal outlook, but it is equally clear that the question, 'Who was the architect of the Henrician "political" revolution?' is *mal posée*, if Henry VIII and Thomas Cromwell are to be our only candidates. Whatever takes its place, the 'King or Minister' debate is dead. Yet as Professor Elton had all along emphasized, Thomas Cromwell was not King Utopus.[63]

---

[63] Elton, 'King or Minister? The man behind the Henrician Reformation', in *Studies*, vol. I, pp. 173-88.

8

Law, Equity and Conscience in Henrician Juristic Thought

John Guy

The relationship of equity and conscience to common law in the Henrician Age is complex and problematical. Concepts of law and equity overlap after 1500 against a background of major changes. First, the rise of Chancery and the conciliar courts galvanized new developments in legal doctrine and procedure, particularly the latter, derived from Roman-canonical practice in the ecclesiastical courts.[1] Second, the invention of printing acted as a catalyst to improved legal citation and the lawyer's burgeoning sense of precedent, as opposed to vaguer perceptions of custom.[2] Finally, the Reformation, by ending duality and interchange between the secular courts and the ecclesiastical forum, which became ossified, and more specifically by abolishing auricular confession, which was the ultimate court of conscience, invited consolidation and near-monopoly of English justice by common lawyers trained at the Inns of Court.

[1] E. W. Ives, *The Common Lawyers of Pre-Reformation England* (Cambridge, 1983), pp. 189-281; M. Blatcher, *The Court of King's Bench 1450-1550* (London, 1978), pp. 63-137; *Reports of Sir John Spelman*, ed. Baker, vol. II. pp. *51-164, 192-208, 220-98*; Guy, *Cardinal's Court*. pp. 51-117; *Public Career*, pp. 50-93; W. J. Jones, *The Elizabethan Court of Chancery* (Oxford, 1967), pp. 177-304. This essay draws in part on some material treated at greater length by Guy, *St German*, pp. 64-94.

[2] Ives, *Common Lawyers*, pp. 147-85; *Reports of Sir John Spelman*, ed. Baker, vol. II, pp. *159-63*.

Throughout these processes the key word is assimilation. New juristic concepts were assimilated within traditional forms; tradition assimilated the new but did not give way to it; reforms were transmitted through traditional systems, not by erection of new ones.[3] The book that reflected and, in some part, itself achieved this assimilation is, of course, *Doctor and Student* by Christopher St German. It is, however, worth examining his book in the light of two controversial tracts composed shortly after St German's two dialogues were printed. The first tract is the *Replication of a Serjeant at the Laws of England* by an unknown writer;[4] the second is the reply to that piece, *A Little Treatise Concerning Writs of Subpoena*, which was written by St German himself.[5] The two tracts, the former especially, coarsen the issues and thus help us to grasp what they really were. In addition, the *Little Treatise* pursues the debates of *Doctor and Student* concerning the relation of the laws of England to equity and conscience with specific reference to the contemporary practice of the Court of Chancery. It had not been the purpose of *Doctor and Student* to discuss the rules and procedures of individual courts in any detail; St German instead provided theoretical analysis of the principles or grounds of the laws of England, and how conscience ought in many cases to be formed in accordance with these axioms. In fact, equity understood according to St German's formulation actually precluded separate courts and special procedures, since 'suche an equytye must alway be obseruyd in euery lawe of man, and in euery generall rewle therof, & that knewe he wel that sayd thus. Lawes couet to be rewlyd by equytye.'[6]

Discussion pivots around the question raised by the student of common law in chapter 19 of the first dialogue of *Doctor and Student*. Should conscience be ruled after the law, or the law be left for conscience?

[3] Ives, *Common Lawyers*, pp. 189-221.
[4] Text printed by Guy, *St German*, pp. 99-105.
[5] Text printed in ibid., pp. 106-26.
[6] *Doctor and Student*, ed. Plucknett and Barton, pp. 3, 95-6.

The lawe wherof mencyon is made in this questyon / that is to saye where conscyence shall be rewlyd by the lawe / is not as me semyth to be vnderstande only of the lawe of reason: and of the lawe of god. But also of the lawe of man that is not contrary to the lawe of reason nor the lawe of god: but that it is superaddyd vnto them for the better orderyng of the common welth / for such a law of man is alwayes to be sette as a rewle in conscyence so that it is not lawfull for no man to go fro it on the one syde ne on the other / for suche a lawe of man hath not only the strength of mannes law / but also of the lawe of reason / or of the law of god / wherof it is dyryuyed / for lawes made by man whiche haue receyued of god power to make lawes be made by god. And therfore conscyence muste be orderyd by that human lawe . . . . But if such a human law is changed by the competent authority, although without sufficient cause, then the conscience which had been previously founded upon it must change likewise.[7]

Within this passage was encapsulated the most fundamental and pervasive feature of St German's own thought. For St German himself held that equity is not outside the law, but resides implicitly in, and should be observed in, every human law. Before approaching equity, however, I should define 'conscience'. In *Doctor and Student*, St German defined it as the driving force within the human soul which inclines a man to pursue good and eschew evil, and which is capable of distinguishing the two at a practical level.[8] Both motive and cognitive in this abstract sense, conscience was an objectivized gauge of ethical evaluation, and it was this gauge that was applied as a theoretical yardstick against the defendant's real-life morality in a particular case in Chancery in order to arrive at a corrective sentence (or decree) should any prove necessary. Hence in concrete terms, conscience became the moral principle which

[7] Ibid., p. 111.
[8] Ibid., pp. 87-95.

gave the chancellor the cognitive and coercive authority to call parties before him, to pronounce decisions in his courts and bind litigants to observe them. Evil must be searched out, and parties could not be allowed to escape the consequences of their wrongful acts because of the excessive rigidity of common law. Conscience, however, operated only in relation to the defendant's conduct and culpability as discerned by the judge in a specific case; it could not otherwise be invoked judicially, as could common law and statute by pleadings and argument. Furthermore, conscience could not touch land or property except indirectly through coercive restraint of the defendant's person.

Turning to equity, we should revert to chapter 16 of the first dialogue of *Doctor and Student*, which was entitled 'What is Equytie'. It is the doctor of divinity who is speaking:

> Equytye is a ryghtwysenes that consideryth all the pertyculer cyrcumstaunces of the dede / the whiche also is temperyd with the swetnes of mercye. And suche an equytye must alway be obseruyd in euery lawe of man / and in euery generall rewle therof / & that knewe he wel that sayd thus. Lawes couet to be rewlyd by equytye. . . And for the playner declaracyon what equytie is thou shalt vnderstande that syth the dedes and actes of men / for whiche lawes ben ordayned happen in dyuers maners infynytlye. It is not possyble to make any generall rewle of the lawe / but that it shall fayle in some case. And therfore makers of lawes take hede to suche thynges as may often come and not to euery particuler case / for they coulde not though they wolde And therfore to folowe the wordes of the lawe / were in some case both agaynst Iustyce & the common welth: wherfore in some cases it is good and even necessary to leue the word is of the lawe / & to folowe that reason and Justyce requyreth / & to that intent equitie is ordeyned / that is to say to tempre and myttygate the rygoure of the lawe. And it is called also by some men epicaia. The whiche is no other thynge but an excepcyon of the lawe of god / or of the lawe of reason / from the generall rewles of the lawe of man: when they by reason of theyr generalytye

wolde in any partyculer case Iuge agaynste the lawe of god /
or the lawe of reason / the whiche excepcion is secretely
vnderstande in euery generall rewle of euery posytyue
lawe.[9]

It will be helpful to trace the history of this formulation, which
is possible thanks to the work of Dr Rueger.[10] St German's
concept of equity as so defined followed the theory of the Parisian Jean Gerson (1363-1429). Although *Doctor and Student*
alludes several times to Aristotle, it seems that St German's
acquaintance with the Greek philosopher's doctrine of *epieikeia*
stems less from first-hand study than from close familiarity with
Gerson's *Regulae morales*. However, the relevant passage in Aristotle says: 'Then when a case arises where the law states a
general rule, and something not covered by the generality
occurs, it is then right when the lawgiver owing to the generality
of his language left a loophole for error to creep in, to fill the gap
by such a modified statement as the lawgiver himself would
make, if he were present at the time, and such an enactment as
he would have made, if he had known the particular circumstances.'[11] *Epieikeia* is essentially this rectification of the law,
'where the law has to be amplified because of the general terms
in which it has to be couched'.[12] But if St German did not know
Aristotle at first hand, he did know St Thomas Aquinas. It is,
however, Gerson who dictates the formulation of chapter 16 of
the first dialogue.[13] Gerson's definition of equity harmonized
epieikeia as presented in the *Ethics*, Book V, with the *aequitas
canonica* as defined by Hostiensis in the *Summa aurea*, Book V:
Aequitas est justitia dulcore misericordiae temperata.[14] As Gerson
explained in the *Regulae morales*, 'Equity is justice [which] having
weighed all the particular circumstances is tempered with the

[9] Ibid., pp. 95-9.
[10] Z. Rueger, 'Gerson's concept of equity and Christopher St German',
History of Political Thought, 3 (1982), pp. 1-30.
[11] Aristotle, *Ethics*, V, x.
[12] Ibid.
[13] Rueger, 'Gerson's concept of equity', pp. 10-13.
[14] Ibid., p. 11.

sweetness of mercy.'[15] Gerson wrote elsewhere: 'For the understanding of human positive law it is necessary to direct one's
attention to the diverse and manifold nature of the human
condition . . . in order that the *epieikeia* or equity may be fully
implemented.'[16] For instance, in governing a monastic society
individual needs must be respected: 'The function of the *praesi-
dens* is to be a sort of living law which moderates the dead laws
. . . in the words of Aristotle he should be a true *epiekes* that is an
interpreter of general laws in their application to singular cases.
This is the virtue which the Psalmist called equity.'[17]

Gerson was, in fact, the source of St German's theory that
equity is not outside the law, but resides implicitly in it, and that
the principle of 'excepcyon', which some men call 'epicaia', is
'secretely vnderstande in euery generall rewle of euery posytyue
lawe'.[18] In lesson five of the *De vita spirituali animae*, Gerson
observed that divine law could be transgressed in various
degrees and in innumerable circumstances. In each case one
must apply 'that virtue which Aristotle called *epieikeia* . . . whose
function is to consider not the bare precept alone, but that
precept in the light of all the particular circumstances'. This
should be done 'in the case of almost every precept'. From such
procedure could be derived 'the method of reconciling the rigour
of the law and austerity of discipline with the gentleness of mercy
and benign mitigation'.[19] In particular, Gerson reasoned in the
De non esu (1401) upon the Carthusian vow of abstinence from
meat. The question was, could the rule be relaxed in case of
'extreme necessity' by means of an excepting clause. Gerson
argued that the laws of God and Nature themselves sufficiently
except: *lex naturalis et divina sufficienter excipiunt*. Moreover, all
general laws 'ecclesiastical as well as divine are subject to

[15] Ibid.; Jean Gerson, *Oeuvres Complètes*, ed. P. Glorieux, 10 vols (Paris, 1960-
73), vol. IX, pp. 95-6.

[16] Rueger, 'Gerson's concept of equity', p. 9; *Conversi estis*, *Oeuvres*, ed. Glorieux, vol. V, p. 175.

[17] Rueger, 'Gerson's concept of equity', p. 11; *A Guillaume Minaudi* (Oct.
1422), *Oeuvres*, ed. Glorieux, vol. II, p. 238.

[18] *Doctor and Student*, ed. Plucknett and Barton, p. 97.

[19] Rueger, 'Gerson's concept of equity', pp. 13-14; *De vita spirituali animae*,
Oeuvres, ed. Glorieux, vol. III, p. 189.

exception which becomes apparent upon examination [of those laws] . . . exception which sufficiently allows itself to be understood or can be drawn from another source need not be expressed.' What is the reason? Anything else would be impossible and unworkable on account of the infinite variety of particular human circumstances.[20]

Gerson's proposition that the principle of exception inherently resides in general rules of law – that equity is part of the law not something outside it – was, nevertheless, controversial. In the *Summa theologiae*, St Thomas Aquinas had maintained that *epieikeia* could be used in exceptional cases only, and that the decision as to when exceptions applied was normally in the sole discretion of the ruler.[21]

> If the decision on the letter of the law is not a matter of immediate danger which requires prompt action, it is not open to anybody to act as interpreter of what is and what is not in the public interest: such decision belongs rightly to rulers, and it is to meet such cases that they have authority to dispense from the law. When, however, danger is so imminent that there is no time to refer the matter to the authorities, necessity itself carries its own dispensation: for necessity knows no law.[22]

Cases of necessity seem, however, to have been rare in Thomist theory. St Thomas quoted the familiar example of the law that the gates of the city must remain closed during a state of siege, but when the enemy pursued some citizens who ran towards the gates, then the gates in such a case should be opened against the letter of the law for the sake of the common welfare which the legislator intended.[23] Yet what is interesting is that when St German gives a similar example in chapter 16 of the first

[20] Rueger, 'Gerson's concept of equity', p. 14; *De non esu carnium, Oeuvres*, ed. Glorieux, vol. III, p. 83.

[21] Rueger, 'Gerson's concept of equity', p. 14, The crucial passages in the *Summa theologiae* are at II, I, q. 96 (art. 6), and II, II, q. 120 (art. 1). St Thomas Aquinas, *Summa theologiae*, ed. P. Caramello, 3 vols (Turin, 1952-62).

[22] *Summa theologiae*, ed. Caramello, vol. I, 439b (II, I, q. 96 [art. 6]).

[23] Ibid.

dialogue of *Doctor and Student*, the case is modified to illustrate not the urgency of necessity, but the principle that 'equytye folowyth the lawe in al partyculer cases where ryght and Iustyce requyreth / notwythstandynge that a general rewle of the lawe be to the contrary.'[24]

Aquinas elsewhere in the *Summa* reinforced his opinion that the interpretation of a legislator's intention was in the sole competence of the ruler.[25] He cited the *Codex Justinianus*: 'It is proper and lawful for us alone to evaluate an interpretation between equity and law.'[26] From this, bald conclusions could be drawn; for instance, in the *Summa* he asserted: '*Epieikeia* does not seem to be a virtue. One virtue does not displace another; yet *epieikeia* displaces virtue, doing away with what is just in law and seeming to be counter to severity. Therefore it is no virtue.' He continued: 'To act under *epieikeia* seems to be to pass judgement on a law, namely in the decision that the law is not to be observed in a certain case. Therefore *epieikeia* is a vice rather than a virtue.' And he concluded: 'The application of *epieikeia* being unlawful, *epieikeia* is thus not a virtue.'[27] Although these were not the last words of Aquinas on the subject, they lead us straight to the *Replication of a Serjeant at the Laws of England*; for whereas in chapter 19 of his first dialogue of *Doctor and Student* St German had suggested that whether or not conscience should be ruled after the law or the law be left for conscience was, ultimately, a question to be analysed in the light of specific examples, the serjeant in the *Replication* was unwilling to discuss particular cases.[28] What he does, in fact, is dogmatically to gloss Aquinas:

> Me thinkithe that the lawe aughte not to be lefte for conscience yn no caas; for the lawe commaundith all thing that is good for the commen welthe to bee doon, and prohibitithe all thing that is evill and that is againste the

[24] *Doctor and Student*, ed. Plucknett and Barton, pp. 97-9.

[25] *Summa theologiae*, ed. Caramello, vol. II, 546-7 (II, II, q. 120 [arts. 1-2]).

[26] *Codex*, I, tit. 14, leg. 1. *Corpus juris civilis*, ed. P. Krueger (Berlin, 1915), II, 67b.

[27] *Summa theologiae*, ed. Caramello, vol. II, 546-7a.

[28] *Doctor and Student*, ed. Plucknett and Barton, pp. 111-21.

commen welle. Wherfore yf ye observe and kepe the lawe, as is yn doying all thing that is for the commen well, and eschewe all thing that is evill and againste the commen well, ye shall not nede to studie so moche upon conscience, for the lawe of the realme is a sufficiente rule to ordre you and your conscience, what ye shall do yn every thing and what ye shall not doo. Yf ye therfore followe the lawe trewly, ye cannot do amys, nor yet offende your conscience, for it is saide, *quod implere legem est esse perfecte vertuosum* (to fulfill the lawe is to be perfitely vertuouse).[29]

In stating that to fulfil the law was to be perfectly virtuous, the serjeant perhaps meant 'sufficiently virtuous', since the notion under review was that of English common law as the basic minimum ethic.[30] Yet even then his assumption that the Englishman's view of common law could be modelled after the Judaic view of Old Testament law reveals a flawed credulity that must eventually be ascribed to invincible ignorance.

At this point in the *Replication*, the student of common law intervenes to observe that perfect virtue was to be understood in terms of conformity with the law of God. But the serjeant retorts: 'Yt is also to be understande by the lawe of man; for the lawe of man is made principally to cause the people to kepe the lawe of God.'[31] But the serjeant plainly felt vulnerable here. He declined to debate individual cases of conscience with the student since, as he claimed, he wished to avoid unnecessary tedium. Instead he turned to attack the chancellor's protection of uses.[32]

It is arguable that the greatest threat to the common law system in the Henrician Age was the 'use'.[33] By 1450 the method was widely recognized as the effective means to evade feudal taxes and the common-law rule prohibiting devises of freehold land. As Sir Edward Coke remarked, 'there were two Inventors

[29] Guy, *St German*, pp. 102-3.

[30] D. E. C. Yale, 'St German's *Little Treatise Concerning Writs of Subpoena*', *Irish Jurist*, new series, 10 (1975), p. 328.

[31] Guy, *St German*, p. 103.

[32] Ibid., pp. 103-5.

[33] Ives, *Common Lawyers*, pp. 197-9, 247-62; see also his article, 'The genesis of the Statute of Uses', *English Historical Review*, 82 (1967), pp. 673-97.

of Uses, Fear and Fraud; Fear in Times of Troubles and civil Wars to save their Inheritances from being forfeited; and Fraud to defeat due Debts, lawful Actions, Wards, Escheats, Mortmains, etc.'[34] Such common-law restrictions as the rule against devises of land applied only to the legal estates; the use was employed in the nature of a trust to separate legal title to land from its beneficial enjoyment, which allowed shrewd property owners to treat the land as their own while escaping the penalties and obligations associated with legal title.[35] In particular, the practice of executing family settlements through the erection of uses became ubiquitous during the fifteenth century, and continued despite some reassertion of feudal rights in the reign of Henry VII.[36] Uses were probably most often invoked to execute the wishes of feoffors after their deaths, achieving in effect the forbidden devises of land by will.

In fact, the ecclesiastical courts had originally enforced and interpreted uses. From the late fourteenth century, such cases were regularly heard in the diocesan courts of Canterbury and Rochester.[37] The probate jurisdiction of the church courts probably justified their intervention in such instances, although it was also a rule of canon law that the ecclesiastical courts should provide justice whenever secular law was inadequate. By 1450, however, the jurisdiction of Chancery over uses was established.[38] The extent to which Chancery's business then became dominated by this species of work, though, is still a matter for debate. One authority suggests that by 1460 nine-tenths of petitions to Chancery concerned uses, but it is far from plain what proportion of these cases involved the protection of equitable interests.[39]

[34] Quoted in Guy, *Public Career*, p. 53. Cf. *Doctor and Student*, ed. Plucknett and Barton, pp. 222-5.

[35] Guy, *Public Career*, pp. 53-9; Ives, *Common Lawyers*, pp. 197-9.

[36] By 4 Hen. VII, c. 17 and 19 Hen. VII, c. 15.

[37] R. H. Helmholz, 'The early enforcement of uses', *Columbia Law Review*, 79 (1979), pp. 1503-13.

[38] M. E. Avery, 'The history of the equitable jurisdiction of Chancery before 1460', *Bulletin of the Institute of Historical Research*, 42 (1969), pp. 129-44.

[39] Ibid. Cf. J. A. Guy, 'The development of equitable jurisdictions, 1450-1550', in *Law, Litigants and the Legal Profession*, ed. A. H. Manchester and E. W. Ives (London, 1983), pp. 80-6.

In the *Replication of a Serjeant at the Laws of England* the writer's assumption is that Chancery's protection of uses was the chief reason for the decline of the central courts of common law in the early sixteenth century. The true situation was more complex. I have shown elsewhere that it was common-law counsel who from the beginning had advised their clients to litigate in Star Chamber and Chancery, rather than in King's Bench and Common Pleas.[40] As a result, general legal business had begun to transfer into Chancery and the conciliar courts, notably real property suits. For doctrinal distinctions apart, the advantage of the 'equitable' forum lay in its use of English bill procedure, notably in the answer which the defendant had to exhibit on oath; this combined with a meticulous analysis of written proofs and powers of recovery and discovery. Many cases succeeded in Chancery which, though theoretically remediable, would have failed at common law – a major attraction. The basic truth ignored by the serjeant in the *Replication* was that litigants were the most potent force for change in the legal system: they did not care whether their judgements were doctrinally orthodox as long as they met immediate needs and were enforceable. Parties wanted results, not lectures in jurisprudence. They flocked to courts that offered a public service. Yet it is also true that some common lawyers, and as time went on the Crown, believed that enfeoffments to uses as a device to engineer the succession to property were *ipso facto* fraudulent.[41] The debate culminated in the Statute of Uses (1536).

Yet whoever wrote the *Replication* deliberately broached the chief issues vexing lawyers in the wake of Wolsey's fall. These issues were the business rivalry of Chancery and the older benches; what conservatives alleged to be the professional apostasy of the practitioners who serviced the chancellor's courts from Sir Thomas More downwards; the relationship between law and conscience, and the theory of equity; the threat of perpetual litigation that would arise if Chancery was ever permitted to review judgements given at common law; the validity of legal doctrine upon such matters as debt under deed and uses;

[40] Guy, *St German*, pp. 65-6.
[41] Ives, *Common Lawyers*, p. 253.

and the Crown's reassertion of its feudal rights in the face of collusive enfeoffments designed to achieve the forbidden succession to property.

The *Replication* was answered by St German: the *Little Treatise Concerning Writs of Subpoena* was drafted in his own hand, though no evidence is known to me that his manuscript was shown to anyone during his lifetime.[42] In defending *Doctor and Student*, St German preferred to review how far equitable rulings and procedures were reasonable in particular cases, though he was prepared to make some general statements. This method was, in fact, necessary, since conscience operated in its juristic context only in relation to the misdeeds of individual defendants. St German examined, for instance, the case of discovery of documents. Since the fourteenth century Chancery had developed its own procedural methods for enforcing common law, and the most popular remedy it offered by Henry VIII's reign was that of discovery of documents. The common-law rule was that legal declarations must be certain, not impressionistic: deeds of title must be properly described in terms of their number, nature and location during pleadings. Yet Chancery held that defendants should not be allowed the unfair advantage of documents not available to the plaintiff, irrespective of whether or not the plaintiff knew the precise details of the deeds he lacked. A fifteenth-century Chancery petition illustrates the form:

> Sheweth unto your good and gracioux lordshipp Robert Draycote that, where he is seased of a mees with thappurtenaunce in Chelmerdon in his demeane as of fee, it is so, gracioux lorde, that divers dedes and evydencys concernyng and apperteynyng to the seid mees be comyn to the handez of oon William Bayly. And howe be it, gracioux lord, that your seid oratour hathe required delyvere of the seid evydences of the seid William, yet that to do he at all tymes hathe refused and yet dothe, contrarie to reason and good conscience. And in so much as your seid suppliaunt knoweth not the certeintye nor nombre of the seid evydences, nor whether they be enclosed in bagg, boxe sealed

[42] Guy, *St German*, pp. 56-62.

or chest loken, he can have no remedy by the common lawe.[43]

In reality, a majority of bills of this type were mainly intended to defend a disputed title or possession before the chancellor.[44] Under Wolsey, 3,042 suitors (41 per cent of the total) had alleged detention of deeds, but only a minority, it is suspected, were aiming to restrict Chancery's intervention to resolving the equitable point.[45] St German, however, did not discuss the use of legal fiction in such circumstances. He wrote of Chancery's powers of discovery: 'And here it is to be ñotyd that it is not ageynste ye common lawe, though ye partye have remedye in ye chauncery in ye seid case, though he can have noone by ye common lawe. For ye common lawe doth not prohybyt, but that there shal be remedye in the chauncery in ye seid case and other lyke.'[46]

St German also treated the question of enforceability of verbal agreements for transfer of incorporeal things and the justifiability of Chancery's intervention by *subpoena* in cases where a deed was lacking to establish grounds of action at common law.[47] St German's opinion was that the real test was consideration. He followed the legal convention that a beneficial transaction of some sort was necessary to the making of a contract, and argued that a bare agreement to do or pay anything on the one side without a *quid pro quo* on the other was as void in equity as in law. Yet where a verbal agreement was reinforced by good and sufficient consideration, a writ of *subpoena* was available.

The principle that what was void in law is void in equity too is crucial. Every text book tells us that a party at common law in the Henrician Age might have right but not remedy. St German said he could not have remedy at equity either if a clear rule of law was at stake. However, let us postpone for a moment scrutiny of what a clear rule, or maxim of law, was in St

---

[43] C1/64/556.

[44] Guy, *Public Career*, pp. 51-3.

[45] F. Metzger, 'Das englische Kanzleigericht unter Kardinal Wolsey, 1515-29' (unpublished Ph.D. thesis, Erlangen-Nürnberg, 1977), p. 333.

[46] Guy, *St German*, p. 108.

[47] Ibid., pp. 108-9.

German's thought. For the moment, it is more important to observe that he had views about what equity *should not* be doing, as well as on what it could do. His position on equity's boundaries is the key to his successful assimilation of law, equity and conscience.

The case of the statute *Quia emptores* was raised in the *Little Treatise*.[48] No rent service could be reserved on conveyance of a fee simple after 1290 because the grantee must hold the land not of the grantor but of the grantor's lord.

> By reason of which statute, yf a man syth that statute make a feffement without dede, or by dede polle, reservynge a rent, that reservacion is voyde, as for any remedy that he shal have by ye commen lawe . . . For there is a maxysme in the lawe that a reservacion of rent shal not stonde in effect, onles he that makyth ye reservacion have a revercion in hym, or ellse that ye lande may be holden of hym by that rent reservyd, as it myght have ben byfore ye seid statute of Quia emptores terrarum.[49]

If, however, it were agreed that a feoffor keeping no reversion and taking no deed should none the less receive a rent, then that agreement was good by the law of reason. St German held that the agreement was enforceable by *subpoena* in Chancery, but the agreement in such a case was only defensible in Chancery because it was not directly against the law. *Quia emptores* had not expressly prohibited reservations of rent service, but simply denied remedy at common law.[50] St German emphasized his position on this important point: 'yf a statute were made that al reservacions of rents out of landes shuld be void, and then a man contrarye to that statute wolde make such a reservacion, that reservacion were void in law and conscyence, for it were dyrectly ageynst ye statute.'[51] As a deleted note generalized the issue: 'A

[48] 18 Edw. I, st. 1.

[49] Guy, *St German*, p. 109.

[50] Yale, 'St German's *Little Treatise*', p. 329. Cf. *Doctor and Student*, ed. Plucknett and Barton, p. 194.

[51] Guy, *St German*, p. 109.

man may have ryght in many cases where he shal neyther have remedye at the common law ne in the chauncerye.'[52]

St German's opinion that equity follows the law was strong in the *Little Treatise*.[53] Common law did not prohibit discovery of documents; it did not deny the validity of verbal contracts reinforced by good and sufficient consideration; it did not directly forbid reservations of rent service. The distinction was always between right and remedy. Yet equity was not unbridled: it could not run against the law.

The bonus derived from reading *Doctor and Student* in the light of the ensuing tracts that debated its contents is, then, that St German reviewed in the *Little Treatise* a series of particular cases in which Chancery's equitable jurisdiction was accounted reasonable. But he was prepared to make negative statements, too: he considered situations in which a *subpoena* should not be made available in Chancery despite the nature of the case and the undoubted existence of some grounds in conscience. The key statement of policy came mid-way through chapter 7 of the *Little Treatise*:

> And then I have hard this taken for a grounde, that when the common law puttyth a man fro his remedye, though he have ryght, for eschewynge of an inconvenience that myght foloo upon it, and that then yf the remedye shuld be had in the chauncery in that same case, the same inconvenyence shuld foloo as shuld have don at ye commen law, that there no sub pena shal lye.[54]

Pleadings in Chancery that contradicted matters on record in the common-law courts were no more permissible at equity than at common law itself. Furthermore, no writ of *subpoena* could run against a statute or against the rules or maxims of common law: if it did, 'then the lawe shuld be juged to be voyd.'[55]

The term 'maxims of law' is crucial to St German's position. We know that the judges and lawyers of his time spoke of

[52] Ibid., p. 110.
[53] Yale, 'St German's *Little Treatise*', p. 332.
[54] Guy, *St German*, p. 117.
[55] Ibid., p. 116.

'maxims' during pleadings in the courts. For instance, Thomas Bryan, chief justice of Common Pleas, said in 1496: 'il est icy comon maxime . . . et pur ceo jeo ne voile arguer a ceo.'[56] Others spoke in Henry VIII's reign of 'le maxime de ley', 'un maxime', and 'Nota que in court baron . . . les maximes et les generalx customes del realme que est le commen ley serra trie per les Justices.'[57] Sir John Fortescue wrote in chapter 8 of his *De laudibus legum Anglie*:

> In the laws, indeed, there is no matter and form as in physical things and in things artificially devised. But, nevertheless, there are in them certain elements out of which they proceed as out of matter and form, such as customs, statutes, and the law of nature, from which all the laws of the realm proceed as natural things do out of matter and form, just as all we read comes out of the letters which are also called elements. The principles, further-more, which the Commentator[58] said are effective causes, are certain universals which those learned in the laws of England and mathematicians alike call maxims, just as rhetoricians speak of paradoxes, and civilians of rules of law. These principles, indeed, are not known by force of argument nor by logical demonstrations, but they are acquired . . . by induction through the senses and the memory.[59]

If, however, maxims were universals, the problem was indeed how to know them, since universals can be inferred from other universals, but not from mere particulars. In 1493 Bryan refused to allow Thomas Kebell to dispute a point 'pur ceo que il est merement inconter nostre comon erudition et est ore in maner un principal, per que per cest mesne nous duissomus transposer

---

[56] *Reports of Sir John Spelman*, ed. Baker, vol. II, p. *161*, n. 3.

[57] Ibid.

[58] Averroës on Aristotle's *Physics*. See *Auctoritates Aristotelis, Senece, Boecii, Platonis*, etc., *De Laudibus*, ed. Chrimes, pp. lxxix, 21, 150; Plummer, *The Governance of England*, pp. 99-100.

[59] *De Laudibus*, ed. Chrimes, p. 21.

touts nostres ancientes presidentes'.[60] The chaos they believed
would follow the negation of their 'common erudition' is the key
to the attitude of the Henrician common lawyers, but this is to
say no more than that the self-proving nature of their axioms
sprang intuitively from their *demi-monde*.

St German took the debate further in chapters 8 and 9 of the
first dialogue of *Doctor and Student*. One of the grounds of English
law was 'in dyuers pryncyples that be called by those learned in
the lawe maxymes / the which haue ben alwayes taken for law in
this realme / so that it is not lawfull for none that is lernyd to
denye them / for euery one of those maxymes is suffycyent
auctorytie to hym selfe to such an extent that it is fruitless to
argue with those who deny them. And whiche is a maxyme / &
whiche not shall alway be determyned by the Juges . . . and not
by men.'[61] In other words, St German paraphrased Bryan,
adding that it was for the judges to adjudicate which parts of
common erudition were 'maxims' and which were not. But he
continued:

> And suche maxymes be not onlye holden for lawe / but also
> other cases lyke vnto them / and all thyngis that neces-
> saryly foloweth vpon the same / ar to be reduced to lyke
> lawe. And therfore moste commenly there be assygned
> [some reasons or] consyderacyon why suche maxymes be
> resonable and ought reasonably to be observed as maxims
> to the intent that other cases lyke may the more conue-
> nyently be applyed to them and judged by the same law.
> And they be of the same strength & effect in law as statutis
> be. And though all those maxims might be conveniently
> numbered among the said general customs of the realm,
> since the generall custome . . . be the strength and war-
> aunte of the sayd maxymes: as they be of the general
> customes of the realme / yet bycause the sayd generall
> customes be in maner diffused throughout the realm of
> England and knowen through the realme as well to them
> that be vnlernyd as lernyd / and may lyghtly be had and

---

[60] *Reports of Sir John Spelman*, ed. Baker, vol. II, p. *161*, n. 4.
[61] *Doctor and Student*, ed. Plucknett and Barton, pp. 57-9.

knowen and that with little stodye in English lawe. And the sayde maxymes be onlye knowen in the kynges courtes or amonge them that take great studye in the lawe of the realme.[62]

It appears, therefore, that maxims are in reality general customs, or particular details of common law, which the lawyers themselves have chosen to elevate into principles for purposes of professional practice. *Doctor and Student* listed twenty-seven specific examples of maxims,[63] from which it is clear that these self-proving axioms subsist apart from customs such as primogeniture, the disinheritance of bastards, or feudal incidents only insofar as they have been received as 'maxims' by lawyers. Exactly this objection was raised by the doctor of divinity in chapter 9 of the first dialogue. St German replied through the mouth of the student of common law:

> Many of the customes [& maxymes] of the lawes of Englande can be knowen by the vse and custome of the realme so apparantly that it nedeth not to haue any lawe wrytten therof . . . The other maxymes and customes . . . may be knowen partly by the lawe of reason: & partly by the bokes of the lawis of Englande called yeres of termes / & partly by dyuers recordis remaynynge in the kynges courtes & in his tresorye. And specyally by a boke that is called the regestre / & also by dyuers statutis wherin [many of] the sayd customes and maxymes be ofte resyted / as to a dylygent sercher wyll euydently appere.[64]

St German's ultimate argument is thus that maxims are customs which the judges have acknowledged as binding in the courts. These customs are justified by the law of reason, but are searched for in practice on the parchment plea rolls, in the Year Books, and in the register of writs and the statute book.

This means, however, that 'maxims' are not universals at all. They are human artifices, or expedients, designed to rationalize custom and to achieve similar results in similar types of case on the basis of presumed principle, but in reality for reasons of

[62] Ibid., p. 59.
[63] Ibid., pp. 59-65.
[64] Ibid., pp. 69-71.

human convenience. The authority of maxims rests entirely upon their reception and usage, and the only method of proving that this or that maxim is a rule of the common law is by showing that it has been the custom to observe it. Yet St German gave maxims equivalent force to statutes: 'they be of the same strength & effect in law as statutis be.'[65] *Lex non scripta* in this scheme had the force of written acts of Parliament, and it was the common-law judges who decided what was and what was not a maxim. The true purpose of this artifice became clear in the *Little Treatise*, where St German applied his theory of maxims to restrict severely the boundaries of equity. He wrote: 'there lyeth no sub pena directely againste a statute, nor directely againste the maxymes of the lawe, for [if] it shuld lye, then the lawe shuld be juged to be voyd, and that may not be don by no courte, but by ye parliament.'[66] The distinction is again between right and remedy, but what St German actually achieves in the *Little Treatise* is to assign to the common lawyers effective control over the boundaries of equitable construction. Without a writ of *subpoena* no one may litigate in a court of conscience; but the *subpoena* cannot run against the maxims of common law acknowledged by the community of lawyers. In short, it is to be common law, not any other species of law civil, Roman-canonical, or papal, that must govern the consciences of Englishmen in the courts. Equity was not to be absolute, but was to be relative to the common erudition of lawyers. It was therefore human and fallible. In particular, it was vulnerable to the political atmosphere of the Inns of Court at a given historical moment.

By stating what equity ought not to be doing, St German tackled the toughest aspect of assimilation. In fact, his views concerning equity's boundaries were essentially those endorsed in practice by the early seventeenth-century judges.[67] In Henrician terms St German was marginally ahead of his time,

[65] Ibid., p. 59.

[66] Guy, *St German*, p. 116. For a qualification to St German's argument, ibid., pp. 111-12, but this applies only to restricted circumstances of debt under deed.

[67] Cf. C. M. Gray, 'The boundaries of the equitable function', *American Journal of Legal History*, 20 (1976), pp. 218-20.

because he formulated the notion that equity follows the law in a progressive sense. Yet it is hard not to see his political motivation. For St German was a man with a mission. He wrote his first dialogue of *Doctor and Student* in Latin, but the second was in English. He explained: 'The cause is this. It is ryght necessary to all men in this realme bothe spyrytuall and temporall for the good orderynge of theyr conscyence to knowe many thynges of the lawe of Englande . . . Therfore for the profyte of the multytude it is put into the Englysshe tonge rather than into the Latyn or Frenche tonge.'[68] What the multitude learned from the second dialogue, however, was St German's anticlericalism. Sir Thomas More, exasperated by his opponent's *Treatise Concerning the Division between the Spiritualty and Temporalty*, rebuked St German for publicising clerical abuses 'in the vulgare tunge'. Gerson, St German's mentor, had written in Latin on this subject out of respect for the clergy: 'he wolde not that a man sholde reproche & rebuke ye prelates before the people'. St German printed the faults of the clergy, More claimed, 'bycause he wolde haue the lay peple both men & women loke on them'.[69]

It is possible, then, that St German's purpose all along in *Doctor and Student* was not to justify common law and to explore equity's functions and boundaries as an exercise in jurisprudence *per se*, but was to do so as the essential precondition to attacking the independent jurisdiction of church courts and clergy in England as guaranteed by chapter 1 of Magna Carta. St German was astute enough to know that the most insidious form of attack was not total destruction, but rather a theoretical campaign in literary form designed to establish the 'principle' that common law, its customs, maxims and statutes, and not the decrees of the Roman Church, should properly inform the consciences of Englishmen. We must never forget that More regarded St German as an enemy of the faith. In reading *Doctor and Student* and the *Little Treatise* it may be completely artificial to distinguish between St German the lawyer and St German the anticlerical polemicist.

[68] *Doctor and Student*, ed. Plucknett and Barton, pp. 176-7.
[69] More, *CW*, IX, p. 60/12-20.

9

Scripture as Authority: Problems of Interpretation in the 1530s

John Guy

Thomas More, mid-way through Book IV of his pleonastic tract *The Confutation of Tyndale's Answer*, paused to survey his objective in one sentence. 'For ye well remember', he prompted his readers, 'that all our mater in this boke, is bytwene Tyndale and me no thynge ellys in effecte, but to fynde out whyche chyrche is the very chyrche.'[1] Two matters were indeed crucial during the 1530s: to define the church and to ascertain its authority over scripture. 'I promyse the[e]', concurred one of Henry VIII's propagandists from a quite different standpoint, 'it is the necessaryest matter to be disputed that can be for the commen welthe, and specyally in the worlde that nowe is. For untyll that be discussed we shall neuer haue peace in Chrystendome.'[2]

The reformers were not alone in identifying the true church by its adherence to the 'Word of God', but interpretations differed

---

[1] R. C. Marius, 'Thomas More and the heretics' (Yale University Ph.D. dissertation, 1962; University Microfilms: Ann Arbor, 1971), p. 199; More, *CW*, VIII, p. 480.

[2] *A dyaloge betwene one Clemente a clerke of the Conuocacyon, and one Bernarde a burges of the parlyament / dysputynge be / twene them what auctoryte the clergye haue to make lawes. And howe farre and where theyr power dothe extende*, sig. D5ᵛ. This tract may be a unique fragment (Selwyn College, Cambridge, Q. 3. 4). Dr H. C. Porter says it has been linked with St German, but this, as he notes, looks pure conjecture. See Porter, 'Hooker, the Tudor constitution, and the *Via Media*', in *Studies in Richard Hooker*, ed. W. Speed Hill (Cleveland and London, 1972), p. 86.

radically. For Luther the 'Word of God' was supreme authority: it expressed God's eternity and redemptive power in Christ. It revealed itself in the church and sacraments, but did so especially in scripture. In fact, More did Luther some injustice by treating his principle of authority as *sola scriptura*.[3] For Luther's 'Word' could judge scripture and find it wanting, as when he said the book of Esther was filled with 'cloudy Jewishness' or the book of James was an 'epistle of straw'.[4] Since, however, scripture for Luther was the objective vehicle of the 'Word', it became in practice the tangible test against which those sacraments which could not be shown to have been instituted by Christ were rejected. None of the reformers thought that scripture on its own was effective: God's spirit had to speak through the writing and inspire faith in men's hearts.[5] Yet scripture in their eyes was the decisive authority in the church's life. The problem of its interpretation accordingly became acute.

William Tyndale reiterated and extended Luther's emphasis on the scriptures. He held that experience of grace was inseparable from scripture which itself mediated the 'Word', thus nothing necessary to salvation was outside the written texts of scripture. Like the Cambridge Lutheran Robert Barnes, he was capable of treating 'scripture' and the 'Word' as synonymous terms. He did so in his *Answer* to More's *Dialogue concerning Heresies*, the work that provoked the *Confutation*. Tyndale argued that scripture was antecedent to the church:

> An other doubt there is, whether the Church or congregation be before the Gospell or the Gospell before the Church, which question is as hard to solue, as whether the father be elder then the sonne or the sonne elder then his father. For the whole Scripture and all beleuing hartes testifie that we are begotten through the word. Wherfore if the word beget the congregation, and he that begetteth is before hym that

[3] More, *CW*, V, pp. 732-74; Marius, 'Thomas More and the heretics', pp. 201-64.
[4] Ibid., p. 202.
[5] Ibid., p. 256.

is begotten, then is the Gospell before the Church . . . And therfore in as much as the word is before the faith, and faith maketh the congregation, therfore is the word or Gospell before the congregation.[6]

Some years later Tyndale said of his translation of the *New Testament*: 'as farre as the scripture approueth it, so farre to allowe it: and if in any place the worde of God dissalow it, there to refuse it, as I doe before our Sauiour Christ and his congregation.'[7] Robert Barnes, attacking the decree of the Council of Constance which forbade the giving of communion in both kinds to laymen, wrote in similar vein: 'Wherfore if I can proue by open Scriptures, of our Mayster Christ, and also by the practise of holy Church, that this counsell is false and damnable, then let all Christen men iudge which of us must be heard and beeleeued, eyther the counsell hauyng no scripture, yea contrary to all scripture, or else I that haue the open worde of God, and the very use and practise of the holy Apostles, and of holy church.'[8]

The heterodoxy of these statements was the idea that scripture stood in opposition to the teaching and practice of the Catholic Church, especially its oral tradition.[9] The crux of the Reformation, in Henry VIII's England as much as on the continent, was the division between the known church and the Word of God which critics regarded as the basis for the attack on Catholicism. Under Henry VIII this issue was debated during June and July 1537 at a synod sitting in the House of Lords that was convoked by Thomas Cromwell as vicegerent in spirituals. The issues at the synod were first, whether sacraments could subsist in the absence of scriptural authority, and second, whether unwritten verities, or traditional doctrines and articles of belief not founded on scripture, were invalid, even if hitherto accepted by the church.[10] Archbishop Cranmer and the

---

[6] *The whole workes of W. Tyndall, John Frith, and Doct. Barnes*, [ed. J. Foxe], 2 vols (London, 1573 [1572]), vol. I, p. 255; *STC²*, no. 24436.

[7] *Workes*, vol. I, sig. B3ᵛ; Marius, 'Thomas More and the heretics', pp. 203-5.

[8] *Workes*, vol. II, pp. 301–2; Marius, 'Thomas More and the heretics', p. 205.

[9] Ibid., pp. 233–6, 241-59.

[10] Guy, *St German*, pp. 46-7.

Scottish theologian Alexander Alesius followed Barnes in resting
the sacraments on scripture. Alesius explained:

> Sacramentes be signes or ceremonys which make us certen
> and sure of the wil of God. But no man's hart can be certen
> and sure of the wil of God with out the word of God.
> Wherfor it foloweth that there be no sacramentes without
> the word of God, and such as can not be proved out of the
> holy scripture ought not to be called sacramentes.[11]

With respect to the second point, Cromwell told the bishops:

> . . . ye will frindly and lovingly dispute among your selves
> of the controversys moved in the church, and that ye wyl
> conclude all things by the word of God without all braul-
> ing, or scolding; neither will his majesty suffer the scripture
> to be wrested and defaced by any glosys, any papistical
> lawes, or by any auctoryte of doctors or councels, and
> moche lesse wil he admit any articles or doctrine not
> conteyned in the scripture, but approved only by conty-
> nuance of tyme and old custome, and by unwritton verytes
> as ye were wont to doo.[12]

By the time these issues were publicly debated at Cromwell's
vicegerential synod, Thomas More was dead. But his views had
been clearly and repeatedly stated in his published writings. He
had defended the supremacy of the Catholic Church and its oral
tradition against the reformers' belief in the sufficiency of scripture. He held the Catholic Church to be so inseparable from the
Word of God that it was itself the sole expression of that Word in
the world. Other manifestations of revelation, including scripture, were subordinate to the church, and were ruled by it.[13]
More saw as his authority the action of the Holy Spirit and two
texts recur in his writings. These are Matthew 28:20, where
Christ assured the disciples, 'Lo, I am with you alway, even

---

[11] Alexander Alesius, *Of the auctorite of the word of God agaynst the bisshop of
London*, sig. B5; quoted by Guy, *St German*, p. 47.

[12] *Of the auctorite of the word of God*, sigs. A5ᵛ-A6ᵛ; quoted by Guy, *St German*,
p. 46 n. 140.

[13] Marius, 'Thomas More and the heretics', p. 233.

unto the end of the world'; and John 14:16-18, 26, in which Christ said, 'And I will pray the Father, and he shall give you another Comforter, that he may abide with you for ever, even the Spirit of truth . . .'.[14]

More believed that Christ's promises had been given to the whole church. Had they been made only to the disciples, their followers would have been abandoned. The visible church was the repository of revelation, and this church was the 'catholyke chyrch', the 'comon knowen chyrch', the church in which Tyndale had 'lerned to know whych is the scripture'.[15] No invisible or 'chyrche vnknowen' comprising only the 'elect' could be believed, 'syth it can not be herd'.[16] The Catholic Church had existed from the Apostles' time to More's, thus it legitimately claimed Christ's promises. More held that the church was antecedent to scripture, not the other way round, as Tyndale had supposed. Indeed the church had itself produced, selected and preserved the texts that together made up the Bible. Without its authority, too, any part of scripture could be questioned at any time. The church, however, prevented this. For instance, if someone proved that St Luke's gospel was not written by St Luke, the truth would still be safe, because the church had validated the gospel's contents when it included the book in the canon. The Holy Spirit inspired consent, which permitted the validation of scripture by the church.[17] Without that essential inspiration, opinions would for ever be divided. Revelation is thus prior to, and more important than scripture. Men have faith because they believe God's teaching, but faith would still subsist if scripture had never been written. The Holy Spirit enters our hearts, guides our endeavours, and inspires faith. Once faith is achieved, 'we byleue as well the chyrch concernynge goddys wordys taught vs by the chyrch and by god

[14] Ibid., p. 210; More, *CW*, V, pp. 100, 364; VIII, pp. 479-80, 999-1000; VI, pp. 108, 114-15, 118-19.

[15] More, *CW*, VIII, pp. 379-82, 477-9, 1004-13, 1029-34.

[16] More, *CW*, VIII, pp. 379-82, 476-9; V, pp. 180-4; Marius, 'Thomas More and the heretics', pp. 211-15.

[17] More, *CW*, V, pp. 242-4; VI, pp. 116-21, 180-2, 253-5; VIII, pp. 377-83, 476-81, 996-1006.

graued in mennys hartys wythout scrypture / as hys holy wordys wryten in hys holy scrypture.'[18]

In fact, More's reliance upon the Holy Spirit quickly placed a protective shield over Catholic practices and beliefs irrespective of their origins. When challenging Luther in the *Responsio*, he had stated his conviction that Christ spoke to the whole church when he said the Holy Spirit would lead men into truth. 'On the heart, therefore, in the church of Christ there remains inscribed the true gospel of Christ which was written there before the books of all the evangelists' – here More reached the kernel.[19] God had imprinted faith so indelibly on the heart of the church that no heretics could erase it. The church's authority was independent of scripture: it did not matter how many scriptural texts, apparently disproving this or that, were adduced by heretics. For the 'true gospel of Christ' was revealed to the church before the bible was written. In short, the 'Word of God' for Thomas More is both written and unwritten: the seven sacraments and articles of faith subsist partly by the written, partly by the unwritten word. Indeed the unwritten 'Word' was in some sense superior to scripture, since it represented 'eternal' revelation, as opposed to written texts limited by the constraints of time and place.[20] More taxed Luther with St Paul's injunction, 'Stand firm and hold the traditions that you have learned whether by word or by letter of ours', and with St John's words, 'Many things were done which are not written in this book.'[21] For More was convinced that necessary articles of faith were among those teachings which the oral tradition transmitted through the church without writing, a process that began with the Apostles and was not restricted in time. He taunted Tyndale with the doctrine of Mary's perpetual virginity, which Tyndale accepted but which he did not prove by scripture.[22] On this point and others, 'the fulnesse of the persuasyon and sure beliefe

[18] More, *CW*, VI, p. 254.

[19] More, *CW*, V, p. 101; VI, pp. 143-4.

[20] More, *CW*, V, pp. 240-2; VI, pp. 115-16, 119-20, 143-4, 172-5, 181, 254; VIII, pp. 377, 381, 476-7, 996; Marius, 'Thomas More and the heretics', p. 249.

[21] More, *CW*, VIII, pp. 99, 105 (2 Thess. 2:15; John 20:30).

[22] Ibid., pp. 479-80, 1005-6.

groweth, by the secrete reuelacion inspyred by the spirite of God into his whole church.'[23] The church came to truth by the 'secret inspyracion' of the Holy Spirit, and this could happen at any time, as More explained in his *Apology*.

> For syth the gospell of Cryste and the wordes of god that are now wryten in bokes, were all wryten in hartes byfore they were wryten in bokes, and yet were at that time of the same strength and authoryte that they be now / we saye to Luther and Tyndale & all such other heretikes, that they say false in that they preche & teche, that men are bounden to byleue nothyng but if it be wryten in bokes / syth god is at his liberty to geue his word in to hys chyrch euen yet at thys daye, by hys owne mouthe, thorow thinspyracyon of hys holy spyryte sent therunto, & by hym selfe abydynge euer therin / & at ye prechyng of the chyrch, wryte it in ye hertes of ye herers, as well & as surely as euer he gaue hys word to his chyrche by hys apostles, and wrote it in the peoples hartes at theyr prechynge, at suche tyme as it was yet vnwryten in any of thapostles bokes.[24]

More ridiculed the reformers' contention that scripture was its own interpreter. The heretics thought 'all thynge is in the scripture as playne as a packe staffe'; everyone could discover 'truth' for himself. 'For they saye that ther is no diffycultye nor hardnesse appearing thereuppon, but that by conferring and comparinge one place wyth an other, euery manne maye fynde out the trouthe well inoughe.' More mocked this claim: 'it wyll make some mannes handes rough with tournyng the booke so often to and fro, before he trye oute euerye suche trouthe on that fashion.'[25] The dangers were transparent. Every man or, even worse, every woman would become his or her own interpreter, and each would have a different reading of the same passage.

In view of Henry VIII's reliance upon scripture as authority for the jurisdictional revolution, it is surprising how little was

[23] Ibid., p. 1006.

[24] More, *CW*, IX, p. 25.

[25] More, *CW*, VIII, p. 997; Marius, 'Thomas More and the heretics', pp. 237-41.

said by his propagandists about the principles of biblical exegesis. Scripture was not the sole authority for the Henrician position: the Fathers Greek and Latin, church councils, popes and
learned 'authors', and the laws and customs of England were all
invoked. Scripture was, however, the key: this is exemplified by
the emphasis on 'truth as revealed in scripture', and the slogan
'We must rather obey God than men', which characterized
Henry's propaganda after the *Glasse of Truthe*.[26] Yet the major
source collection known as *Collectanea satis copiosa*, and learned
defences of the new orthodoxy such as Edward Foxe's *De vera
differentia* (1534) and Stephen Gardiner's *De vera obedientia*
(1535), did not address the problem of exegesis.[27] However,
Gardiner made various relevant statements in his book. He
wrote: 'God's pronouncements (*eloquia*), which are enshrined in
Holy Scriptures brought forth by the declaration of the Holy
Spirit himself, report to us the most certain Word of God
(*certissimam dei vocem*).'[28] He thought there were no exceptions
from obedience to the prince, since none was mentioned in
divine law.[29] In the matter of Henry VIII's divorce, 'the judgement of the divine Word (*divini verbi*) might have sufficed.'[30] It is
far from clear, however, that Gardiner repudiated tradition in
1535, and these passages do not prove he did. In fact, Gardiner
recognized the pope's pastoral role as a teacher and preacher in
De vera obedientia: he was 'primus ante alios' in that function, and
should long continue so.[31] *A litel treatise ageynste the mutterynge of
some papistis* (1534) was more oblique, saying that if the pope was

---

[26] Pocock, *Records of the Reformation*, vol. II, pp. 385-421, 546, 551; P. Janelle
(ed.), *Obedience in Church and State* (Cambridge, 1930), p. 72. *De vera differentia*,
sigs. A2-B1. R. Sampson, *Richardi Sampsonis, regii sacelli decani oratio, qua docet,
anglos, regiae dignitati ut obediant* (London, [?1535]); *STC*[2], no. 21681.

[27] The *Collectanea* is British Library, Cotton MS Cleopatra E. vi, fos. 16-135;
see above, pp. 123–31. Gardiner's *De vera obedientia* is reprinted by Janelle,
Obedience in Church and State, pp. 68-170.

[28] Ibid., p. 82.

[29] Ibid., p. 100.

[30] Ibid., p. 86.

[31] Ibid., pp. 140-8.

truly a man of Christ as the Apostles had been, his preaching would have converted pagans to Christianity.[32] Both tracts were, however, printed before the statute of 1536 (28 Henry VIII, c. 10) extinguished residual papal authority in England.

The Henrician theorist who did tackle the problem of exegesis at length was Christopher St German. Chapter 7 of *An Answer to a Letter* (1535) asked who might interpret scripture and whose exposition should be deemed authoritative.[33] In St German's view, the clergy were disqualified from interpreting texts disputed between church and state, because passages touching their power, jurisdiction, liberties, and possessions would inevitably prove most controversial. Only a priest who through special grace had cast aside worldly ambition could offer impartial guidance, but St German seemed to doubt that any such person existed. He thus proposed that in difficult cases kings and princes should oversee the interpretation of the bible, 'For it appereth. Psalm ii. that it is said thus to kynges and princes, "O ye kynges, understande ye: be ye lerned that iudge the worlde".'[34] The role of rulers, however, was to be supervisory: their intervention was only necessary to avoid 'dyversyties of opinyons and unquyetnesse amonge the people' and to ensure that subjects did not wilfully break divine law. St German withheld from Henry VIII as supreme head the right to construe the meaning of scripture, for this was the preserve of the 'catholyque churche'.

This brings us back to the definition of the church. Gardiner in *De vera obedientia* had defined it as the body (*corpus*) of people united in the profession of Christ, but he elucidated it by reference to provincial boundaries.[35] The *ecclesia anglicana* was in his opinion rightly called 'English': it comprised the communion of Christians in the realm of England. The Gallican and Spanish Churches existed in France and Spain in the same manner, and even the Roman Church in Rome, as he maintained. Gardiner

[32] Pocock, *Records of the Reformation*, vol. II, p. 548.
[33] *STC*[2], no. 21558.5; see Guy, *St German*, pp. 17-18, 41-5, 139-43.
[34] Sig. G3.
[35] Janelle, *Obedience in Church and State*, pp. 92, 94, 114.

defined the English Church as the gathering (*congregatio*) of Christian men, women, clergy and laity in England.[36] The king's headship, he argued, derived from scripture and the consent of the realm, thus he visualized England as a unitary sovereign state in which the secular ruler was also the supreme spiritual authority. Gardiner, however, was a little disingenuous here. He said that the king's supremacy existed by God's law, but claimed, too, that the people gave Henry VIII the authority by their free votes in Parliament.[37] In fact, these propositions contradict each other. If royal supremacy existed by divine law, its authority preceded Parliament's approval of the Act of Supremacy; the extent of Parliament's consent was limited to the declaration of pre-existent truth. On this reading Henry VIII's supreme headship was 'imperial' despite the use of Parliament. Henry as king was bound by the laws and customs of the realm, but as supreme head he was a 'pope' and not bound by them. The realm's assent in Parliament was the link between Henry's two functions, but political change was needed to alter the nature of his supremacy.

St German took a different position to Gardiner. He defined the 'catholyque churche' in *An Answer to a Letter* as 'emperours, kynges and princes with their people as well of the clergye as of the lay fee'. This church, however, could not conveniently be assembled when scriptural exegesis was required: 'therfore it semeth that kynges and princes' whom the people have chosen and agreed to be their rulers and governours, and which have the whole voyces of the people, maye with theire counsell spirytuall and temporall make exposycyon of such scripture as is doutfull'.[38] The representative ideal is strong here: St German visualized consent as a continuous process that did not cease once the 'correct' definition of the church was realized. Power ascended as well as descended, and St German reasserted vigorously the 'constitutional' theory of Sir John Fortescue which he believed to be endangered by 'imperial' theory and Henry VIII's attraction to theocratic kingship.[39] St German explained:

[36] Ibid., p. 94.
[37] Ibid., p. 90.
[38] Sig. G5.
[39] Plummer, *The Governance of England*, pp. 109-16.

There be two maner of powers that kynges and princes have over theire subjectes: the one is called *Jus regale*, that is to saye a kyngely governaunce; and that hathe that power maye with his counsell make lawes to bynde his subjectes, and also make declaration of Scrypture for the good order of his subjectes as nede shall requyre for appeasyng of varyance. The other is called *Jus regale politicum*, that is to saye a kynglye and a polytyke governaunce. And that is the most noble power that any prince hath over his subjectes, and he that ruleth by that power maye make no Lawe to bynde his subjectes without their assent; but by their assent he maye, so that the lawes that he maketh be nat agaynste the lawe of God nor the lawe of reason. And this power hathe the kynges grace in this Realme, where he by assente of his lordes spirytuall and temperall, and of his commons gathered togyther by his commaundement in his parlyamente maye make lawes to bynde the people. And of those lawes there nedeth no proclamation, bicause they be made by all the people, for the parliament so gathered togyther representeth the estate of al the people within this realme, that is to say of the whole catholyque churche therof.[40]

St German agreed with Fortescue that government in England was *dominium politicum et regale*. Henry VIII was not to be an autocrat in respect of his ecclesiastical polity. For 'the whole catholyque churche' came together in Parliament, an equating of the 'church' with Parliament that echoes William Marshall's marginal glosses in his English edition of Marsilius of Padua's *Defensor Pacis*.[41] (Marshall's translation was printed in the same year as St German's *Answer to a Letter*.)[42] In fact, the formulation based on Parliament was theoretically convenient for St German. First, 'the estate of al the people within this realme'

[40] Sigs. G5ᵛ-G6; quoted by Guy, *St German*, pp. 43-4.

[41] *The defence of peace: lately translated out of laten in to englysshe* (London, 1535); *STC*², no. 17817. Marshall glossed Marsilius's citizen legislative body as meaning Parliament on fos. 27ᵛ, 28ᵛ, 35, 91ᵛ, 138.

[42] Marshall's translation had been ready for a year, but was delayed by lack of money: Elton, *Policy and Police*, p. 186. This was not, however, the first printed edition of *Defensor Pacis*; there had been a Basel edition of 1522.

included Henry VIII, who as king was himself an estate. Second, the equating of the church with Parliament implied that Henry's supremacy was bounded by English law and custom. So might scripture legitimately be expounded in Parliament? Or in St German's own words, 'Why shuld nat the parlyament than whiche representeth the whole catholyke churche of Englande expounde scrypture'?[43] The combination of functions within England's premier representative institution would not only liberate the community from clerical bias, but would also assure the smooth assimilation of the changes of the Reformation into English constitutional thought without the reverberations that might otherwise derive from the discovery of 'empire' and royal supremacy.

St German's question about Parliament remained unresolved, and *An Answer to a Letter* was his last treatise to be printed. However, he wrote more in manuscript. A copy of 'A Dyaloge shewinge what we be bounde to byleve as thinges necessary to Salvacion, and what not' is deposited among Thomas Cromwell's papers at the Public Record Office.[44] It was a 'third' dialogue between doctor and student, and I have identified it as St German's work on the basis of his autograph corrections, after the manner of his parliamentary draft of 1531 and *Little Treatise concerning Writs of Subpoena*.[45] This new dialogue is not, however, concerned with legal questions, but sets out to anatomize the points of controversy raised at Cromwell's vicegerential synod of 1537. The roles of the protagonists were accordingly reversed from what appears to have been St German's previous method. It is to be suspected that in *Doctor and Student* and *New Additions* the student of common law had spoken frequently, if not exclusively, for the author, especially in *New Additions*, but in the new 'Dyalogue' the doctor of divinity, the authority on

---

[43] *An answere to a letter*, sig. G6^v.

[44] SP 6/2, pp. 89-168; see Guy, *St German*, pp. 17, 40, 47-54.

[45] Ibid., pp. 8-9, 17, 56. St German's handwriting appears in the 'Dyalogue' on pp. 91, 93, 95, 97, 99, 100–1, 104-8, 110, 112-29, 131, 133-7, 139, 141-3, 146-7, 149-52, 154-63, 165-8. St German's holograph letter to Cromwell is Public Record Office, SP 1/152, fo. 249.

theological matters, voiced what I take to be St German's own views.[46]

The debate opened with a clear statement that scripture 'is fully to be beleved as a thing necessary to salvacion', but the 'sayinges of doctours' did not inspire belief 'oonles theire seyinges be grounded of Scripture and may be deryvied owte therof in a probable consequence'.[47] St German gave an example to illustrate his point. St Augustine had said 'the synne is not forgyven but the thing taken awaye be restored'. This was worthy of belief, since it followed the tenth commandment.[48] Non-scriptural assertions were not, however, valid: 'it cannot be assuredly knowen that the doctours said it, for thoughe it be in his bookes as they be called, yet it mighte be put in by some other man.'[49] The writings of the Fathers were subject to interpolations and posthumous additions, and there was no adequate means of verifying them.

The practical objections to an epistemology which rested on textual criticism were obvious, and the student of common law raised the issue in terms of the histories, chronicles, and legal records that were the daily routine of the Inns of Court. 'By that reason', he exclaimed, 'no man shulde be bounde to byleve nor to gyve faithe to legendes, cronicles, [hi]stories, deedes, writinges or yet recordes, and that shulde be a greate confusion and disordre, and in maner a distruccion of all the politique ordre and Civile governaunce.'[50] St German argued that to adjudicate upon *meum et teum* and to ensure the workings of the courts of law, 'deedes, writinges, prouffes and recordes ar[e] to be bileved, and faith muste be geven to theym.' But it was necessary to take a pragmatic view: in doing justice to our neighbour, 'we be boun-

---

[46] St German did not write dialogues after the manner of Plato or More's *Utopia*. One character generally asks questions, nods assent, and covers awkward shifts of subject matter or tone, while the other advances the argument. It does not seem unreasonable to equate the latter with the author.

[47] SP 6/2, p. 89. It is possible that the 'Dyalogue' was commissioned in 1536; see *LP*, XI, no. 84.

[48] SP 6/2, pp. 89-90.

[49] Ibid., p. 90.

[50] Ibid., p. 91.

don to bileve many thinges that we be not necessarilie boundon
to bileve in oure herte as articles of oure faithe.' Chronicles,
legends and histories were in that category. Hence a man might
say with impunity that there was no pope called Cletus or that
King Lear was not the founder of Leicester.

> He were no heretique nor he aughte not to be punysshed
> therfore: for the [hi]stories therof be not sufficiente to bynde
> any man to a full belyve of it . . . but yet trewthe it is that if
> a man denye any suche [hi]storie or common opynyon
> wherby hurte maye growe to any other, he offendeth oonles
> he have a sufficiente cause to move hym to it . . . and suche
> avermentes no man maye with conscience take to the hurte
> of iustice or of the righte of his neighbour oonles he have
> sufficiente profe of his avermente, but where suche aver-
> mentes be not to the hurte of any other, if he that make the
> the avermente thinke that he saithe trewlie, he may speke it
> withoute offence of conscience, thoughe it be againste
> legendes, cronicles, or seyinges of doctours, or againste the
> common oppynyon, so his saying be not againste scripture,
> nor against that that is dirivied upon scripture, nor
> againste the lawe of nature.[51]

St German thus applied juristic formulae to the debate on
textual exegesis. Within the limitations of human justice a pragmatic approach to belief of written documents is the precondition of conducting affairs, and methodology at this level is
directed to the need to avoid inflicting wrongs on others as a
consequence of men's assertions. Providing a man's statements
did not hurt another, and providing he did not speak against the
law of God (scripture) or that of Nature, he might seek to
confute – whether correctly or incorrectly – the authority of
learned doctors, chronicles, or histories, if he believed that what
he said was well founded. Applying the idea of 'conscience' in a
juristic sense, St German argued that the test of a man's morality in challenging incompletely proven beliefs rested upon an
objective calculation of the hurt he did to another, if he made his
assertions without sufficient cause. Should any 'murmoure or
unquyetnes' erupt among the people by virtue of men's opinions,

[51] Ibid., pp. 91-4.

'kinges and princes mighte prohibite theym: but the Clergie hathe no powere to prohibite theym.' The acid test of public policy was to be sedition, not heresy.[52]

Yet the central issue at stake was the epistemology of scripture. Salvation depended upon knowledge of the 'Word of God', 'but howe that worde may be perfitly knowen I doo not yet perceyve'. The question was whether 'scripture' meant the Bible, or whether an oral tradition supplemented or was superior to the written word, as More had argued. The doctor explained: 'surelie by that worde scripture hathe ben alwaye understande the bookes conteyned in the bible whiche be called canonycall and non but they'. Christ, he thought, would not have left his people without 'an infallible rule of scripture', and by scripture he understood 'the bodie of the bible canonised, and that noon other manner of writing maye be called scripture'. No other opinions or revelations were authorized, even though they might have been accepted as binding by the clergy.[53]

St German did not, however, believe that scripture was antecedent to the church, as did Tyndale and Barnes. His interpretation rested on his analysis of the process whereby the texts of scripture had been validated by the primitive church. This part of the 'Dyalogue' opened with an assertion by the student that there had, in fact, been an oral tradition during two historical periods. The first was in the Old Testament from Adam's time to that of Moses. The second ran from the Crucifixion until St Matthew wrote his gospel, 'whiche was abowte viij yeres after the passion of Criste'. After the Crucifixion there was no written word, but the student knew that many people were converted to the faith then 'by hearing and by relac[i]on of thappostles' without any scripture. Furthermore, those persons 'were boundon to bileve as they were taughte'.[54] He quoted at this point one of More's favourite texts, 'Stand firm and hold the traditions that you have learned whether by word or by letter of ours.'[55] It was obvious that St Paul had said many things he had not written down and his hearers were required to believe them. The

[52] Ibid., pp. 92-3.
[53] Ibid., pp. 99-100, 148.
[54] Ibid., pp. 107-8.
[55] 2 Thess. 2:15.

doctor's immediate reply was unsatisfactory: 'For the Thessolo-
nians herde his wordes and therfore they were boundon to bileve
theym, but we herde theym not nor scripture witnessithe not
what they were.'[56] Hence the student reiterated his case, which
obliged the doctor to concede an oral tradition. It was, however,
restricted in time. Before scripture was validated by the church,
there was no other means save an oral tradition whereby the
faith might be propagated, hence 'every man was then boundon
to bileve it generallye or specially by hearing of other.'[57] But
after faith was reduced to writing, a process 'auctorised by the
instincte of the holie ghoste as shulde suffise to salvac[i]on', it
was no longer permissible to define the articles of faith other
than by the written word. This was expedient, 'for els many
supersticious articles and untrewe invenc[i]ons' might be added
to those articles. Nothing outside the written word could stand
as a basis of belief, argued St German, and nothing outside it,
however meritorious, should be so adduced, because even a
single such addition would constitute a precedent which might
'doo greate hurte to the universall churche and to all cristen
religion'.[58] On this matter of scripture versus tradition, St German may have drawn upon the thought of Jean Gerson, who
had affirmed that nothing necessary to salvation was preserved
outside the canonical scriptures.[59]

St German's opinion, then, was that the oral tradition of the
early church had been superseded by the written word, which
became the decisive authority. Yet this account did not elucidate
the mechanism whereby scripture had been validated. The
doctor thus explained that the law of the New Testament was
'firste canonised in the hertes of the people' by the teaching of
the Apostles and their immediate successors.[60] The people
trusted these 'diligente shepardes', who fed them the 'trewe
worde of god'. This had been a 'blessed tyme', when 'the holie

---

[56] SP 6/2, p. 108.
[57] Ibid., pp. 109-10.
[58] Ibid., pp. 110-11.
[59] Marius, 'Thomas More and the heretics', p. 245.
[60] SP 6/2, p. 126.

goste wroughte so in the hertes of the people that theire owne conscience witnessed that the doctryne that they had was trewe, for it speke inwardlie to theire hartes and it was also many tymes confirmede by miracles.'[61] All this had occurred before kings were converted to the faith. The earliest Christians, however, were anxious that future generations should learn the faith. By 'full assente' it was therefore 'put in writing and canonysed by the vniuersall [people *scored out by St German*] chyrch as a thing necessarie to be bileved of all men that shalbe saved, as it was to theym that firste receyved it'.[62]

Revelation was thus prior to scripture, but once the books of the Bible had been canonized by the church, the articles of belief depended on the written, not the unwritten, word. Revelation was imprinted on the hearts of the faithful by the Holy Spirit, but this inspiration had led to the New Testament, which became the sufficient authority for faith. The conversion of kings and princes to Christianity was, however, a key element in St German's account. The process whereby the written word was validated by the church was accompanied by the conversion of rulers. The exact chronology was uncertain, but once this conversion of rulers was achieved, the 'vniuersall churche had power to ordre scripture and to maynteyn the vnitie of the faithe', but it exercised its authority 'vnder kinges whiche were hedes of that church nexte vnder god'.[63] In other words, the primacy of the Apostles ended when kings were converted to Christianity. St German's proof was scriptural. Before the birth of Christ, kings were heads over the people, and if the Apostles and their successors should be heads of the church, 'then shulde they be the highe iudges and the highe commaunders of the worlde, and therupon shulde folowe a contradicc[i]on betwene the olde testamente and the newe'. Such contradiction was impossible. Christ had said, 'I come not to breke the lawe but to fulfill it', from which it followed that 'the power that kinges had before his cummyng shulde contynue'.

[61] Ibid., pp. 125-6.
[62] Ibid., p. 126.
[63] Ibid., p. 127.

> And if the vniuersall churche shulde oon tyme haue power
> under the hedship of kinges and princes to order the
> churche and to expound the doubtes of scripture, and to do
> suche thinges as perteyne to a generall counsaile, and an
> other tyme it shulde haue like powere under the hedship of
> the successours of the Appostles to doo likewise, there
> mighte followe a contradicc[i]on betwixte theire sentences
> and determynac[i]ons, whiche it is not to doubte but that
> oure maister Criste prevented. Neuertheles when riches
> encreased yn the clergie . . . many of theym endevoured
> theym self more thoroughlie then they had done bifore, to
> sette fourthe the powere of the clergie, and pretendid still
> that the power and auctoritie . . . contynued in the succes-
> sours of the Appostles.[64]

Kings had taken too little heed of such matters, and had listened
to the clergy's biased interpretations of scripture. The result was
that 'not oon generall counsaile be gathered and holdon to all
intentes according to thauctoritie of scripture' since the time of
the Apostles. For church councils were properly summoned by
emperors and kings, and they should represent the whole
church: that is, laymen should have 'voices' at them.[65] Here St
German reinforced his definition of the 'church' given in *An
Answer to a Letter*: it comprised emperors and kings with their
clergy and laity.

Just as St German accepted More's view that revelation
preceded scripture, so he agreed, too, that the authority that
vouchsafed the truth of scripture was the church. We recall that
More thought it did not matter if someone suggested that St
Luke had not written 'his' gospel: the church had validated its
contents. St German wrote: 'I thinke verilie that the gospelles
nor any other parte of scripture be not of auctoritie bicause the
Evangelystes or othere writers therof were of suche holynes that
they mighte not erre, but bicause the seyd evangelystes and the
other scryptures were accepted, allowed, and canonised by the
vniuersall churche, as thinges necessary to be bileved.'[66] It could

[64] Ibid., pp. 129-30.
[65] Ibid., pp. 130-3.
[66] Ibid., p. 136.

not be proved that one particular author wrote this or that gospel, that St Luke wrote the Acts of the Apostles, or that St Paul wrote the Epistle to the Hebrews.[67] St German conceded, however, that the exact historical moment when the canon of scripture was established was uncertain, and the books of the Apocrypha caused him difficulty. There was no 'auctentique wryting' to prove what had been done: 'so that the common assente of the people is at this daye the moste chief recorde therof'. Yet who would doubt but that those concerned had authority to do what they had done?[68] (Such rhetoric St German had previously employed in *New Additions* to justify the anticlerical legislation of the Reformation Parliament.)[69] The books of the New Testament were canonized by those 'that had sufficiente auctoritie therto'.[70] Furthermore, the people had consented: through the workings of the Holy Spirit, 'a full assente hathe risen yn the hertes of the people to bileve and to thinke theym self bounde to bileve suche thinges as were written of the instincte of the holy ghoste as thinges necessary to be bileved for theire salvac[i]on.'[71] In the last analysis, however, St German was willing to cite as specific authority for the canonization of scripture the text of St Matthew, 'Whatsoever thou shalt bind on earth shall be bound in heaven: and whatsoever thou shalt loose on earth shall be loosed in heaven.'[72]

One of St German's main objects in writing the 'Dyalogue' was to deny the validity of 'unwritten verities' as reviewed at Cromwell's vicegerential synod in 1537. The term itself was first attacked by the doctor on the grounds of inherent obfuscation: a 'verity' was a 'true thing', but if unwritten verities were accepted as truth then 'I shulde estop my self to speke any thing againste theym.'[73] The phrase 'opinions not written in scripture' was thus agreed between doctor and student as the basis for discussion, and several examples were selected for detailed scrutiny: Mary's

[67] Ibid., pp. 137-8.
[68] Ibid., pp. 142-3.
[69] *Doctor and Student*, ed. Plucknett and Barton, p. 317.
[70] SP 6/2, pp. 142-3.
[71] Ibid., p. 142.
[72] Ibid., p. 143 (Matt. 16:19).
[73] SP 6/2, p. 95.

perpetual virginity, whether the Apostles devised the creed, whether the clergy 'make' the church, whether the pope might summon general councils, whether he and the clergy alone might expound doubts of scripture, whether bishops have authority to make holy oil and cream, the use of images, and so on.[74] St German accepted some opinions on some of these points as matters sufficiently supported by scripture, but flatly rejected others because they had no basis in the written word. For instance, Mary's virginity and the contents of the creed were matters sufficiently founded on scripture to be believed 'of necessitie'; but to define the church as the clergy without the laity, to affirm the pope's right to summon general councils, and to invoke the personal authority of the Apostles for the format of the creed, as opposed merely to its doctrinal contents, and for existing levels of episcopal power and the use of images – these were opinions devoid of scriptural backing, and thus invalid.[75]

Unwritten verities had often been confirmed later by the decrees of church councils, and this led St German to attack the errors of past councils. He allowed that the decrees of former councils carried greater weight than the opinions of individuals, but decrees were binding only if they were 'deryvied owte of scripture and be warraunted by scripture'. Otherwise 'they were not made by auctoritie of the churche.'[76] It was, however, permissible for unwarranted decrees to be upheld not as decrees but as 'lawful customs' of the people. St German was ambiguous about the means of verifying the 'lawfulness' of customs: his argument was probably directed against the 'unlawfulness' of attempts by the clergy to claim as justified by divine law what, in practice, they enjoyed solely on the basis of human acceptance, 'and that somtyme by lawes made by theymself, and where they had no auctoritie to have made any lawe'.[77]

St German clearly wanted a general council to examine the Bible, particularly the Apocrypha, in order to settle beyond any doubt which were the books of canonical scripture: 'I thinke that

[74] Ibid., pp. 96-7.
[75] Ibid., pp. 97-120.
[76] Ibid., pp. 133-4.
[77] Ibid., pp. 134-5.

nothing perteynethe to the vniuersall churche more appropriat-
lie then that dothe, and it perteynethe to the churche . . . to
expo[u]nde the doubtis of scripture wherby diversitie of opy-
nyons have risen in tyme paste in suche playne and charitable
manner that no diversitie be therin after.'[78] St German agreed
with Gerson that while scripture was entirely sufficient for faith,
authoritative interpretation came from the church. His idea of a
general council was, however, one 'gathered and kepte by auctoritie of kinges and princes, and wherin notable men of the
temporaltie, as they be callede, shulde have voices'.[79] Yet his
switch from proposing Parliament in *An Answer to a Letter* as the
institution representative of the English Church, to advocating a
general council as the appropriate organ for determining the
canonical scriptures in his 'Dyalogue', is striking. St German
thought the church could not make new articles of faith by
exercising its authority to interpret scripture, but he quite distinctly visualized reform in a 'universal' context in 1537:

> Trouthe it is that the church may not make newe articles of
> the faithe ne bynde the people to bileve any newe thing . . .
> but yet it may declare the doubtis of scripture, and what
> necessarilie followethe upon scripture, and what ministrac-
> [i]ons and powers the bisshops and clergie have by the
> lawe of god, and what not. And if any doubte rise whether
> any booke that is in the bible be to be taken for a booke
> canonysed or not, it perteignith to the vniuersall churche
> gathered according to scripture to determyn that doubte . .
> . and therfore as it semythe a catholique generall councel
> shulde doo righte well if they made theym [the books of the
> Apocrypha] of like auctoritie as the scripture is, and yet
> therbie they shulde make no newe articles of the faithe, nor
> but oonly stablishe that that as many men thynke aughte
> to have ben stablisshed bifore.[80]

To sum up. More, Gardiner, and St German defined the
church in radically different ways, but none agreed with the

[78] Ibid., pp. 160-1.
[79] Ibid., p. 122.
[80] Ibid., pp. 163-5.

reformers that scripture was antecedent to the church. Of the Henrician propagandists, St German wrote most about scripture, but his 'Dyalogue' was not printed; it remained among Thomas Cromwell's papers in manuscript, and may not have been much read. How far St German spoke for the regime between the Act of Supremacy and 1537 is arguable. His 'universal' solution was not a plausible policy option, and his views signalled disquiet over caesaropapism, rather than support for it. In particular, St German for some reason abandoned his notion of the church 'represented in Parliament'. This idea had doubtless been too strong for Henry VIII, since it assumed a restricted interpretation of the supreme head's prerogative. The 'imperial' theory of the supremacy was not commensurate with St German's conviction that the real test of the legitimacy of government was the consent of the governed. To opt for conciliarism, however, was to chase a dream: there was not the remotest chance of the general council St German had in mind actually taking place. Since Gardiner wrote *De vera obedientia* before papal authority was finally extinguished, no useful comparison can be made with St German's 'Dyalogue'. St German's *An Answer to a Letter* and Gardiner's book were, however, written in the same year, and the differences between them suggest that there was no one 'Henrician' position on scripture as authority. Furthermore, what happened in practice supports this view. The issues were not resolved during Henry VIII's lifetime. Attitudes as to the church's relationship to scripture remained ambivalent in England until his death: the terms of the debate were thereafter dictated by the reformers.

Select Bibliography

MANUSCRIPTS

Bodleian Library, Oxford, MS Laud Misc. 597
Bodleian Library, Oxford, MS Rawlinson C. 813
British Library, London, Cotton MS Cleopatra E. vi, fos 1–15; 16-135
British Library, London, Cotton MS Vitellius B. xxi, fo. 60
British Library, London, Lansdowne MS 639, fos 34ᵛ–5ᵛ
British Library, London, Lansdowne MS 762
British Library, London, Sloane MS 2578
Folger Shakespeare Library, Washington DC, Loseley MS L.b.546
Henry E. Huntington Library, San Marino, California, Ellesmere MS 2652
Lambeth Palace Library, London, MS 527
Public Record Office, London, PC 2/1
Public Record Office, London, SP 1/152, fo. 249
Public Record Office, London, SP 2/R, fos 24-5
Public Record Office, London, SP 6/2, pp. 89-168
Public Record Office, London, STAC 10/4

PRINTED BOOKS AND ARTICLES

Adams, Robert P., *The Better Part of Valor: More, Colet, and Vives, on Humanism, War, and Peace, 1496-1535*, Seattle, 1962
Alesius, Alexander, *Of the auctorite of the word of God agaynst the bisshop of London*, n.p., n.d. (*STC* 292)
Alexander, Paul J., 'The diffusion of Byzantine Apocalypses in the medieval West and the beginnings of Joachimism', in *Prophecy and Millenarianism: Essays in Honour of Marjorie Reeves*, ed. Ann Williams, Harlow, Essex, 1980, pp. 55-106, esp. pp. 62-5

Aquinas, Thomas, *Summa theologiae*, ed. P. Caramello, 3 vols, Turin, 1952-62

Auctoritates Aristotelis, Senece, Boecii, Platonis, etc., *Gesamtkatalog der Wiegendrucke*, Leipzig, 1928

Avery, M. E., 'The history of the equitable jurisdiction of Chancery before 1460', *Bulletin of the Institute of Historical Research*, 42 (1969), pp. 129-44

Baker, J. H., ed., *The Reports of Sir John Spelman*, Selden Society, 2 vols, London, 1977-8

Baldwin, J. F., *The King's Council in England during the Middle Ages*, Oxford, 1913

Barclay, Alexander, *The myrrour of good maners*, London, ?1518 (*STC*² 17242)

—, *Stultifera nauis, qua omnium mortalium narratur stultitia. The ship of fooles*, London, 1570 (*STC* 3346)

Bayne, C. G. and Dunham, W. H., eds, *Select Cases in the Council of Henry VII*, Selden Society, London, 1958

Berdan, John M., *Early Tudor Poetry, 1485-1547*, New York, 1920

Blatcher, M., *The Court of King's Bench, 1450-1550*, London, 1978

Bornstein, D., ed., *The Middle English Translation of Christine de Pisan's* Livre du corps de policie, Heidelberg, 1977

Bouck, Constance W., 'On the identity of Papyrius Geminus Eleates', *Transactions of the Cambridge Bibliographical Society*, 2 (1958), pp. 352-8

Bouwsma, William, *The Interpretation of Renaissance Humanism*, 2nd edn, Washington, 1966

Bradshaw, Brendan, 'The Christian humanism of Erasmus', *Journal of Theological Studies*, new series, 32.2 (1982), pp. 411-47

Brodie, D. M., ed., *The Tree of Commonwealth*, Cambridge, 1948

Burton, K. M., ed., *A Dialogue between Reginald Pole and Thomas Lupset*, London, 1948

Bush, Douglas, *The Renaissance and English Humanism*, Toronto, 1939

—, 'Tudor humanism and Henry VIII', *University of Toronto Quarterly*, 7 (1937), pp. 162-7

Calendar of State Papers, Spanish, ed. G. A. Bergenroth and others, 13 vols, London, 1862-1954

Campana, Augusto, 'The origin of the word "Humanist"', *Journal of the Warburg and Courtauld Institutes*, 9 (1946), pp. 60-73

Caspari, Fritz, *Humanism and the Social Order in Early Tudor England*, Chicago, 1954

Challis, C. E., *The Tudor Coinage*, Manchester, 1978

Chambers, R. W., *Thomas More*, London, 1935

Chatterjee, Kalyan K., *In Praise of Learning: John Colet and Literary Humanism in Education*, New Delhi, 1974

Clarke, Basil, ed., *Life of Merlin: Geoffrey of Monmouth, Vita Merlini*, Cardiff, 1973

Clarke, M. V., *Medieval Representation and Consent*, London, 1936

Coleman, C. and Starkey, D. R., eds, *Revolution Reassessed: Revisions in the History of Tudor Government and Administration*, Oxford, 1986

Colet, John, *Joannis Coleti enarratio in epistolam S. Pauli ad Romanos: An Exposition of St Paul's Epistle to the Romans*, ed. J. H. Lupton, London, 1873

A Collection of Ordinances and Regulations for the Government of the Royal Household, Society of Antiquaries, London, 1790

The Complaynt of Scotlande vyth ane Exortatione to the Thre Estaits to be vigilante in the Deffens of their Public veil. 1549, ed. James A. H. Murray, Early English Text Society, extra series, nos 17-18, London, 1872

Condon, M. M., 'Ruling elites in the reign of Henry VII', in *Patronage, Pedigree and Power*, ed. C. Ross, Gloucester, 1979

Corpus juris civilis, ed. P. Krueger, Berlin, 1915

Le debat des heraulx darmes de Fra[n]ce et de[n]gleterre, Rouen, 1515

Le débat des hérauts d'armes de France et d'Angleterre, ed. L. Pannier, Paris, 1877

The Debate betwene the heraldes of Englande and Fraunce, compyled by Jhon Coke, clarke of the kynges recognysaunce, or vulgerly, called clarke of the Statutes of the staple of Westmynster, and fynyshed the yere of our Lorde. M.D.L., London, 1550 (*STC* 5530)

Derrett, J. Duncan M., 'The affairs of Richard Hunne and Friar Standish', in More, *CW*, IX, pp. 213-46

The determinations of the moste famous and mooste excellent vniuersities of Italy and Fraunce, that it is so vnlefull for a man to marie his brothers wyfe, that the pope hath no power to dispence therwith, London, 1531 (*STC²* 14287)

Dickens, A. G., review of McConica, *English Humanists and Reformation Politics*, *History*, 52 (1967), pp. 77-8

Dodds, Madeleine Hope, 'Political prophecies in the reign of Henry VIII', *Modern Language Review*, 11 (1916), pp. 276-84

—, and R. Dodds, *The Pilgrimage of Grace 1536-1537 and the Exeter Conspiracy 1538*, 2 vols, Cambridge, 1915

Dolan, John P., tr. and ed., *The Essential Erasmus*, New York, 1964

Donner, H. W., 'The Emperor and Sir Thomas Elyot', *Review of English Studies*, new series, 11 (1951), pp. 55-9

Duff, E. G., *A Century of the English Book Trade*, London, 1905

A dyaloge betwene one Clemente a clerke of the Conuocacyon, and one Bernarde a burges of the parlyament / dysputynge be / twene them what auctoryte the clergye haue to make lawes. And howe farre and where theyr power doth extende, n.p., n.d.

Edwards, A. S. G., *Stephen Hawes*, Boston, 1983

Edwards, H. L. R., *Skelton: The Life and Times of an Early Tudor Poet*, London, 1949

Ellis, H., ed., *Original Letters Illustrative of English History*, 1st series, 3 vols, 2nd edn, London, 1825

Elton, G. R., *England under the Tudors*, London, 1955

—, 'Henry VII's Council', in *Studies*, vol. I, pp. 294-9

—, *Policy and Police: The Enforcement of the Reformation in the Age of Thomas Cromwell*, Cambridge, 1972

—, *Reform and Reformation: England 1509-1558*, London, 1977

—, 'King or Minister? The man behind the Henrician Reformation', *Studies*, vol. I, pp. 173–88

—, *Reform and Renewal: Thomas Cromwell and the Common Weal*, Cambridge, 1973

—, 'Reform by statute', *Proceedings of the British Academy*, 54 (1968), pp. 165-88

—, review of McConica, *English Humanists and Reformation Politics*, *Historical Journal*, 10 (1967), pp. 137-8

—, 'Sir Thomas More and the opposition to Henry VIII', in *Studies*, vol. I, pp. 155-72

—, *Studies in Tudor and Stuart Politics and Government*, 3 vols, Cambridge, 1974, 1983

—, 'Thomas Cromwell redivivus', *Archiv für Reformationsgeschichte*, 68 (1977), pp. 198-203

—, 'Thomas More, Councillor', in *Studies*, vol. I, pp. 129-54

—, 'The Real Thomas More?', ibid., vol. III, pp. 344-55

—, ed., *The Tudor Constitution: Documents and Commentary*, 2nd edn, Cambridge, 1982

—, 'Tudor government: the points of contact, the Council', in *Studies*, vol. III, pp. 21-38

—, *The Tudor Revolution in Government: Administrative Changes in the Reign of Henry VIII*, Cambridge, 1953

—, 'Why the history of the Early Tudor Council remains unwritten', in *Studies*, vol. I, pp. 308-38

Elyot, Thomas, *The Boke Named the Governour*, ed. H. H. S. Croft, 2 vols, London, 1883

—, *The Castel of Helth*, London, 1539 (*STC* 7644)

—, *The Bankette of Sapience*, in *Four Political Treatises*, ed. Lillian Gottesman, Gainsville, Florida, 1967

—, *The Letters of Sir Thomas Elyot*, ed. K. J. Wilson, *Studies in Philology*, 73.5 (1976), pp. 1-78

—, *Of the Knowledge which Maketh a Wise Man*, ed. Edwin Johnston Howard, Oxford, Ohio, 1946

—, *Pasquil the Playne*, London, 1533 (*STC* 7672)

Erasmus, Desiderius, *Collected Works of Erasmus*, various editors, 78 vols, Toronto, 1974–

—, *The Education of a Christian Prince*, tr. and ed. Lester K. Born, New York, 1968

—, *Opera omnia Desiderii Erasmi Roterodami*, ed. J. H. Waszink and others, Amsterdam, 1969–

—, *Opus epistolarum Des. Erasmi Roterodami*, ed. P. S. Allen and others, Oxford, 1906-47

—, *Praise of Folly*, tr. Betty Radice with an introduction by A. H. T. Levi, Harmondsworth, 1971

Ferguson, Arthur B., *The Articulate Citizen and the English Renaissance*, Durham, N.C., 1965

Fleisher, M., *Radical Reform and Political Persuasion in the Life and Writings of Thomas More*, Geneva, 1973

Fletcher, A., *Tudor Rebellions*, 2nd edn, London, 1979

Fortescue, John, *The Governance of England*, ed. C. Plummer, Oxford, 1885

—, *De laudibus legum Anglie*, ed. S. B. Chrimes, Cambridge, 1942

—, *The Works of Sir John Fortescue, Knight, Chief Justice of England and Lord Chancellor to King Henry the Sixth*, ed. T. Fortescue (Lord Clermont), privately printed, 2 vols, London, 1869

Fox, Alistair, 'Stephen Hawes and the political allegory of *The Comfort of Lovers*', *English Literary Renaissance*, (forthcoming)

—, *Thomas More: History and Providence*, Oxford, 1982

Foxe, Edward, *Opus eximium. De vera differentia regiae potestatis et ecclesiasticae*, London, 1534 (*STC* 11218)

—, *The true dyffere[nce]s betwen y[e] regall power and the ecclesiasticall power*, tr. Henry, Lord Stafford, London, 1548 (*STC* 11220)

Gairdner, J., ed., *The Historical Collections of a Citizen of London in the Fifteenth Century*, Camden Society, new series, no. 17 [4], London, 1876

Gerson, Jean, *Oeuvres complètes*, ed. P. Glorieux, 10 vols, Paris, 1960-73

Giustiniani, Vito R., 'Homo, humanus, and the meanings of "humanism"', *Journal of the History of Ideas*, 46 (1985), pp. 167–95

A Glasse of the truthe, [1532] (*STC* 11918–19)

Gottesman, Lillian, ed., *Four Political Treatises by Sir Thomas Elyot*, Gainsville, Florida, 1967

Gravissimae atque exactissimae illustrissimarum totius Italiae et Galliae Academiarum censurae, London, c. 1531 (*STC*² 14286)

Gray, C. M., 'The boundaries of the equitable function', *American Journal of Legal History*, 20 (1976), pp. 218-20

Griffiths, R. A., *The Reign of King Henry VI*, London, 1981

Guy, John A., *The Cardinal's Court*, Hassocks, 1977

—, *Christopher St German on Chancery and Statute*, Selden Society, suppl. series, vol. 6, London, 1985

—, *The Court of Star Chamber and its Records to the Reign of Elizabeth I*, Public Record Office Handbooks, no. 21, London, 1985

—, 'The court of Star Chamber during Wolsey's ascendancy', unpublished Ph.D. dissertation, University of Cambridge, 1973

—, 'The development of equitable jurisdictions, 1450-1550', in *Law, Litigants and the Legal Profession*, ed. A. H. Manchester and E. W. Ives, London, 1983, pp. 80–6

—, 'Henry VIII and the praemunire manoeuvres of 1530-1531', *English Historical Review*, 97 (1982), pp. 481-503

—, 'The legal context of the controversy: the law of heresy', in More, *CW*, X

—, 'The Privy Council: revolution or evolution?', in *Revolution Reassessed*, ed. C. Coleman and D. R. Starkey, Oxford, 1986

—, *The Public Career of Sir Thomas More*, Brighton, 1980

—, 'Wolsey, the Council and the Council courts', *English Historical Review*, 91 (1976), pp. 481-505

Haigh, Christopher, *Reformation and Resistance in Tudor Lancashire*, Cambridge, 1975

Harcourt, Vernon, *His Grace the Steward*, London, 1907

Harrison, C. J., 'The petition of Edmund Dudley', *English Historical Review*, 87 (1972), pp. 82-99

Hawes, Stephen, *The Pastime of Pleasure by Stephen Hawes*, ed. William Edward Mead, Early English Text Society, original series, no. 173, London, 1928 for 1927

Helmholz, R. H., 'The early enforcement of uses', *Columbia Law Review*, 79 (1979), pp. 1503-13

Herrmann, Erwin, 'Spätmittelälterliche englische Pseudoprophetien', *Archiv für Kulturgeschicte*, 57 (1975), pp. 87-116

Herrtage, Sidney J., ed., *England in the Reign of Henry the Eighth: Life and Letters and A Dialogue between Cardinal Pole and Lupset by Thomas Starkey*, Early English Text Society, extra series, nos 12, 32, London, 1878, repr. 1927, New York, 1975

Hill, L. M., ed., *The Ancient State, Authoritie, and Proceedings of the Court of Requests by Sir Julius Caesar*, Cambridge, 1975

Hoak, D. E., *The King's Council in the Reign of Edward VI*, Cambridge, 1976

Hogrefe, Pearl, *The Life and Times of Sir Thomas Elyot, Englishman*, Ames, Iowa, 1967

Hook, W. F., *The Lives of the Archbishops of Canterbury*, 12 vols, London, 1860-76

Hughes, P., *The Reformation in England*, 3 vols, London, 1950-4

Huizinga, Johan, *Erasmus and the Age of Reformation*, New York, 1957

Ives, E. W., *The Common Lawyers of Pre-Reformation England*, Cambridge, 1983

—, 'Crime, sanctuary, and royal authority under Henry VIII: the exemplary sufferings of the Savage family', in *Of the Laws and Customs of England*, ed. M. S. Arnold and others, Chapel Hill, 1981

—, 'The genesis of the Statute of Uses', *English Historical Review*, 82 (1967), pp. 673-97

Jacob, E. F., *The Fifteenth Century 1399-1485*, Oxford, 1961

Jaech, Sharon L. Jansen, 'English political prophecy and the dating of MS Rawlinson C. 813', *Manuscripta*, 25 (1981), pp. 141-50

Janelle, P., ed., *Obedience in Church and State*, Cambridge, 1930

Jones, W. J., *The Elizabethan Court of Chancery*, Oxford, 1967

Joye, George, *Supper of the Lord*, 1533 (*STC*² 24468)

Kelley, D. R., ed., *The Monarchy of France*, New Haven, 1981

Kelly, H. A., *The Matrimonial Trials of Henry VIII*, Stanford, 1976

Kenyon, J. P., *The Stuart Constitution*, Cambridge, 1966

Kingsford, Charles Lethbridge, *English Historical Literature in the Fifteenth Century*, New York, 1913

Knecht, R. J., 'The episcopate and the Wars of the Roses', *University of Birmingham Historical Journal*, 6 (1957-8), pp. 108-31

Koebner, R., 'The imperial crown of this realm', *Bulletin of the Institute of Historical Research*, 26 (1953), pp. 29-52

Kristeller, Paul Oskar, *Renaissance Thought and its Sources*, ed. Michael Mooney, New York, 1979

—, 'Studies on Renaissance Humanism during the last twenty years', *Studies in the Renaissance*, 9 (1961), pp. 7-30

Lander, J. R., 'Council, administration and councillors, 1461 to 1485', *Bulletin of the Institute of Historical Research*, 32 (1959), pp. 138-80

—, 'The Yorkist Council and administration', *English Historical Review*, 73 (1958), pp. 27-46

Lapsley, G. T., 'The parliamentary title of Henry IV', *English Historical Review*, 49 (1934), pp. 423-49, 577–606

Lehmberg, Stanford E., *The Reformation Parliament, 1529-1536*, Cambridge, 1970

—, *Sir Thomas Elyot, Tudor Humanist*, Austin, Texas, 1960

Letters and Papers, Foreign and Domestic, of the Reign of Henry VIII, ed. J. S. Brewer and others, 21 vols and Addenda, London, 1862-1932

Lewis, C. S., *English Literature in the Sixteenth Century Excluding Drama*, London, 1954

A litel treatise ageynste the mutterynge of some papistis, 1534 (*STC*² 24219.5)

Logan, F. D., 'The Henrician canons', *Bulletin of the Institute of Historical Research*, 47 (1974), pp. 99-103

Lupton, J. H., *A Life of John Colet, D. D.* London, 1909

—, ed., *Joannis Coleti enarratio in epistolam S. Pauli ad Romanos: An Exposition of St Paul's Epistle to the Romans*, London, 1873

McConica, James Kelsey, *English Humanists and Reformation Politics under Henry VIII and Edward VI*, Oxford, 1965

McFarlane, K. B., *England in the Fifteenth Century: Collected Essays*, London, 1981

McKenna, J. W., 'How God became an Englishman', in *Tudor Rule and Revolution: Essays for G. R. Elton from his American Friends*, ed. D. J. Guth and J. W. McKenna, Cambridge, 1982, pp. 25-43

Major, John M., *Sir Thomas Elyot and Renaissance Humanism*, Lincoln, Nebraska, 1964

Marius, Richard, *Thomas More*, New York, 1984

—, 'Thomas More and the heretics', unpublished Ph.D. dissertation, Yale University, 1962, Ann Arbor, 1971

[Marshall, William, tr.], *The defence of peace; lately translated out of laten in to englysshe*, London, 1535 (*STC*² 17817)

Mayer, Thomas F., 'Faction and ideology: Thomas Starkey's *Dialogue*', *Historical Journal*, 28.1 (1985), pp. 1-25

Metzger, F., 'Das englische Kanzleigericht unter Kardinal Wolsey, 1515-29', unpublished Ph.D. thesis, Erlangen-Nürnberg, 1977

More, Thomas, *The Correspondence of Sir Thomas More*, ed. E. F. Rogers, Princeton, 1947

—, *The Debellation of Salem and Bizance*, London, 1533 (*STC²* 18081)

—, *The answere to the fyrst parte of the poysened booke*, 1534 (*STC²*18077)

—, *The Latin Epigrams of Sir Thomas More*, tr. and ed. Leicester Bradner and C. A. Lynch, Chicago, 1953

—, *St Thomas More: Selected Letters*, ed. Elizabeth Frances Rogers, New Haven and London, 1961

—, *The Yale Edition of the Complete Works of St Thomas More*, 14 vols, New Haven and London, 1963–: vol. IV: *Utopia*, ed. J. H. Hexter and E. L. Surtz, 1965; vol. V: *Responsio ad Lutherum*, ed. J. M. Headley, 2 parts, 1969; vol. VI: *A Dialogue concerning Heresies*, ed. Thomas M. C. Lawler and others, 1976; vol. VIII: *The Confutation of Tyndale's Answer*, ed. Richard Marius and others, 3 parts, 1973; vol. IX: *The Apology*, ed. J. B. Trapp, 1979; vol. X: *The Debellation of Salem and Bizance*, ed. John Guy and others (forthcoming); vol. XII: *A Dialogue of Comfort against Tribulation*, ed. Louis L. Martz and Frank Manley, 1976; vol. XIII: *A Treatise on the Passion*, ed. Garry E. Haupt, 1973

Morison, Richard, *A remedy for sedition*, London, 1536 (*STC²* 18113.5)

Murphy, Virginia, 'The debate over Henry VIII's first divorce: an analysis of the contemporary treatises', unpublished Ph.D. dissertation, University of Cambridge, 1984

Murray, James A. H., ed., *The Romance and Prophecies of Thomas of Ercildoune*, Early English Text Society, original series, no. 61, London, 1875

Myers, A. R., ed., *English Historical Documents, 1327–1485*, London, 1969

Nicholson, G. D., 'The nature and function of historical argument in the Henrician Reformation', unpublished Ph.D. dissertation, University of Cambridge, 1977

Nicolas, N. H., ed., *Proceedings and Ordinances of the Privy Council of England, 1368–1542*, 7 vols, London, 1834–7

Olin, John C., ed., *Christian Humanism and the Reformation: Selected Writings of Erasmus*, revised edn, New York, 1975

Pace, Richard, *De fructu qui ex doctrina percipitur (The Benefit of a Liberal Education)*, tr. and ed. Frank Manley and Richard S. Sylvester, New York, 1967

Phillimore, J. S., 'The arrest of humanism in England', *Dublin Review*, 153 (1913), pp. 1-26

Plucknett, T. F. T. and Barton, J. L., eds, *St German's Doctor and Student*, Selden Society, London, 1974

Pocock, Nicholas, ed., *Records of the Reformation: The Divorce, 1527-1533*, 2 vols, Oxford, 1870

Pole, Reginald, *Apologia ad Carolum V*, in *Epistolae Reginaldi Poli S. R. E. Cardinalis et aliorum ad se*, ed. A. M. Quirini, 5 vols, Brescia, 1744-1757

Pollard, A. F., 'Council, Star Chamber, and Privy Council under the Tudors', *English Historical Review*, 37 (1922), pp. 337-60, 516-39; 38 (1923), pp. 42-60.

Porter, H. C., 'Hooker, the Tudor Constitution, and the *Via Media*', in *Studies in Richard Hooker*, ed. W. Speed Hill, Cleveland and London, 1972, pp. 77-116

—, *Reformation and Reaction in Tudor Cambridge*, Cambridge, 1958

Prestwich, M., 'The *Modus tenendi parliamentum*', *Parliamentary History*, 1 (1982), pp. 221–5

Pronay, N. and J. Taylor, eds, *Parliamentary Texts of the Later Middle Ages*, Oxford, 1980

—, 'The use of the *Modus tenendi parliamentum* in the Middle Ages', *Bulletin of the Institute of Historical Research*, 47 (1974), pp. 11-23

Quinn, D. B., 'Henry VIII and Ireland', *Irish Historical Studies*, 12 (1960–1), pp. 318–44

Reeves, Marjorie, *The Influence of Prophecy in the Later Middle Ages: A Study in Joachimism*, Oxford, 1969

Reynolds, E. E., *The Life and Death of St Thomas More*, London, 1968

Rice, Eugene F., 'John Colet and the annihilation of the natural', *Harvard Theological Review*, 45 (1952), pp. 141-63

—, *The Renaissance Idea of Wisdom*, Cambridge, Mass., 1958

Robbins, Rossell Hope, 'Poems dealing with contemporary conditions', in *A Manual of the Writings in Middle English, 1050-1500*, ed. Albert E. Hartung, New Haven, 1975

Roper, William, *The Lyfe of Sir Thomas Moore, Knighte*, ed. Elsie Vaughan Hitchcock, Early English Text Society, original series, no. 197, London, 1935

Rueger, Z., 'Gerson's concept of equity and Christopher St German', *History of Political Thought*, 3 (1982), pp. 1-30

St German, Christopher, *An answere to a letter*, London, [?1535] (*STC²* 21558.5)

—, *A lytell treatise called the newe addicions*, 1531 (*STC²* 21563–4)

—, *Salem and Bizance*, 1533 (*STC²* 21584)

—, *The addicions of Salem and Byzance*, 1534 (*STC²* 21585)

—, *A treatise concernynge the diuision. . .* , [?1532] (*STC²* 21586–7.7)

Sampson, R., *Richardi Sampsonis, regii sacelli decani oratio, qua docet, anglos, regiae dignitati ut obediant*, London, [?1535] (*STC²* 21681)

Sayles, G. O., '*Modus tenendi parliamentum*: Irish or English?', in J. F.

Lydon ed., *England and Ireland in the Later Middle Ages*, Dublin, 1981, pp. 122–52

Scarisbrick, J. J., 'Thomas More: The King's good servant', *Thought*, 52 (1977), pp. 249-68

Scattergood, V. J., *Politics and Poetry in the Fifteenth Century*, New York, 1971

Seebohm, Frederic, *The Oxford Reformers, John Colet, Erasmus, and Thomas More*, 2nd edn, London, 1869

Shennan, J. H., *The Parlement of Paris*, London, 1968

A Short-Title Catalogue of Books Printed in England, Scotland, and Ireland, and of English Books Printed Abroad, 1475-1640, by A. W. Pollard and G. R. Redgrave and others, 2 vols, London, 1926

A Short-Title Catalogue of Books Printed in England, Scotland, and Ireland, and of English Books Printed Abroad, 1475-1640, 2nd edn, ed. W. A. Jackson, F. S. Ferguson and K. F. Pantzer, vol. II, London, 1976

Skelton, John, *John Skelton: The Complete English Poems*, ed. John Scattergood, New Haven and London, 1983

Skinner, Quentin, *The Foundations of Modern Political Thought*, 2 vols, Cambridge 1978

Slavin, Arthur J., ed., *Humanism, Reform, and Reformation in England*, New York, 1969

—, 'Profitable studies: humanists and government in Early Tudor England', *Viator: Medieval and Renaissance Studies*, 1 (1970), pp. 307-25

Starkey, D. R., 'The King's Privy Chamber, 1485-1547', unpublished Ph.D. dissertation, University of Cambridge, 1973

—, 'Which Age of Reform?', in *Revolution Reassessed*, ed. C. Coleman and D. R. Starkey, Oxford, 1986

Starkey, Thomas, *A Dialogue between Reginald Pole and Thomas Lupset*, ed. K. M. Burton, London, 1948

State Papers during the Reign of Henry VIII, Record Commission, 5 parts in 11 vols, London, 1830-52

Storey, R. L., *Diocesan Administration in Fifteenth-Century England*, 2nd edn, Borthwick Papers no. 16, York, 1972

Stubbs, W., *Select Charters*, ed. H. W. C. Davis, 9th edn, Oxford, repr. 1962

Talbert, R. J. A., *The Senate of Imperial Rome*, Princeton, 1984

Taylor, Rupert, *The Political Prophecy in England*, New York, 1911, repr. 1967

Thompson, Craig R., 'The humanism of More reappraised', *Thought*, 52 (1977), pp. 231-48

Thorpe, Lewis, tr. and ed., *Geoffrey of Monmouth: The History of the Kings of Britain*, Harmondsworth, 1966

Throop, P. A., *Criticism of the Crusade* (forthcoming)

Trapp, J. B., 'John Colet and the *Hierarchies* of the Ps-Dionysius', *Studies in Church History*, 17 (1981), pp. 130-3

Trevor-Roper, H. R., 'Tudor Humanism', *History Today*, 6 (1956), pp. 69-70

Ullmann, W., *Principles of Government and Politics in the Middle Ages*, 2nd edn, London, 1966

—, 'This Realm of England is an Empire', *Journal of Ecclesiastical History*, 30 (1979), pp. 175-203

Wegg, Jervis, *Richard Pace: A Tudor Diplomatist*, London, 1932

Weiss, Roberto, 'Learning and education in Western Europe from 1470-1520', in *The New Cambridge Modern History*, Cambridge, 1957, vol. I, pp. 95-126

Whibley, C., ed., *Henry VIII* [an edition of Edward Hall's *Chronicle*], 2 vols, London, 1904

The Whole Prophesie of Scotland, 1603, repr. for the Bannatyne Club, vol. 44, Edinburgh, 1833

The whole workes of W. Tyndall, John Frith, and Doct. Barnes [ed. J. Foxe], 2 vols, London 1573 [1572] (*STC*^{2} 24436)

Wilkins, D., ed., *Concilia Magnae Britanniae et Hiberniae*, 4 vols, London, 1737

Wilkinson, B., *Constitutional History of Medieval England*, 3 vols, London, 1948-58

—, 'The deposition of Richard II and the accession of Henry IV', *English Historical Review*, 54 (1939), pp. 215-39

Williams, P. and Harriss, G. L., 'A revolution in Tudor history', *Past and Present*, 25 (1963), pp. 3-58; 31 (1965), pp. 87-96

Yale, D. E. C., 'St German's *Little Treatise Concerning Writs of Subpoena*', *Irish Jurist*, new series, 10 (1975), pp. 324-33

Zeeveld, W. Gordon, *Foundations of Tudor Policy*, Cambridge, Mass., 1948

Index

A litel treatise ageynste the mutterynge of some papistis, 206
Alesius, Alexander, 202
Alexander III, King of Scotland, 81
Ambrose, St, 156
Amicable Grant, the, 135
Aquinas, Thomas, St, 183, 186
on equity, 185
Ariosto, Ludovico, 178
Aristippus, 71
Aristotle, 17, 122, 183–4
Armstrong, Clement, 24
Arthur, Prince, 155
Articles devised by the Whole Consent of the King's Most Honourable Council, 116–17
Arundel, Earl of (Thomas fitz Alan d. 1524), 130–1
Arundel, Earl of (William fitz Alan d. 1544), 135
Arundell, Thomas, 90
Ascham, Roger, 22, 30
Assembly of the Gods (Lydgate), 12
Audley, Thomas, 138, 144, 145, 161
Augustine, St, 17, 156, 211
Augustus, Emperor, 137, 178

Bacon, Nathaniel, 146
Bainbridge, Christopher, 41
Baker, John, 165
Bale, John, 11–12
Barclay, Alexander, 11, 15
and humanism, 15
Egloges, 15
The Shyp of Folys, 16
Barnes, Robert, 22, 200–2, 213
Barnet, Battle of, 126
Barton, Elizabeth ('the Nun of Kent'), 96, 118
Becket, Thomas, St, 166
Bede, the Venerable, 157
Berners, Lord (John Bourchier), 135
Berthelet, Thomas, 112, 115–16, 118, 119, 138
Bibliotheca historica (Diodorus Siculus), 13
Bilney, Thomas, 37
Boleyn, Anne, Queen of England, 59, 60, 61, 118, 163
Bosworth, Battle of, 85, 130
Bowes, Robert, 121
Bracton, Henry de, 159
Brandt, Sebastian, 16
Broughton, John, 90

Bryan, Thomas, 194–5
Buckingham, Duke of (Edward Stafford), 134–5, 141
Bullock, Henry, 37
Burgavenny, Lord (George Neville), 130–1, 135
Burgo, Nicholas de, 153–4
Bush, Douglas, 19

Cade, Jack, 125
Campeggio, Lorenzo, 154–5
Caspari, Fritz, 25
Castiglione, Baldassare, 43
Catherine of Aragon, Queen of England, 59–60, 61, 63, 111, 117, 155
Chancery, court of, 119, 136, 179–81, 189–93
    and discovery of documents, 190
    jurisdiction over uses, 188
Chapuys, Eustace, 59–61
Charles V, Emperor, 37, 46, 58–60, 65, 92, 178
Charles I, King of England, 146
Chaucer, Geoffrey, 82
Cheke, John, 11, 22, 30
Cicero, 17, 41, 42, 122
Clarence, George, Duke of, 81, 125
Clement VII, Pope, 117, 155
Clerk, John, 134, 136, 168
Coke, Edward, 99, 187
Colet, John, 10, 23, 28, 36–7, 42
    educational programme of, 25
    and Erasmus, 12, 14, 22, 27, 36
    and humanism, 21
    sermon to Convocation, 168
Collectanea satis copiosa, 58, 156–61, 163–6, 171–2, 175, 206
Common Pleas, court of, 189, 194
Constantine, Emperor, 160, 171

Constitutions of Clarendon, the, 171
Council, Fifth Lateran, 166
Council, King's, 20, 46, 54, 58, 70, 96, 108, 110, 114, 115, 116, 117–18, 121–47, 167, 174, 175
    the 'inner' council, 136–7, 144
    the Privy Council, 142–3, 145–6
    theories of, 142
Council of Carthage (Sixth), 161
Council of Constance, 117, 161, 201
Council of Nicaea, 161
Council of Toledo, 161
Cranmer, Thomas, 46, 58, 61, 63–4, 69, 117, 138, 144–5, 153–6, 159–62, 201
Croke, Richard, 37
Cromwell, Thomas, 2, 33, 47, 50, 55–61, 63–4, 90, 92, 93, 101, 111, 113, 115–17, 120, 122, 136–8, 143–5, 151–78, 210, 220
    and the Act of Appeals, 172
    and the *Collectanea*, 161
    and the Council, 58, 142–3
    his political creed, 152–3
    and the political revolution, 151
    and vicegerential synod of 1537, 201–2, 210, 217
Cumberland, Earl of (Henry Clifford), 135

Dacre of Graystock, William, Lord, 135
Darcy, Thomas, Lord, 135
Das Narrenschiff (Brandt), 16
David I, King of Scotland, 80
David II, King of Scotland, 82
de Bohun, Humphrey, Earl of Hereford, 123, 141

De fructu qui ex doctrina percipitur
   (Pace), 41, 43
De Guilleville, Guillaume, 12
De laudibus legum Anglie
   (Fortescue), 126, 194
De non esu (Gerson), 184
De Puebla, Gonsalvo, 60
De senectute (Cicero), 122
De unitate ecclesiastica (Pole), 47
De vera differentia (Foxe), 156–7,
   170–2, 177, 206
De vita spirituali animae (Gerson),
   184
Debate of the Heralds, 176
Defensor Pacis (Marsilius of
   Padua), 209
Derby, Earl of (Thomas Stanley
   d. 1504), 130–1
Derby, Earl of (Thomas Stanley
   d. 1521), 135
Desmond, Earl of, 60
Despenser, Hugh, 122
*Determinations of the moste famous
   and mooste excellent universities
   of Italy and Fraunce*, 155–6
Dionysius, King of Sicily, 70
'Discourse of the Laws and
   Government of England'
   (Bacon), 146
Docwra, Thomas, 135
Dodds, Madeleine Hope, 93
Donation of Constantine, the, 160
Dorset, Marquis of (Thomas
   Grey), 134–5
Dudley, Edmund, 124, 131, 133

Eden, Richard, 55–6
Eden, Thomas, 56
Edgar, King, 167, 171, 172
Edward I, King of England, 124,
   151, 159–60, 171–2
Edward II, King of England,

122–3, 125, 137, 145
Edward IV, King of England, 85,
   125, 127, 129, 133
Edward VI, King of England, 93
Eleates, Papyrius Geminus, 55
Eleutherius, Pope, 158, 160, 163
Eltham Ordinance, the, 135, 136,
   143, 145
Elton, G. R., 1, 47, 151, 178
Elyot, Margaret, 54, 61
Elyot, Thomas, 2, 24, 26–7, 30,
   33, 34, 43–7, 52–73, 124, 143
   as ambassador, 46, 58–62
   and Boleyn faction, 56, 59–60
   as Clerk to the Council, 54–5
   as Clerk to the Justices of
     Assize, 54
   on the Council, 142
   on counsel, 138–40
   dismissal as ambassador, 71
   Erasmianism of, 25, 43, 52, 68
   and More, 64, 66
   political career, 46, 53, 57
   political thought of, 43, 45
   relations with Cromwell, 57–8
   works: *Dictionary*, 52–3, 57;
     Hermathena, 55; *Of the
     Knowledge which Maketh a Wise
     Man*, 46, 63, 65–6, 69–73;
     Pasquil the Playne, 46, 63–70,
     73, 138–9; *The Bankette of
     Sapience*, 52; *The Boke Named
     the Governour*, 25, 43–5, 52,
     56–9; *The Castel of Helth*, 52;
     The Doctrinal of Princes, 52;
     The Image of Governance, 25,
     45, 52
Epistolae obscurorum vivorum (Von
   Hutten), 31
Erasmus, Desiderius, 12, 14,
   19–23, 27, 30, 32, 34–51, 53,
   73

and Christian-humanist
synthesis, 28
and Colet, 12, 14, 22, 27, 36
and the Reformation, 21, 29
works: *Antibarbari*, 35; *De pueris
instituendis*, 43; *De ratione
studii*, 43; *Enchiridion militis
christiani*, 29, 35; *Institutio
principis christiani*, 37, 43, 73;
Letter to Martin Dorp, 28;
Moriae encomium, 19–20, 28,
39; *Novum instrumentum*, 14,
19, 37; *Querela pacis*, 39
Erceldoune, Thomas of ('the
Rhymer'), 81
Essex, Earl of (Henry Bourchier),
135
Ethics (Aristotle), 183
Eucolpius, 45
Exeter, Marquis of (Henry
Courtenay), 135

Facta et dicta memorabilia (Valerius
Maximus), 122
Faerie Queene (Spenser), 178
Febribus infectus, 80
Ferguson, A. B., 27
Fisher, John, 9, 55, 96, 116, 118,
161, 168
Fitzwalter, Viscount (Robert
Ratcliffe), 135
Flodden, Battle of, 85–6
Fortescue, John, 99, 119, 124,
126–9, 133, 137, 169–70,
208–9
on the Council, 126–7, 129, 142
works: *De laudibus legum Anglie*,
126, 194; *De natura legis
naturae*, 126; *The Governance of
England*, 126–7, 129, 133
Fox, Richard, 37, 175

Foxe, Edward, 58, 138, 153–4,
156–7, 159–62, 171–2
De vera differentia, 156–7, 170–2,
177, 206
on regal power, 170–1
Francis I, King of France, 178
Frith, John, 22
Fyneux, John, 167

Gardiner, Stephen, 27–8, 154,
219–20
De vera obedientia, 27, 206–7, 220
on the English Church, 207–8
on the royal supremacy, 208
Gaveston, Piers, 122
Germanus, St, 97
Gerson, Jean, 113, 169, 198, 214,
219
on equity, 183–5
on the principle of exception,
185
Gibson, Thomas, 92–3
Glasse of Truthe, 157–8, 172, 206
Glendower, Owen, 81
Gravissimae censurae, 153, 155–7,
172
Gregory's Chronicle, 125
Grimani, Domenico, 37
Grosseteste, Robert, 177

Hackett, John, 63–4
Hagen, H., 32
Hales, John, 165
Hastings, George, Lord, 135
Hawes, Stephen, 11–12, 14
'Henricus Octavus', 154, 157, 172
Henry I, King of England, 171
Henry IV, King of England, 81
Henry V, King of England, 151
Henry VI, King of England,
125–6

Henry VII, King of England, 77, 85, 130–1, 133, 155, 174–6, 178, 188

Henry VIII, King of England, 19, 28, 33, 46–7, 56–64, 69, 70, 77–8, 85, 89, 91–4, 95–6, 98–101, 111–12, 114–19, 121, 128–31, 133–8, 141, 143–5, 154–64, 166, 169, 172–8, 199, 201, 205–10, 220

and Act of Appeals, 163

and the clergy, 175

and the *Collectanea*, 157–9

and the Council, 135–6

and the English Church, 172–3

his imperial ambitions, 175–6

and the Kidderminster affair, 166

and Pauncefote case, 167

and the Pilgrimage of Grace, 144–5

and power of Parliament, 172–3

regal sovereignty, his view of, 166–7

supreme headship of, 208

Historia regum Britanniae (Geoffrey of Monmouth), 79, 82, 86

Hooker, Richard, 102

Hughes, P., 166

humanism

and Christianity, 27–8, 30

and humanists, 11, 31

definition of, 23, 31

English, 43, 50: 'arrest theory' of, 19, 30; definition of, 33; diversity of, 32; and Erasmianism, 37; as a movement, 18, 22; and politics, 33; views of, 9–10, 18

Erasmian, 9, 22, 34, 43, 53; and Christianity, 35; influence of, 33; and politics, 44, 46, 50; and reform, 34

Hussey, John, 165

Innocent IV, Pope, 177

James I, King of England, 51

Jewel, John, 102

Joachim of Fiore, 83

John, King of England, 94, 163

Joye, George, 97, 116

Julius II, Pope, 155

Justinian, Emperor, 160, 171

Kebell, Thomas, 165, 194

Kelly, H. A., 153

Kent, Earl of (Richard Grey), 135

Kidderminster, Richard, 166

King's Bench, court of, 119, 165, 189

'King's Book', 153, 155

Knight, William, 136

Kowe, Robert, 90

Kristeller, Paul Oskar, 31

Laertius, Diogenes, 70

Lancaster, Thomas of, 123

Lee, Edward, 154

Legate, Robert, 90

Leges Anglorum, 158, 163

Leges Edwardi Confessoris, 158

Lehmberg, Stanford E., 59

Leo X, Pope, 166

Linacre, Thomas, 11

Lisle, Viscount (Arthur Plantagenet), 135

Locher, 16

Lovell, Thomas, 134

Lucian, 17, 39, 44

Lucius I, King, 158, 160, 163, 171

Lupset, Thomas, 37

Luther, Martin, 29, 204–5
  on the Word, 200
Lydgate, John, 12, 82
*Lyfe of Sir Thomas Moore, Knighte,
  The* (Roper), 65

McConica, James K., 34
McKenna, J. W., 176
Magna Carta, 166, 198
Malmesbury, William of, 157, 171
Mantuanus, 15
Margarita philosophica (Reisch), 12
Marney, Henry, 134
Marshall, William, 17, 25, 209
Marsilius of Padua, 160, 169, 209
Matilda, Empress, 80
Matilda, Queen of England, 80
Maximilian, Emperor, 176
Maximus, Valerius, 122
Menippus (Lucian), 39
Methodius, St, 79
Miseriae curialium, 15
Modus tenendi parliamentum, 123–4,
  141–2
Monmouth, Geoffrey of, 79–80,
  82, 86, 157
Montfort, Simon de, 123
More, Thomas, 1, 9–10, 13–14,
  17, 19, 22, 23, 25, 30, 32, 34,
  37, 54, 56, 61, 63, 65, 70, 91,
  95–100, 104–20, 124, 132–4,
  136–7, 154, 156, 161, 163–4,
  168, 170, 177, 189, 198,
  199–200, 202, 213, 216, 219
  as anti-propagandist, 112
  on canon law, 105–8
  on the church, 202–5
  on the clergy, 104–6
  on the clerical jurisdiction, 107
  on common law, 106
  on the Council, 142

  and Erasmianism, 19–20, 37,
    39, 41
  on heresy, 105–7, 109–11
  and humanism, 14, 19, 21, 29,
    40–1, 44
  on the oral tradition of the
    church, 204
  political thought of, 133
  resignation of, 21, 64–5, 95, 115
  on scripture, 202–3, 205
  and Star Chamber, 138
  works: *A Dialogue Concerning
    Heresies*, 29, 41, 200; *A
    Dialogue of Comfort against
    Tribulation*, 29; *A Treatise upon
    the Passion of Christ*, 10; *An
    Answer to the Poisoned Book*, 96,
    117; *Letter to Oxford University*,
    29, 40; *Responsio ad Lutherum*,
    204; *The Apology*, 96–8,
    104–7, 111–12, 114–15, 119,
    168, 205; *The Confutation of
    Tyndale's Answer*, 116,
    199–200; *The Debellation of
    Salem and Bizance*, 96–9, 109,
    111–12, 114–15, 119, 168;
    The History of King Richard III,
    44; *Utopia*, 17, 19, 37–40, 44,
    49, 53, 56, 60, 62, 67, 131–3
More, treaty of the, 135
Morison, Richard, 26
Mortimer, Edmund, Earl of
    March, 81
Morton, John, 174
Mountjoy, John, third Lord, 130
Mountjoy, Lord (William
    Blount), 135
Murphy, Virginia, 153–4

Neville, George, 125
Neville, Thomas, 134

Nicholson, Graham, 157
Norfolk, Duke of (Thomas
    Howard d. 1524), 134
Norfolk, Duke of (Thomas
    Howard d. 1554), 135
Northumberland, Earl of (Henry
    Algernon Percy), 135

On Rhetoric (Aristotle), 122
Orlando furioso (Ariosto), 178
Ormond, Earl of (Piers Butler),
    130–1
Oversole, George, 90
Oversole, Richard, 90
Oxford, Earl of (John de Vere
    d. 1526), 135
Oxford, Earl of (John de Vere
    d. 1540), 145

Pace, Richard, 34, 41–3, 55
Paris, Matthew, 157
Parlement of Paris, 138, 144
Parliament, 50, 100–1, 111, 114,
    120, 123–4, 126–9, 136,
    140–1, 143, 145–6, 163–4,
    169, 172–3, 208–10, 217, 219,
    220
  Act of Appeals (1533), 98, 101,
    151–2, 156–8, 161–3, 165,
    171–3, 175
  Act Extinguishing the
    Authority of the Bishop of
    Rome (1536), 207
  Act of Supremacy (1534), 101,
    119, 163, 170, 208, 220
  De heretico comburendo (1401), 99
  Dispensations Act (1534), 164
  First Act of Succession (1534),
    99, 118
  Heresy Act (1534), 99
  Mortuaries Act (1529), 100

Quia emptores (1290), 192
  Statute of Uses (1536), 189
Pastime of Pleasure (Hawes), 12
Patrizi, Franceso, 43
Paulet, William, 145
Pauncefote, John, 167
pèlerinage de la vie humaine, Le (De
    Guilleville), 12
Percy, Henry, 81
Pilgrimage of Grace, the, 93, 121,
    143–5
Pisan, Christine de, 122, 131
Plato, 12, 17, 70
Pole, Reginald, 47, 140–1
Privy Chamber, the, 134–5
Privy Council *see* Council, King's
prophecies, 77–94
  in Bodleian MS Rawlinson C.
    813, 78, 80, 92
  of Bridlington, 80
  in British Library MS
    Lansdowne 762, 78, 80, 88,
    91, 92, 93
  'The Cock in the North', 80, 88,
    90
  in Folger Loseley MS L. b. 546,
    93
  function of, 78, 89–90
  of Merlin, 79
  'Prophecia Johannis Merlyon',
    81
  'The Prophecy of Methodius',
    79, 88
  'The Prophisies of Rymour,
    Beid, and Marlyng', 81, 83,
    85, 88, 91
  'Tomas of Ersseldoune', 81–3

Rastell, William, 96–7, 116–17
Rawlinson, William, 90
Redman, Richard, 175

Regulae morales (Gerson), 183
Reisch, Gregorius, 12
Replication of a Serjeant at the Laws of England, 180, 186–7, 189–90
Requests, court of, 99
Richard II, King of England, 122, 124–5, 127, 146, 151
Riche, Richard, 144–5, 164
Rochford, Viscount (Thomas Boleyn), 135
Roper, William, 65
Rueger, Z., 183
Rutland, Earl of (Thomas Manners), 135

Sadler, Ralph, 145
St German, Christopher, 1, 24, 50, 97–115, 118–20, 124, 128–9, 142, 168–70, 177, 183–6, 207–20
  on Chancery, 191–3
  on the church, 208, 210, 214, 216, 219–20
  on clerical jurisdiction, 98, 103–5, 198
  on common law, 102–4, 168, 197–8
  on conscience, 180–2, 197, 212
  on custom, 218
  and the divorce, 101
  on equity, 102, 104, 180–2, 186, 191, 193, 197
  on general councils, 218–19
  on heresy laws, 99, 108–9
  influence of Gerson on, 113, 169, 183, 198, 214, 219
  on maxims, 193–7
  and 1531 parliamentary draft, 17, 100–1, 111, 113–15, 128, 210
  political role of, 100

  on power of Parliament, 101–2, 111, 119, 169
  on property, 103
  and reform, 17
  on scripture, 207–8, 210–17
  on unwritten verities, 217–18
  works: 'A Dyalogue shewinge what we be bounde to byleve as thinges necessary to Salvacion, and what not', 4, 210–20; *A Little Treatise concerning Writs of Subpoena*, 4, 113–14, 180, 190, 192–3, 197–8, 210; *A Treatise concerning the Division*, 97, 104–5, 108, 112–15, 118–19, 128, 168, 198; *An Answer to a Letter*, 4, 207–10, 216, 219–20; *Doctor and Student*, 4, 16, 99–100, 102–4, 107, 113–14, 168–70, 180–3, 186, 190, 193, 195–6, 198, 210; *New Additions*, 100–1, 111–14, 128–9, 168–9, 210, 217; *Salem and Bizance*, 17, 97–9, 107–8, 112–15, 118–19, 128, 168; *The Additions of Salem and Bizance*, 98, 112–14, 128
Sallust, 15
Sampson, Richard, 136, 145
Sandes, William, Lord, 135
Segrave, Nicholas, 122
Selden, John, 146
Severus, Alexander, Emperor, 45–6
Seyssel, Claude de, 125
Shrewsbury, Earl of (George Talbot), 134–5, 145
Siculus, Diodorus, 13
Silvius, Aeneas, 15
Skelton, John, 11–12, 14
  and humanism, 13

Replicacyon, 15
Speculum principis, 13
Speke Parrott, 13–14
Why Come Ye Nat to Courte, 14
Skot, John, 122
Smith, Thomas, 11
Smith, William, 175
Spagnolo, Baptista, 15
Spenser, Edmund, 178
Stafford, Edward *see* Buckingham, Duke of
Stapleton, Thomas, 54
Star Chamber, 55, 99, 109, 114, 119, 134–9, 143, 189
Starkey, Thomas, 24–6, 32, 34, 124, 138
   A Dialogue between Lupset and Pole, 47–8, 140–2, 143
   on the Council, 142
   on counsel, 140–1
   humanism of, 48
   political thought of, 47, 49
   view of kingship of, 26
Stephen, King of England, 80
Stokesley, John, 153–5
Submission of the Clergy, 95, 113, 115, 128
Suffolk, Duke of (Charles Brandon), 134–5
Suffolk, Duke of (William de la Pole), 125
Summa aurea (Hostiensis), 183
Summa theologiae (Aquinas), 185–6
Supper of the Lord (Joye), 97, 116
Surrey, Earl of (Thomas Howard d. 1554), 135
Surtz, Edward, 153

Tacitus, 137
Tempest, Thomas, 121–2, 124, 138, 144, 147

Thérouanne, siege of, 85, 86
Thwenge, John, Prior of Bridlington, 80
Tournai, siege of, 85, 86
Trapp, J. B., 97
'Treatise on the Steward', 123
Tree of Commonwealth (Dudley), 131
Tunstall, Cuthbert, 177
Tyndale, William, 20, 22, 199, 204, 213
   Answer to More's Dialogue, 200
   on scripture, 200–1
   his translation of the New Testament, 201

uses, 187–90

Vaughan, Stephen, 115–16
Vita Merlini (Geoffrey of Monmouth), 79, 80, 86
Voigt, Georg, 32

Wambar, king of the Visigoths, 161
Warbeck, Perkin, 86
Warwick, Earl of (Richard Neville), 125, 126, 127
Welden, Robert, 90
Wells, Viscount John, 130–1
West, Nicholas, 168
William I, King of England, 171, 172
Wiltshire, Earl of (Henry Stafford), 135
Wolsey, Thomas, 13, 14, 16, 27, 41, 43, 53–6, 60, 67, 133–7, 139, 154–5, 166, 173, 175, 177, 189
   and Chancery, 191
   and the Council, 134–5

and the Eltham Ordinance
(1526), 135–6, 143, 145
Worcester, Earl of (Charles
Somerset), 135
Wriothesley, Thomas, 145

Wyatt, Thomas, 15

York, Duke of (Richard
Plantagenet), 85